"*World-Class Teams* is an invaluable resource for any company executive looking to break through functional and cultural walls to compete effectively in the global marketplace."
> —Vic Micati, Executive Vice President, Pfizer
> Pharmaceuticals Group

"As a global company, we know what it takes to compete in the international marketplace. This book offers valuable answers and practical strategies for doing just that. *World-Class Teams* is in a class by itself."
> —Cathie Black, President, Hearst Magazines

"A well-focused book with immediate practical application for global businesses. The toolkits will help avoid reinventing best practice and enable teams to get off to a running start. Everyone is setting up teams but hardly anyone is setting them up well—this book will help you do that."
> —Andy Owen-Jones, General Manager, Information Services,
> Virgin Atlantic

"While there are many books written about 'teams,' *World-Class Teams* is the best book I have read recently. It provides practical insights for creating and leading teams that are highly diverse and, perhaps, geographically dispersed. A must read!"
> —Julie O'Mara, O'Mara & Associates, Past President,
> American Society for Training and Development

"The practical strategies and tools contained in *World-Class Teams* make it a must read for those who create, lead and work in the complex and exciting world of team-based structures."
> —Rob Norton, Senior Vice President, Employee Resources,
> Pfizer Pharmaceuticals Group

"It's great—easy to read, practical, punchy. I predict *World-Class Teams* will be a best-seller."
> —Richard A. Levine, Managing Director, BT Wolfensohn—
> Bankers Trust

"A comprehensive, insightful and practical compendium of everything you need to know to set up World Class Teams. Sage, sound, and practical advice accompanied by tools to make it happen. A very valuable contribution to the field. Many thanks!"
> —Paul Maloney, Ph.D., Paul Maloney & Associates, Former
> Director, Management Development, NBC

"Terrific! *World-Class Teams* is user friendly, practical, experienced-based and comprehensive . . . [it is] a veritable toolkit for both team leaders and consultants."
> —Donna McNamara, Director, Global Education & Training,
> Colgate-Palmolive Company

WORLD-CLASS TEAMS

Working Across Borders

LYNDA C. McDERMOTT

NOLAN BRAWLEY

WILLIAM W. WAITE

John Wiley & Sons, Inc.
New York • Chichester • Weinheim • Brisbane • Singapore • Toronto

Library of Congress Cataloging-in-Publication Data:

McDermott, Lynda C. (Lynda Caryl)
    World class teams : working across borders / Lynda C. McDermott,
  Nolan Brawley, William W. Waite.
      p.   cm.
    Includes bibliographical references and index.
    ISBN 0-471-29265-6 (hardcover : alk. paper)
    1. Teams in the workplace.   2. International business enterprises—
  Management.   I. Brawley, Nolan.   II. Waite, William W.
  III. Title.
  HD66.M385   1998
  658.4′ 036—dc21   98-15211

To Carylyn and Sasha,
who provide balance and love to our team,
and to Prakong,
who has the patience of Job.

ACKNOWLEDGMENTS

The origins of this book date back to July 1996, at a place called Chateau Limelette, just outside of Brussels, Belgium. We had just completed the successful launch of our third European product team for Pfizer Europe and were feeling quite pleased with the results of our "High-Performance Team Development" process and the accolades we had been receiving from our clients. In his strong Texan drawl, Nolan turned to Lynda and said, "By damn, I think we're on to something here—and I don't think anyone has put it all together—at least not in writing. . . . Why don't we write a book?"

Lynda, having already authored one book that took a year and a half of weekends out of her life, was less than enthusiastic. Bill, who had consulted on and supported her in that effort, was also clearly not interested in losing his partner to another long project. But as the summer went on and we continued to work with other teams in various companies worldwide, the three of us continued to talk about a book. Finally, in the spirit of "global teamwork," we developed our book proposal via e-mail when Bill and I were in China adopting our daughter and Nolan was working in Turkey. We found an agent who was enthusiastic about the concept and, before we knew it, we were committed to sharing with the world our extensive work and experiences with cross-functional/cross-cultural teams.

As with all of our projects, this one could not have been successfully completed without much help along the way. We went back to our clients for insights and feedback, and we sought help from new contacts—in surveys and interviews, and on the Internet—as we developed our ideas. Although many of them are named in the book, we have used pseudonyms for others who preferred anonymity. We are grateful to all those who contributed to these chapters in so many ways. These wonderful folks include Frank Hickson, Dick Levine, Paul Maloney, Mike Halloran, Julie O'Mara, Vivian Eyre, Paul Habegger, and our colleagues at Management Research Group.

Special thanks go to John Willig, our agent (and Kathryn Hall, our wise publicist who suggested him to us), who somehow knew that despite the proliferation of books on "teams," this one would fill a unique niche in the marketplace. He wisely guided us from the book proposal phase right through to final hard copy.

From the very beginnings of the book proposal, we have had the continued support of our colleagues. At EquiPro International, Steve

Monaghan has helped to keep our business growing and our clients' needs met. He deserves a gold medal for having lived through two book projects since joining our staff in 1991. Stefanie Robinson was in on the ground floor of researching other companies' experience with global teams, and Steve Potter also lent a helping hand. Our heartfelt thanks also go to our colleagues at Pfizer: Willy Hernandez, Iraj Ajir, Jeff Blakely, and Angella Jones, and to all the Pfizer teams that helped us to learn and develop our ideas. Our sincere appreciation to all of them.

This book would not have happened were it not for the effort of a global team. We are deeply grateful to Karen Petty, a premier writer and editor with expertise in management development topics, who joined our team to help pull the final product together. As you will learn in this book, teams can only achieve high performance if they recognize their own limitations and then reach out for help. Thank goodness Karen was available. Much credit for our "performance results" goes to her wordsmithing talents and her steadfast commitment to the team.

Finally, we want to thank our families and personal support group who helped us meet our deadlines while still having fun along the way. To Prakong Brawley, Nolan's dear sweetheart and loving wife, who immersed herself in New York University studies while we labored. To Carylyn, Lynda and Bill's precious daughter, who, with the loving help of her caregiver, Lora Yusupova, has grown into a joyful two-year-old while we completed the book. And particular thanks to Rick Beck for his moral support during a critical phase of the writing.

We all agree that writing a book is a bit like being a parent. As we close the pages on the writing stage, with both incredible joy and some sadness, we will now move on to the next stage of our own team development.

LYNDA CARYL MCDERMOTT
NOLAN BRAWLEY
WILLIAM W. WAITE

New York City
August 1998

THE AUTHORS

Lynda C. McDermott is President of EquiPro International, Ltd., an international strategic and organizational consulting firm headquartered in New York City. She and her firm are recognized by clients and colleagues as experts in leadership and team development.

The firm's client list of corporations and professional service firms includes Pfizer Inc., Coopers & Lybrand, Hearst Magazines, Virgin Atlantic Airlines, Mobil Oil, and Consolidated Edison Company.

Before starting her own firm in 1987, Ms. McDermott spent over eight years as a management consultant with Ernst & Young and KPMG Peat Marwick. Prior to that, she was a line manager and internal organization development consultant for Ohio Bell and AT&T.

Ms. McDermott has a BS degree in psychology from Miami University and a Master of Science in organizational development from Bowling Green State University. She served over ten years on the National Board of Directors of the American Society for Training and Development, the world's leading and largest professional organization. Ms. McDermott received the ASTD's Torch Award in 1986 for outstanding contributions to the profession and, in 1983, was selected by *Working Woman* magazine as one of "73 Women Ready to Run Corporate America." She is a frequent author for the *Training and Development Journal* and *Accounting Today,* and her first book, *Caught in the Middle: How to Survive and Thrive in Today's Management Squeeze,* was a bestseller and designated as a main selection for the Newbridge Executive Book Club.

Ms. McDermott has been a featured speaker for over fifteen years at international professional and trade conferences, such as ASTD's International Conference. She is sought out as an interviewee by media such as CNBC, Wall Street Journal Radio, *The Chicago Tribune, The Washington Post, Boardroom Reports, Training Magazine, New York, Newsday, Working Woman, New Woman,* and *Executive Directions.*

Nolan Brawley is Associate Director of Pharmaceutical Development and Training for Pfizer, Inc., a leading pharmaceutical company. Mr. Brawley specializes in the design and implementation of programs and processes aimed at improving field force productivity. He consults regularly with 52 international subsidiaries on a wide range of organizational issues.

During a career at Pfizer that spans 18 years, Mr. Brawley has held numerous positions. Initially a field sales representative in Dallas, Texas, he has since served in several key positions in domestic and international sales development and training along with professional relations.

Mr. Brawley began his career in the public education arena and at one point became the youngest athletic director in Texas at a major high school in Fort Worth. He supervised a staff of 13 people.

Mr. Brawley has a Master's degree in biology and a BS degree in mathematics and biology from Texas Christian University.

William W. Waite is Executive Vice President of EquiPro International, Ltd., headquartered in New York City. Over the past several years with EquiPro, Mr. Waite has specialized in leadership, coaching, and development, and has consulted extensively with international executive teams.

Prior to joining EquiPro, Mr. Waite was Director of Corporate Management Development and Training for the CIGNA Corporation. During his years with CIGNA, he managed a staff of 40, with whom he developed training programs that were recognized throughout the industry as being leading-edge. Mr. Waite and his staff also consulted with senior management on a wide variety of business issues.

Mr. Waite began his career as a field sales representative with Procter and Gamble. He was then recruited by the Ohio Bell Telephone Company into a high-potential line management program. Over the next eight years, he held increasingly responsible management positions in large divisions such as network operations and customer service.

Mr. Waite made a major shift in his career when he became Director of Manpower Utilization for the entire company. In this position, he developed and implemented Corporate Human Resource Utilization Systems for overall performance management, career development, and human resource planning. After eighteen years with Ohio Bell, Mr. Waite accepted the position of Director of Corporate Management Education and Training for the American Can Company, where he directed his staff in evaluating, implementing, and revising existing core programs and designing and introducing new pilot programs. Mr. Waite then went on to Connecticut General Life Insurance Company as Director of Corporate Training. During a two-year period, he and his staff developed a corporate training plan that resulted in the formulation of an entirely new curriculum for first-line management programs up to and including programs for senior management.

Mr. Waite has a Master's degree in human resource development and a BA degree in business administration from Baldwin-Wallace College.

CONTENTS

STRATEGY 3
Leading World-Class Teams

STRATEGY 4
Measuring, Managing, and Rewarding World-Class Team Performance

STRATEGY 5
Managing the Functional and Cultural Borders of World-Class Teams

HOW TO USE THIS BOOK

Companies that want to compete successfully in the global marketplace must be able to develop innovative products and services and get them into the hands of their customers in record time. This requires organizations that are lean, flexible, and responsive to local customers and customs.

To meet the need for *creative, quick,* and *customized* organizations, companies are increasingly rejecting hierarchical, functionally driven pyramidal structures and replacing them with flatter, team-based organizations that pull together people with diverse backgrounds and skills and set them to work on critical business issues. These *cross-functional teams* are very powerful tools for strengthening strategic problem-solving capabilities.

For multinational organizations, it is becoming evident that not only must people move across the "functional silos" within their companies, but they must also learn to work in teams that cross regional and national borders. Much has been learned and written about cross-functional teams, but there is little shared knowledge about best practices for *cross-cultural teams,* whose members not only represent different functions but also bring different national and cultural values and experiences to the team.

Many organizations today are jumping on the team bandwagon. Teams are addressing a multitude of business issues, from "How do we reengineer our information systems throughout the company?" to "How do we launch a product in the Pacific Rim?" However, the authors' own experiences in consulting with a wide variety of organizations around the world suggest that although many organizations are investing time and resources in setting up *cross-functional/cross-cultural teams,* few are harvesting *real success.*

World-Class Teams will benefit organizations that want to initiate or have already established cross-functional teams, as well as those that seek to form teams to address business issues that cut across regional/national borders. The book is designed to provide specific advice and practical "how-to" tools and techniques that can make these teams *"world class."* It is not a collection of anecdotes about teams; no "top ten" world-class teams are cited that do everything so well that the rest of the world has only to benchmark them for best practices. The book, instead, offers detailed help for those who will lead, facilitate, and support world-class teams. It will answer such questions as:

➤ What are the economic, cultural, and technological forces that are spawning cross-functional/cross-cultural teams?

➤ What business and performance challenges can these teams address?

➤ How should senior management set up cross-functional/cross-cultural teams for success?

➤ What is the best way to "start up" these teams so as to maximize their chances of success?

➤ What are the critical elements of *world-class performance* and how can a company diagnose whether a team is succeeding or failing?

➤ How should the successes of world-class teams be measured and rewarded?

➤ What is the impact of functional, language, and cultural diversity on team dynamics and performance—that is, what is the effect of having team members who:

  —work 4,000 miles from each other?

  —speak different languages?

  —work for different functional bosses (who continue to want *their* work performed)?

  —have different work and cultural norms and values?

➤ What kinds of technology facilitate the work of cross-functional/cross-cultural teams?

➤ What roles and skills are necessary if team leaders and team members are to be effective? How are those roles and skills selected and developed?

➤ How should the "stakeholder borders" of cross-functional/cross-cultural teams be managed?

➤ How is cross-functional and cross-cultural collaboration developed?

➤ How can a balance between "high tech" and "high touch" be achieved on world-class teams?

➤ The Audience

We wrote this book for people who are looking for *answers and practical strategies*. It is written as a handbook. Its concepts, learnings, and exercises are taken directly from "the field"—which has been our workplace in over thirty countries. Several types of people will want to read *World-Class Teams* and keep it handy for reference:

➤ *Executives and senior managers* who are considering whether and how to establish cross-functional/cross-cultural teams and are looking for guidance from and lessons learned by other organizations. They will be particularly interested in Chapters 1 and 3.

➤ *Cross-functional/cross-cultural team leaders and members* who are looking to maximize their chances of success and their contributions, and want a methodology and framework for diagnosing how their team is performing. These team leaders and members will want to read the entire book!

➤ *Human resources and organization development professionals* who have been given the responsibility to assist in launching or developing cross-functional/cross-cultural teams. They will want to focus on those chapters that will help them facilitate the teams that are expected, by management, to become "high performing."

➤ *World-class team stakeholders* such as the functional bosses, the "clients," the sponsors, the support specialists, and others who contribute to or benefit from the work of these teams. They will want to absorb Chapters 3, 5, 15, and 16 to understand their role in participating with and supporting their team from the very beginning, so that needs and expectations can be addressed.

➤ Start at the Top and Then Go Anywhere

This book does not need to be read in strict chapter order. Instead, you could read Chapters 1 and 2 to get an overview, and then select those sections or chapters that have the most relevance to your need to better understand particular areas—for example, World-Class Team Launch, Team Development, Team Measurement, Team Technology, or Team Border Management.

➤ Practice as You Go

We encourage you to mark up the pages as you read. Write your ideas in the margins or in a notebook. Much of what we have experienced in the field (and included in the book) will only come alive for you as you think about and, in fact, apply and practice world-class team performance in your own organization.

➤ Icons

Throughout the book, we use various icons to indicate different types of material:

Individual Exercise. A thought-provoking exercise to encourage you to reflect on your own experiences or to practice a concept or technique alone, before you try it out with the team.

Team Exercise. An exercise that you will want to apply with a group of people, facilitated either by a team leader or an external consultant.

Learning Lights. Principles, concepts, and ideas that we have found to be meaningful and worth remembering.

Toolkits. Techniques, models, sample documents, and other practical accoutrements—a world-class team "toolbox" that you can put to use with your team.

➤ World-Class Team Learning Continues

We certainly do not know all there is to know about managing the complexity of cross-functional/cross-cultural teams. Much more can be learned, and we want to continue refining our models, tools, and lessons. If you want to stay connected to our work and/or provide us with feedback, you can write or call us at the following locations:

Lynda McDermott, President
Bill Waite, Executive Vice President
EquiPro International, Ltd.

Business Address:
420 Lexington Avenue
Suite 1712
New York, NY 10017
Tel. (212) 573-9046
Fax (212) 573-9049
www.equiproint.com

Nolan Brawley
Associate Director of Pharmaceutical
   Development and Training
Pfizer, Inc.

Home Address:
71 Wayne Street
Jersey City, NJ 07302
Tel. (201) 332-4630

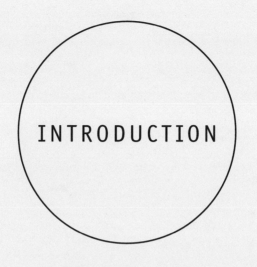

INTRODUCTION

The Quest for World-Class Teams

Chapter 1

Teamwork as a Global Competitive Strategy

A critical factor in the success of companies competing in the global marketplace is their ability to develop innovative products and services and get them into the hands of their customers in record time. To reduce cycle time and react to ever-changing opportunities, while still emphasizing innovation, quality, and service, organizations must be lean, flexible, and responsive to local customers and customs—or risk obsolescence. As Jack Welch, CEO of General Electric, once observed: "When the rate of external change exceeds the rate of internal change, the end [of your business] is in sight."

The organization of the future—which is *now*—will be built around a few guiding principles:

➤ *Continuous change.* The concept of the "light at the end of the tunnel" is moot. Stability is out and "organizational whitewater" is in. To survive, companies and individuals must be willing to learn how to change the tires while their car is moving.

➤ *Knowledge workers.* Today, less than 10 percent of the workforce is involved in direct labor. The growing asset that must be leveraged is the knowledge worker, the person whose intellectual capital will fuel future success.

➤ *Global scope.* Whether or not your company is multinational, you cannot ignore reality: We are now operating in a global economy. National boundaries are no longer barriers to product innovation, services, and sources of production. Competition will be liberated from time and space and, by definition, will be global.

➤ *Networked cross-specialization.* The smokestack organization of the Industrial Era is dead. Specialization continues to be of value, but not in isolation. Future success will depend on how efficiently you can link sources of expertise to create value and share learnings, whether within or across borders.

➤ *Speed.* There is an old fable (see the "Learning Light" below) that ends with the suggestion that no matter where you live in the world, when dawn breaks, if you don't want to die, you had better be prepared to move *fast.* In today's world, where products can be copied in record time, those who get to the market first have a flat-out advantage.

Every morning, in Africa, a gazelle wakes up and knows it will have to run faster than a lion today—or else it will be killed.

Every morning, in Africa, a lion wakes up and knows that it must outrun the slower gazelle today, and if it doesn't do that, it will starve—and eventually die.

So you see, it doesn't really matter if you're the lion or the gazelle. When the sun comes up—you'd better be running.

■ SILOS 'R'NT US: THE "TRANS-INFORMATION/FAST COMPANY" ERA

As we move toward the 21st century, we are indeed using the promised power of the Information Age to transform the way we do business. The migration into cyberspace has enabled us to communicate and work across functions, locations, country borders and cultures, companies, and industries. Just about any "wall" seems penetrable.

To be a successful *fast company,* an organization must:

➤ Develop fluid work structures and processes.

➤ Think global and act local—what the Japanese call "glocalize."

➤ Encourage empowerment and "bottom-up" thinking.

➤ Encourage flexible employee work patterns.

➤ Value and maximize diversity for knowledge and learning.

➤ Keep employees focused on just-in-time results.

It is not enough for people to move across the functional silos or chimneys within their own companies; if they are part of a multinational organization, they must also learn to work across their national borders and respond more effectively to global market realities. They must learn to work with people from different countries, and maybe even from different companies through strategic intercompany alliances.

Organizational experts Edward Lawler and Susan Cohen conducted a study among the Fortune 1000 in the early 1990s that describes just how pervasive teams have become in America over the past decade. Their findings include:

➤ As early as 1991, nearly 87 percent of all Fortune 1000 companies were using parallel teams—groups of individuals working parallel to the existing organizational structure as temporary problem-solving units to improve a specific business process, such as quality.

➤ Nearly 100 percent of all companies were using project teams— usually, cross-functional teams brought together to complete a clearly defined set of tasks within a clearly defined time frame. A product development team is a typical example.

➤ Of all the companies surveyed, 47 percent were experimenting with permanent work teams comprised of cross-functional team members for whom the functional silo had become an anachronism.[1]

Current research suggests that the use of teams continues to grow. Data on teams in the American workplace, reported by *Training and Development Journal* in 1996, revealed that:

➤ Most (six out of ten) employees prefer to work in teams rather than independently.

➤ Two-thirds of women prefer teamwork, compared with 54 percent of men.

➤ Adult workers, on average, spend 61.5 percent of their time working in a team environment.

➤ Most workers (90 percent) have some exposure to working on teams, but only half receive team training.[2]

All over the world, companies such as ABB, Unilever, Westpac Banking, General Electric, Bankers Trust, Mobil Oil, IBM, Sanofi Pharmaceuticals, Colgate, Royal Dutch Shell, and Pfizer are forming a matrix of international teams. Jeff McHenry, director of executive development at Microsoft, has commented that "basically all of our work is done in some sort of team. Our people have to work very closely together to develop and market our software products. We're about 50 percent bigger today than we were a few years ago. And so we're trying to find ways to link teams together more tightly."[3]

Mike Halloran, business development executive for IBM, notes the challenges that IBM faced in capitalizing on unique market opportunities in the Asia-Pacific region for network-centric computing. To successfully market IBM's services to industry-leading companies, it was necessary to put together "virtual" project teams that had expert knowledge of the industry and of technological applications, but also were capable of adapting the service offerings to local customs and regulations.

"From headquarters in Armonk, New York, we are not in a position to call people in from all over the world, pick their brains, send them home, and tell them to wait until we develop the solution for their marketplace," says Halloran. "The speed of change and the competition are requiring that we create teams that can operate with just-in-time readiness to develop the *right* solutions for their customers."

■ WHAT IS A "WORLD-CLASS TEAM"?

Much has been learned and written about cross-functional teams, but there is little shared knowledge about how to set up and sustain the high performance of cross-functional/cross-cultural teams. In these world-class teams, which represent one of the most complex forms of team-based organizational structures, team members:

> ➤ Are from cross-functional units (such as marketing, sales, R&D, engineering, finance, information technology).
>
> ➤ Either serve in a full-time assignment (reporting directly to a Team Leader) or report part-time to Team Leaders and part-time to their functional bosses.
>
> ➤ Work at different locations and perhaps in different countries.
>
> ➤ Work on global projects that have strategic impact on the company's results, whether the company is national or multinational.
>
> ➤ Are "knowledge workers": Their intellectual capital is the asset that needs to be leveraged by the organization.

Such teams have been variously referred to as "virtual teams" or "geographically dispersed teams" or "remote teams." However, we have coined the term "world-class team" because it also implies that this type of team has aspirations to become a true high-performance team. In world-class team organizations, much of the core work of the organization is produced by teams, in a lateral fashion. People work with their peers on the team as well as across teams to make decisions and get results. This lateral approach is much different from the vertical, hierarchical way of working that most people have grown accustomed to.

In addition, although membership on the team is not necessarily permanent, team leaders and members are expected to serve on the team for at least a year or for the duration of the project. However, these teams should not be thought of as task forces, formed to be temporary and focused on highly discrete and time-specific issues.

Nor should world-class teams be confused with a working group (see the definitions in Toolkit 1.1). As noted previously, a world-class team is committed to "high performance." Like a football team, it should have

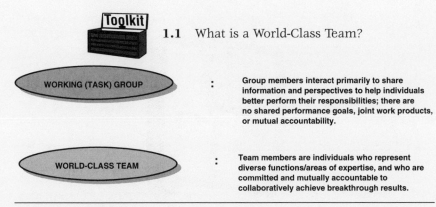

clearly defined roles for every team member, measurable goals, a visible purpose around which the team can unite, and a coach. A working group, on the other hand, is a loose group of individuals, many of whom may not be sure where they or others fit in; often, the goals of the group have never been spelled out. As much competition exists inside the group as outside of it. Typically, the group is left to its own devices with no coaching or support. We often refer to working groups as "FYI" (For Your Information) groups. People may come together for meetings, but they walk away from the experience wondering why they were there.

Although we are strong proponents of world-class teams, we do not believe they are for everyone. In fact, we believe that numerous myths and misconceptions are floating around about the "magical powers" that teams supposedly possess. Here are some of those myths:

➤ *Teams are the answer whenever there is an issue to be resolved.* Not all work or decisions can or should be made by teams. In fact, some teams are formed in an effort to avoid dealing with a performance issue.

➤ *Teams eliminate hierarchy.* Impossible. Someone always has a boss and there's nothing wrong with that. Managing the politics of hierarchy is one of the team's toughest assignments.

➤ *Everyone should be on a team.* Not the case. Some people can't function on and don't belong on teams. It takes too much of an investment to work with them, and they are better off working on their own.

➤ *Just setting up teams is all it takes to create high-performance results.* Think again. The entire premise of this book is that while you need

The Chinese Characters for the Word "Team"

to focus on the basics and do those well, world-class team development takes time, dedication, perseverance, blood, sweat, and, yes, sometimes tears!

➤ *Teams don't need leaders.*　As Microsoft's Jeff McHenry points out: "We have very achievement-oriented people who often just want to do something on their own. Teamwork takes time. I would say that if [you] take care of two basics—having clear goals and strong leadership—[you] are 99 percent of the way home toward having strong teams."[4]

World-class teams, like world-class racing yachts, face turbulent waters on their journey. They are not for the unskilled, unprepared, or fainthearted. For most organizations, world-class teams represent such a different and complex way of working, thinking, and behaving that when they are initially set up, those who work on and with them find it hard to figure out why anybody thought that a team was such a good idea in the first place!?! They are complex. They do require work. They do *force change.* But if you can set them up, develop them, and support them well, the payoffs will be there.

■ JUMPING ON THE TEAM BANDWAGON

Imagine the following scenario. You are a Team Leader for a French-owned financial services company that has offices worldwide. It is Wednesday morning in your country, and you are waiting to begin a videoconference; each month, you hook up with your team members for a team meeting. It has been very difficult to have these meetings because serving on your team are individuals from Tokyo, Istanbul, Vancouver, New York, Brussels, and Sydney. Even satisfying everyone with the right time for the meeting is hard; invariably, it cuts into someone's sleep! In addition, the meetings are used not only to share information, but also to try to resolve issues, and everyone on the team, because of the uniqueness of the markets and customers each represents, has a different opinion. Try problem solving over this distance with people who are cranky to begin with! For a moment, you wonder what it would be like to work with a team you play softball with every Saturday and have conversations with in the coffee room on a regular basis.

Unfortunately, many organizations view teams as a panacea for whatever ails them. Nothing could be further from the truth. In fact, because of their rampant misuse, teams have begun to get a bad rap and may, to some, be looking like another management fad. Our own experience in consulting with a wide variety of organizations around the world suggests that teams can be a very powerful way to organize people to perform work and address business issues, yet very few organizations invest the thoughtful time and resources needed to set up teams for success.

Before jumping on the bandwagon, consider why companies are choosing to develop increasingly complex team-based organizational structures:

> ➤ To address constantly changing business needs that compel organizational structures to be fluid; team members can be moved like modular furniture to where their expertise is required.

> ➤ To focus and integrate the competencies and perspectives of a diverse set of people on a problem, an opportunity, a product, a set of customers or markets that our increasingly sophisticated marketplaces demand.

> ➤ To create, among the maximum number of employees, a spirt of high involvement, accountability, and ownership of the business.

> ➤ To efficiently and effectively allocate and leverage resources lower in the organization, in order to reduce cycle time, improve quality, and encourage innovation.

Such business and performance challenges are not unfamiliar to Pfizer, a multinational pharmaceutical company. Like others in its industry,

Pfizer has for years used cross-functional/cross-cultural teams in R&D efforts. However, its experience with teams in its country organizations has, by comparison, been relatively limited. In 1996, senior management in the European organization introduced a new "Euroteam" concept, which was designed to maximize the potential for Pfizer's new and existing products throughout Europe.

The product teams, whose members would come from different countries and functions (such as marketing, medical, sales), were formed as a strategic response to this business issue: "How can we maximize our efficiency, work more creatively, leverage our resources, and provide more of a 'one company' focus as we meet the changing demands of the healthcare marketplace throughout Europe?" The Euroteams were designed to contribute a unique European perspective and to optimize resources and innovation among the European countries so that product performance could be enhanced.

Frank Hickson, executive director of new product planning in Europe, expressed the cautious optimism with which Pfizer Europe introduced the team concept: "The Euroteams represent the single most important organizational 'experiment' we've embarked upon. We have traditionally been a functionally siloed organization and our countries have operated within strong border walls. When we form cross-functional/cross-cultural teams, we are changing not only the infrastructure, but the culture of the company. We must find new ways to cross-pollinate and leverage our resources across borders—not just country borders, but the borders we have created between sales, marketing, and medical or between New York [headquarters for the corporation] and Europe."

Not all of Pfizer's teams cross national borders. For example, Pfizer Canada, under the direction of Alan Bootes and John Stewart, restructured its marketing-driven product teams into a therapeutic class team structure. Louis Couillard, Director of Marketing, comments: "Undoubtedly teams have been a key driver of our strong and sustained growth. We, therefore, started this process [of setting up 'high-performance teams'] thinking we had teams, but came to realize we had working groups that were falling short of operating at high potential—not because of our people, but because they were not structured to be high-performing teams. We have now named Team Leaders and core team members and are ready to make the investment in training that both Team Leaders and team members need to effectively operate in a high-performance team structure."

Apple Computer is another company that has made use of world-class teams to address specific business challenges. "As the company's international sales grew to approach our domestic revenues, the need to provide a more uniform response [to the marketplace] increased," says

Cole Hamlin, an organizational development and human resources consultant for Apple. The company identified materials procurement as one area that was particularly in need of a "global organization"—by our definition, the equivalent of a world-class team. The global materials organization that was formed, reports Hamlin, "leveraged the collective resources of a multisite, multicultural organization while retaining the local strengths that had made the company so responsive in the past."

None of this happened without time and effort. Hamlin points out that "the design and implementation of a global team concept requires a great deal of commitment on the part of the leadership of an organization. The company must be prepared to challenge sacred institutions, suffer political assaults from any quarters, redistribute personal power, and subordinate some local autonomy."[5]

Breaking down the old (and the sacred) to make way for the new sometimes means reconstructing the very foundation. A case in point is the Chrysler Corporation. "Perhaps the most insidious, damaging example of our thinking was reflected in how we were organized. Chrysler, like most large corporations, had for decades been organized along functional lines," reports Robert Lutz, president and chief operating officer. "And, while functional hierarchies have been around since at least the inception of the Catholic Church and of the Roman military, our functional hierarchies at Chrysler had become ossified, inter- and intracompetitive, self-serving, self-indulgent, and self-possessed." The company's response? According to Lutz, they essentially "toppled the old functional chimneys" and replaced them with cross-functional product development teams that were truly empowered to make decisions and thereby enable Chrysler to produce new cars that were faster and cheaper.[6]

In an article titled "Global Teams: The Ultimate Collaboration," author Charlene Marmer Solomon effectively conveys the "why" of using world-class teams: "Global teams address certain problems and affect the bottom line. They maximize expertise from a variety of people, provide companies a more accurate picture of international customers' needs and profit by the synergy necessary to unify the varying perspectives of different cultures and different business functions."[7]

At Intel, which has been using global teams for more than a decade, teams are used for "a medley of projects: they formulate and deliver sales strategies for specific products; they develop new products; they manufacture and produce microprocessor elements." Sharon Richards, intercultural training program manager at Intel's headquarters, decided to study these global teams to determine their success factors. According to Richards, "One of the most important discoveries we made is that teams need very simple basic processes and procedures. . . . It's very important to set clear expectations and to have clearly defined goals, roles, and responsibilities."[8]

As we noted earlier, however, teams are not the ultimate "get-well" pill. In a *Fortune* article, "The Trouble with Teams," author Brian Dumaine notes that teams are not without their problems and cites DEC as an example of how one company lost its competitive edge as a result of going too far on the team bandwagon: "The problems at DEC, America's second-largest computer maker, stand as a striking illustration. [The company] announced . . . it was abandoning its matrix team structure. Under the old system, workers in functional areas—engineering, marketing—also served on teams organized around product lines like minicomputers or integrated chips. The team spent endless hours in meetings trying to build a consensus between the two factions in the matrix: the functional bosses and the team bosses. Its sheer organizational weight left DEC a laggard in the fast-moving technology sector."[9]

Although the process of adopting a team-based structure does have a warning label attached, one of the many advantages of world-class teams—one that is perhaps not obvious—is that *they are key to organizational learning.* Management expert Peter Senge refers to "adaptive" learning and double-loop learning as processes for discovering what does and doesn't work in the organization, then making changes accordingly. When you are forming a world-class team and bringing together people from different functions and different locations within the company, you can begin to uncover (if you *listen*) valuable information about how the organization is really functioning that previously was unknown or was ignored.[10]

For example, with one team development we facilitated, as we were trying to put team members in place, we encountered much resistance from a particular senior executive who had reluctantly agreed to sponsor the team at the insistent suggestion of his boss. Through the process of working with the team, we uncovered many examples of tight controls and a lack of collaboration within the executive's organization which was affecting the team's ability to function. Before the team spotlight was turned on, he had been able to control his fiefdom as he chose. Now he was in the spotlight.

■ ARE YOU READY FOR WORLD-CLASS TEAMS?

One day we received a call from a prospective client who was well down the road toward setting up world-class teams. Senior management had committed to the endeavor and endorsed a task force to identify what projects should be placed in the hands of these teams. Team Leaders had been named, and a big meeting was scheduled to diagnose the challenges these teams would face (for example, apparently not everyone at the top was on board—already a senior functional head was vocally active in denouncing the team structure). We were asked several questions about the work we'd done with teams, and they listened politely to a few of our stories until we shook things up by saying, "What you're really trying to have happen is a change in culture—which doesn't happen overnight."

That remark prompted a lengthy discussion that brought out hesitancy on the part of one of the task force members: perhaps they *were* moving too fast, or the culture wasn't yet ready to *really* support these teams, or people were not willing to give up their power and control. This led us to our "lecturette on culture change." Ultimately, they did take the plunge, but not before taking a good hard look at their "readiness issues."

If you're considering setting up world-class teams, have you given any thought to all the *problems* they will create? Are you ready to tackle:

➤ Helping teams who must manage their internal team processes as well as their external borders with key stakeholders, both inside and (perhaps) outside the organization?

➤ Competition among and between world-class teams for resources and recognition?

➤ Information, budgeting, and communications systems that were designed for traditional hierarchical organizations and are thus insufficient for multifunctional, multicultural, need-to-be-networked teams?

➤ Performance appraisal and compensation systems that are more aligned to individual than to team performance?

➤ A lack of commitment from team members who may be juggling multiple roles, cultures, and stakeholder expectations, and want to know what their "real" job is?

➤ Functional unit heads who are politically threatened by the role and authority of the world-class team and refuse to give their support?

➤ Functional or country bosses who still think they "own" their employees who are serving on world-class teams?

➤ Team members who may have a stronger allegiance to their functional boss than to the team because the boss controls their performance appraisal and salary/bonus recommendations?

➤ The difficulties of building interpersonal relationships and trust among people who speak different languages and have only periodic and possibly limited face-to-face contact?

➤ Stereotypes about professions (engineers are "nerds" and sales reps are "pushy") and cultures (Germans are stubborn and Italians are temperamental)?

➤ Individual "star" contributors who value their independence and don't really want to play the interdependent "team game"?

➤ World-class Team Leaders and team members who are not skilled in team processes (decision making, conflict management, and so forth), yet who (like their bosses) think teamwork just comes "naturally" and wonder why they must attend team skills training?

➤ Managing the tensions of differentiation and integration that world-class teams create in relation to other organizational units?

➤ The gap between the organization's espoused value of "teamwork" and the behavior that actually gets rewarded?

➤ World-class teams that take you seriously when you say they are "empowered"?

That's a lot to tackle—and it's not even a complete list. So how do you know whether your organization is ready to handle all this?

Before answering that question, we probably need to say that if your company has a long history of "smokestacking" (or silo/turf-war management), the answer may be *"Never."* On the other hand, if there's a strong performance or business challenge that now requires multidisciplinary or multilocation perspectives, *and* top management is strongly endorsing a team-based structure, then go for it—don't wait. If you wait until the organization is "ready," you're focusing on the wrong sequence of events.

The fact remains that, if world-class teams are to be successful, the organization's culture needs to be supportive of them. The culture—the prevailing collection of beliefs, values, norms, and practices—ultimately governs the "talk and walk" of the group of individuals who comprise the organization. How do you change the culture? By motivating a critical mass of people to *behave* and *think* differently. Notice the order of those two words. There are many theories about change management, most of which could be divided into two camps based on this fundamental question: Do you get people to change by first altering their attitudes about an issue, or by first motivating (encouraging or coercing) them to behave differently?

After years of observing both individual and organizational change, it's our profound belief that if you can't initially convince people about an issue (change their beliefs), but you can get them to change their behavior, this will enable you to provide them with a new set of experiences (hopefully positive) that eventually will lead to a change of

1.2   Why Change Efforts Fail

x No Sense of Great Urgency

x No Guiding Coalition of Influencers

x No Clear and Compelling Vision

x Not Enough Vision-Focused Communications

x No Clear Strategies for "Closing the Gap" (Vision - Current Reality)

x No Plan for "Quick-Hits/Short-Term Wins"

x Seeking and Declaring Victory Too Soon

x No Performance Accountability or Anchoring of Change in the Culture

x No "Buy-In" for the Need for Change

Adapted from John Kotter's *LEADING CHANGE*, EquiPro International, Ltd.

attitude. We do believe that until the changes to a person's belief system are internalized, there will not be a chance of long-term change.

In reply to the question "How do you achieve cultural change?" someone once said: "By getting a lot of people to change direction one step at a time."

Now, back to how you get an organization's culture to accept a potentially foreign entity like a world-class team. One "change leader" expert whose research and writings we have found valuable in this regard is John Kotter, the Konosuke Matsushita Professor of Leadership at Harvard Business School. In Toolkit 1.2, we've adapted Kotter's theories as they relate to world-class teams to show why change efforts fail.

Another model we use for assessing how to change an organization to support teams, is based on McKinsey and Company's "7 S's" model:

1. *Strategy.* A coherent set of actions aimed at gaining a sustainable advantage over competition, improving position vis-à-vis

customers, or allocating resources. Will world-class teams significantly contribute to corporate strategy?

2. *Structure.* The organization chart and accompanying baggage that show who reports to whom and how tasks are both divided up and integrated. How will teams integrate with the current organizational chart? Are you willing to make them visible, put them in the spotlight, give them something important to do?

3. *Systems.* The processes and flows that show how an organization gets things done from day to day. (Information systems, capital budgeting systems, manufacturing processes, project management systems, and performance measurement systems would be good examples.) Can these systems be readily adapted to accommodate world-class teams?

4. *Style.* Tangible evidence of what management considers important: how it collectively spends time and attention and uses symbolic behavior. It is not what management says that is important; it is the way management behaves. Does senior management's style serve as a role model for world-class teams?

5. *Staff.* The people in an organization. Do we have enough of the right people to work on world-class teams, both as Team Leader(s) and team members?

6. *Shared values (or superordinate goals).* The values that go beyond, but might well include, simple team goal statements, or the degree to which management supports teams with their walk, not just with their talk. Does management continue to send messages of accountability that things must change around here?

7. *Skills.* Skills are those capabilities that are possessed by an organization as a whole, as opposed to the people in it. McKinsey's concept of corporate skills, as distinct from the skills of individuals within the organization, seems difficult for many to grasp. However, some organizations that hire only the best and the brightest cannot get seemingly simple things done, while others perform extraordinary feats with ordinary people. What is the history of your organization in learning and acquiring new skills? Do team competencies require too large a jump?

We adapted this model to focus on the critical elements that must be examined to determine whether an organization is ready for world-class teams. Our "Readiness Checklist," in Toolkit 1.3, shows how we've expanded the seven elements of the McKinsey model into fifteen dimensions of organizational readiness.

1.3 World-Class Team Readiness Checklist

General Considerations	No Concern	Mild Concern	Moderate Concern	Significant Concern	Critical Concern
My perceptions about:					
1. Senior management's proactive participation and support for world-class teams.	12	9	6	3	0
2. How well the business need for world-class teams has been communicated and understood.	12	9	6	3	0
3. Our people's tradition of practicing "silo" behavior.	8	6	4	2	0
4. Our employees' competencies to work effectively in world-class teams.	4	3	2	1	0
5. Senior management's ability to role-model being a high-performance team.	12	9	6	3	0
6. Our organization's history of not just starting, but sustaining change initiatives.	8	6	4	2	0
7. Our performance management and reward system's ability to support individual and team performance.	4	3	2	1	0
8. Our organization's willingness to measure the success of change initiatives.	4	3	2	1	0
9. Our willingness to really become a learning organization; i.e., honest dialogue, creative cross-functional and cross-cultural problem solving, etc.	4	3	2	1	0

(Continued)

Toolkit 1.3 *(Continued)*

General Considerations	*No Concern*	*Mild Concern*	*Moderate Concern*	*Significant Concern*	*Critical Concern*
My perceptions about:					
10. Our organization's commitment to high performance standards, best practices, and continuous improvement.	8	6	4	2	0
11. Our organization's commitment to empowerment.	12	9	6	3	0
12. Our organization's willingness to invest in developing employees' competencies to work effectively in world-class teams.	12	9	6	3	0
13. Our organization's capabilities or willingness to invest in systems, processes, and technologies to enable teams to work effectively.	4	3	2	1	0
14. How well people are working together today across borders, even informally.	8	6	4	2	0
15. The degree to which our employees share a common understanding of and are committed to the company's overall direction and goals.	12	9	6	3	0
				Total Readiness Score	

A score of less than 50 indicates you should strongly consider the wisdom of setting up world-class teams without first addressing the issues.

A score of 50–70 indicates enough organizational readiness to warrant a "pilot."

A score over 70 indicates you have a culture that strongly supports world-class teams.

World-class teams may look like simply a change in *structure,* but organizations need to change their *systems* as well. For example, in the setup of Apple Computer's materials procurement team, mentioned previously, Cole Hamlin notes how they learned that "accountability is a critical element. . . . " One of their initial tasks was to develop a set of metrics measuring the worldwide supplier management organization in the areas of availability, cost, and quality. They then tied these metrics into their performance reviews and annual bonus plans. Team members, who continue to reside in their countries, receive their reviews and salary decisions from their local site managers, but these are based on the evaluations of their Team Leaders. But this local focus provides flexibility for differences in compensation systems worldwide, cultural biases, and other local norms."[11]

"The people factor"—everything from organizational politics to valuing diversity to managing borders—cannot be neglected when adopting world-class teams. In doing background research for a study on why cross-functional teams are successful, researchers Daniel R. Denison, Stuart Hart, and Joel Kahn found that: "Teams that were isolated, passive or overly technical were far less successful than teams that proactively managed the political dynamics of their client organization." They cited several studies to support their contention that effective new product development occurs when two conditions are present: "First, the requisite diversity of viewpoints, disciplines and functional specialties is represented in a team, and second, the team is able to span organizational boundaries and integrate the functional expertise represented by team members."[12]

A specific example cites a team in which the "chimney representatives who were members of the team came to this meeting with instructions from their bosses (who, incidentally, did their performance appraisals . . .) *not* to make any compromises, but to make certain that their chimney 'got what it needed' and didn't lose out." Their research strongly suggests that if a team is going to be successful, it must manage team members' needs to be functional representatives as well as team problem-solvers who take "collective responsibility for resolving a diverse set of demands."[13]

If you want to operate effectively on a world-class team (which, according to our definition, is both cross-functional and cross-cultural), you must become comfortable in working relationships that are fraught with ambiguity, with complex and multiple interconnections, and with potentially conflicting agendas; and, even when you have no formal authority and power, you must learn how to influence others to get what you need to deliver the results you promised. But, paraphrasing the lyric Frank Sinatra so often crooned about New York: "If you can make it there, you'll make it anywhere." Those who succeed on world-class teams are on a fast track to the future.

We asked members of a cross-functional/cross-cultural Pan-European team, after they had been working together for a year, to describe "What Euroteams Feel Like" using the categories indicated below. Here's what they said:

Sports

It's like cross-ocean/world-tour sailing (a sport that demands high-performance teams well versed in strategic planning, high-tech expertise and equipment, crisis management, ownership, flexibility, and team and individual responsibility).

Monuments

It's like the Atomium (a structure built for the Brussels World's Fair and familiar to all Europeans; represents strong and energetic structure, reflects matrix relationships).

Cities

It's like a "Europolis" (newly created city; represents "Champion City," multicultural, dynamic, loving change; empowered and fully employed employees).

A Natural Wonder

It's like Mont Blanc, the Mediterranean Sea, and the Blue Danube River (respectively, highest mountain in Europe, Mother of Europe, and longest river cutting across the maximum number of countries; as the team members indicated, "From the mountains to the sea via the river, Euroteams bridge the gap").

■ CRITICAL SUCCESS FACTORS FOR WORLD-CLASS TEAMS: LESSONS LEARNED

World-class teams require courage, persistence, and the ability to deal with ambiguity. There are no carved-in-stone rules and very few guidebooks to map out both their challenges and the strategies that will make them successful. The logic that guides world-class teams is different from that of traditional organizations, which valued hierarchy and authority of level. As we have expressed within this chapter, for world-class teams to succeed, we must change not only the structure, but also the processes and systems and, most important, *the way we think and act.*

For the most part, you will act as your own mapmaker when building your world-class teams, but you won't be traveling in entirely uncharted waters. Others have come before you, and their experiences point to several critical success factors. Before moving on to the nuts and bolts of building world-class teams, consider the following "Lessons Learned."

➤ Before teams start their work, senior executives need to participate in a systematic process to set teams up for success.

➤ Senior executives (sponsors) must provide visible support and commitment to the team.

➤ Teams need a clear Charter (mission) and set of Boundaries (roles and responsibilities).

➤ Key stakeholders need to participate in and support the team's Charter, Boundaries, and Goals, as well as projects, budgets, and so forth.

➤ Teams must develop their own internal roles, operating agreements, and guidelines for border management with key stakeholders.

➤ Country management/functional bosses of the team members must be committed to honoring/supporting team members' roles and responsibilities.

➤ Decisions must be made as to how the team's success will be measured.

➤ Team Leaders/members must be selected for their diversity and competency.

➤ Teams need communication processes and technologies.

➤ Teams must be held accountable for value-added results.

➤ The team and individual team members must receive rewards and recognition.

➤ Teams must receive training/development in teamwork skills, such as team communications, team goal setting, team problem solving, team decision making, and team facilitation.

➤ Individual team members, who must balance ongoing individual and team roles and responsibilities, must receive performance feedback and professional development opportunities.

➤ A territorial/silo culture threatens the formation and short-/long-term viability of cross-functional/cross-cultural teams.

➤ Not all work requires "real teams." However, if the work requires a real team structure, then a significant investment must be made in ongoing team development.

Chapter 2

World-Class Teams:
A Model for High Performance

Congratulations! So you're going to embark on the journey to create a world-class team. Where do you begin? Should you just name a Team Leader, choose some team members, and call a meeting? Given the "Lessons Learned" in the previous chapter, we hope you'll think twice about doing that!

But where and how do you begin? Over the years, we have taken the lessons *we* have learned and turned them into what we call a "World-Class Team Performance System." So much of the literature and tools for teams focus on the inner workings of the team. The system that we have found to be very useful with our client organizations is, in fact, comprised of interlocking components that integrate the process of how the team works within itself and the team's external relationships. In this chapter, we introduce you to the system and its key components. In later chapters, we will provide you with the "how-to" details of using the system to set up your world-class teams.

The World-Class Team Performance System can be used to:

➤ Help establish the structure and purpose of world-class teams.

➤ Provide guidelines for selecting team leaders/members.

➤ Launch new world-class teams.

➤ Establish a process for teams to work with key stakeholders in meeting their expectations.

➤ Assess the effectiveness of established teams (those that have been up and working for some time).

➤ Establish metrics for measuring a team's effectiveness.

➤ Provide guidance in helping world-class teams develop and manage themselves for high performance.

Toolkit 2.1 provides a graphic depiction of the World-Class Team Performance System, which is a series of progressive phases that world-class teams will go through to develop into high-performing teams.

Old Chinese saying: "When is the best time to plant a tree? Twenty years ago. When is the second best time to plant a tree? Today."

The first critical step in developing world-class teams is to "set them up for success." In the Senior Executive Team Set-Up stage, the sponsor and other key stakeholders hold team planning discussions to reach consensus on such issues as:

➤ The team's performance and business challenge.

➤ The team's structure.

➤ The team's Charter and Boundaries.

➤ Team Leader and team member selection.

➤ Strategies for management support and commitment.

➤ The team's measures of success.

➤ The team's key stakeholders' expectations and Operating Agreements.

Toolkit **2.1** World-Class Team Performance System

This process launches New Teams, who then go through a series of initial meetings to develop their team processes and structure and to determine the competencies needed for starting up their teams. Among the questions addressed are:

➤ What is the Team Charter? What are the Boundaries?
➤ What are the Team Goals?
➤ How will we manage borders with key stakeholders?
➤ What are our Team Values and Operating Agreements?
➤ What are our roles and responsibilities?

As world-class teams begin to work on their Team Goals and tasks, they concurrently should focus on how they will continuously improve their team competencies through some form of Team Development:

➤ How will we develop the Team Leader?
➤ What are the critical team member competencies and how should we develop them?
➤ How will we orient new team members?

As the team begins its work, members will want to periodically assess their performance not only in terms of *what they are accomplishing,* but also in terms of *how they are working.* The team may want to use the following tools and methodologies as aids:

➤ Team metrics (ROI, impact, and value) analysis.
➤ Team Process Survey.
➤ Team member 360° surveys.
➤ Linkage to MBO/compensation and incentives.

Finally, if you are an Established World-Class Team with some history, it may be helpful to take a more formal "time out" to assess your overall effectiveness through the use of:

➤ Senior Management/Stakeholder Assessment.
➤ Team Diagnostic Workshop.
➤ Team Effectiveness Plan of Action.

To complement our World-Class Team Performance System, we also have developed a Navigational Model (see Toolkit 2.2), which focuses on

2.2 Navigating World-Class Team Performance

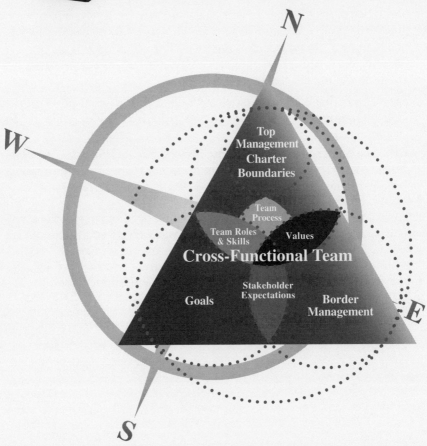

the fundamental principles that govern the success of world-class teams from the time of their "launch" and through their "life cycle":

➤ Top management must be intimately and consistently supportive of the team's Charter and Boundaries.

➤ There must be clarity and consensus—among the team, its Sponsors, and key stakeholders—about the team's Charter and Boundaries.

➤ The team's stakeholders must be clearly identified and their expectations of the team must be made explicit.

➤ There must be agreed-on goals and working arrangements between the team and its stakeholders in order to effectively manage the team's borders with those stakeholders.

➤ Each team member must know what roles he or she will play on the team and what knowledge, skills, and abilities he or she will need to perform and/or develop for success on the team.

➤ There must be specific team goals and clear accountabilities of team members for goal achievement.

➤ The team's Values must be explicit and translated into specific team Operating Agreements that will help the team manage its relationships.

➤ The team should have clearly identified Team Processes (communications, decision making, project management, and so forth) to help the team manage its tasks.

Again, these principles were developed through our research of successful world-class teams and others that have "failed." Highly successful world-class teams pay attention to and continuously manage and improve these core elements so as to navigate their journey through the uncharted and often turbulent waters created by their formation.

STRATEGY

1

Launching World-Class Teams

Chapter 3

The Role of Senior Executives
in a World-Class Team Setup

Too often, someone gets the idea to form a team, selects a Team Leader and some team members, issues a memorandum giving a few vague directives about what the team is supposed to accomplish, and essentially says, "Go ye forth and be a team." That's one way to go about it—but certainly not the *best* way if you want your world-class team to succeed.

Among the most critical factors that contribute to the success of world-class teams is how they are initially set up by the senior executives who will be their Champions and Sponsors. By actively involving senior management in the setup process, we can clarify the team's purpose, demonstrate top-level support and commitment to the team, and help anticipate boundary and border conflicts that may arise with other teams or functional units in the organization.

Among the issues that need to be resolved in the Team Setup phase of launching world-class teams are:

➤ Why has the team been formed? What business and performance challenges is this team intended to address?

➤ What is the organizational context in which this team will be operating? What are the competitive opportunities? How will the team prevent, fix, or enhance these opportunities?

➤ Who is the team's Sponsor or Champion?

➤ What is the broad outline of the team's Charter and Boundaries, i.e., its reason for existence and its levels of empowerment?

➤ Regarding the team's structure:
— What are the team's composition and size? Will these change over time?
— What are the team's, the Team Leader's, and the team members' reporting relationships?
— What amount of time is the Team Leader and each of the team members expected to contribute to the team?

—Who will select the Team Leader and team members, and on what basis?

—Who are *core* team members and who are *Associate* or *support* team members?

—How will we ensure an appropriate and relevant diversity of skills, knowledge, and representation on the team?

➤ Who are the team's key stakeholders? How should we involve them in the team's "launch" or formation?

➤ What kind of support and commitment must we initially provide to ensure a successful launch of this team?

➤ How will the team's performance be measured, managed, and rewarded?

The strategic process by which these issues are resolved is vital to the team's success. The process should be tailored to reflect the experience that the organization and its people have in setting up and launching world-class teams.

■ SETTING UP WORLD-CLASS TEAMS

So, you want to set up *teams*. . . .

Today, teams are "hot" and there are many good reasons why they are chosen as a competitive business strategy. Teams have proven to be a very effective tool for addressing complex organizational problems and achieving breakthrough results.

Once a decision has been made to move toward a team-based organizational structure, or even to develop one world-class team, a meeting of the senior executives who will be the Sponsors, the Champions, or the key stakeholders of the team(s) should be held to discuss and resolve issues that will ultimately affect the team's success.

Establishing a Team Setup Committee—including not only the team's Sponsor, but the highest ranking senior management group possible—not only guides the team's initial launch but is also a valuable way to build management's commitment to, and understanding of, the team's structure and process.

For example, at the start of a major team reorganization that created over fifteen global product teams, we facilitated a meeting of the senior management Sponsors of these teams, all the Global Product Team Leaders, and the Sponsor and Team Leaders for the product teams in the European region. This was the first time that these major stakeholders in the new team-based organizational structure had met in the same room to clarify their respective Charters (i.e., Mission Statements) and their roles and responsibilities. Senior management left that meeting with an appreciation for the complexity of the new team structure and an awareness of the need to establish clear guidelines, a mutually aligned goal-setting process, and other strategic elements.

Another example for setting up a team-based (cross-functional/cross-cultural) organizational structure stems from our work with the Latin America division of a major pharmaceuticals company. The countries within the division were facing the launch of many new products over the next several years. The Latin America Area President had determined that having a product team for each product would be unworkable. He recognized the need for product teams that would be responsible for coordinating the countries' product prelaunch and launch planning activities. His first action was to form a Steering Committee to design the team structure that would be required for Latin America.

In the Canadian division, we used yet another process, initiated by the country manager. We facilitated a diagnostic process by enlisting approximately 20 representatives from across the company to examine what a high-performance team organization would look like and what "performance gap" existed today. As a result of ongoing discussions among this group, which addressed key issues over a six-month period, the decision was made to move toward a radically different team-based organizational structure.

The sections below describe in more detail the issues that need to be resolved by senior executives and key stakeholders during the World-Class Team Setup phase.

➤ Identifying a Team's Performance and Business Challenge

Teams are groups of individuals who are committed to achieving a specific *Performance and Business Challenge.* In essence, this challenge is the business issue for which a world-class team has been selected and which it is chartered to address. Individuals who serve on teams want to believe that their contributions will make a significant difference to their organization's success. Therefore, the Performance and Business Challenge must be seen as aligned with and supporting the business's mission/vision.

For example, the Performance and Business Challenge established by one company's European product teams is: "To optimize product growth and P&L for Europe." Within the same company, Latin America Area Product Teams, which were formed to support five new products, stated their business rationale in this way:

> Our primary objectives for creating Area Product Teams in Latin America are to provide a structure for directing and coordinating all new product development activities in the Area, to enable all

our countries to ensure rapid and successful market penetration, and to serve as a coordinative partnership role with other strategic units (Headquarters R&D) in the global product development process.

With a mandate such as this, the Area Product Teams were clear from the outset about the critical importance of their work to the corporation.

Making the most of an organization's talent—wherever in the world it resides—is one of the potential benefits of cross-functional/cross-cultural teams. Conversely, one of the real dangers of the trend toward team-based organizations is to overdo their use. One regional manager in Argentina expressed this very cynically when he said that, in his mind, "Teams = Meetings ≠ Results." However, he added that his organization was facing many business challenges—improvement of productivity per employee, sales, market share, competitive ranking, and so forth—and if teams could create and achieve objectives to directly address these challenges, then he would be the first to support those teams.

➤ Defining the Team's Charter and Boundaries

The team's *Charter* sets forth the overall mandate of the team and the performance results the team is expected to accomplish. When a team is formed, the Sponsor(s) and possibly other key stakeholders should establish a broad Charter. At the same time, it is important that the team have "space" to customize the Charter and make it their own.

The team's Charter meets the following criteria:

➤ It describes why *this* team was selected to address the performance and business challenge.

➤ It defines the primary customer or client needs and expectations that the team's results will fulfill.

➤ It describes in broad terms the team's goals and responsibilities, and the processes by which the team will operate.

➤ It provides enough leeway to allow flexibility in implementation.

The team's *Boundaries* define the "playing field" on which the team operates:

➤ They define to whom the team *reports* and what it is specifically accountable to do (i.e., not only identifying to whom the Team Leader reports, but also making it clear that the team—not just the Team Leader—is accountable for team results).

➤ They define a "nonnegotiable" team operating framework that states:

   —Financial requirements.

   —Time-frame requirements.

   —Quality/Quantity requirements.

   —Resource limitations.

   —External/Internal regulations/policies.

   —Technical/Organizational requirements.

   —Team and cross-functional communication requirements.

➤ They define by whom and how the team and individual team members will be evaluated.

(See Chapter 4 for more detailed examples of how to develop a team's Charter and Boundary statements.)

The *Boundaries* also define the team's authority, i.e., its level of empowerment. They must explicitly state whether the team will be empowered to:

➤ Make its own decisions (and which ones).

➤ Manage its own budget.

➤ Provide recommendations.

➤ Implement decisions without further approval.

One world-class Team Leader summarized the essence of this issue when she asked: "Are we supposed to be *planning, doing,* or *facilitating?*" Nothing is more demotivating and discouraging to teams than to learn that they have assumed a higher level of team empowerment than their Champions/Sponsors believe they have been given.

Research indicates that the number one source of conflict on cross-functional teams centers on *goal or priority definition.* In today's multiproject environment, individuals find themselves serving on a variety of project teams while continuing to report to their functional managers. When organizational and team priorities are unclear, are not communicated effectively, or are ignored or frequently changed by senior executives, people become less productive team members. Therefore, agreeing to the team's Charter and Boundaries is a pivotal role for senior executives in the team's setup phase.

■ WHAT'S THE BEST TEAM STRUCTURE?

Before embarking on reorganizing your company, or a particular region or country, to a team-based structure, or before merely establishing one high-performance team, it is critical that you go through some process and dialogue to answer these questions:

> ➤ What structure is the "best fit" for your organization's strategies?

> ➤ What structure is most compatible with your organization's culture?

Keep in mind the organizational adage that "Form follows function." There is no one best team structure. Elements such as the team size, membership, and reporting relationships should be determined based on the team's Charter (why it exists in the first place) and the organizational context within which it will operate.

For example, one company formed a Latin America product team and assigned three to four marketing and medical representatives part-time to the team. The Team Leader was also part-time and reported to an Area Business Development Director. On the other side of the world, a similar product team was formed in Asia with a Team Leader and a medical representative, both of whom were full-time. This Team Leader reported to the Area President. In the end the Asian product team had a faster and more productive team launch, which may have been the result of early team-structure decisions.

➤ Team Size

How large can a world-class team be? Among those forming teams, often the tendency is to think, "The bigger the better." They are assuming that:

> ➤ More team members means more ideas and resources.

> ➤ The more important the project, the more people want to be, and should be, part of the team.

> ➤ The more people involved, the more buy-in the team will have for its existence/work.

> ➤ Having more people means less risk of leaving some important people off the team.

Despite those common assumptions, both experience and research indicate that the ideal size for a working team (the "core team," where final recommendations and decisions are made) is from six to ten people.

If a larger team is needed to accommodate expertise (or political) issues, subteams can be formed with core team members as the "chairs." For example, one European product team named its specialty marketing core team representative as the chair of a Specialty Sales Subcommittee that was made up of sales representatives from all over Europe and was charged with developing specific sales strategies for a new emerging market. When a core team expands into subteams, at any one time the number of people working on a team's issues or work products may be as large as thirty people who meet periodically to review team progress.

One Team Leader we work with was so concerned about maximizing participation on her team that she wanted to have a representative from each of the countries in her region, which would have resulted in an 18-member team. We encouraged her to create a core team of six to eight team members. She then created Associate members from the other countries. They were invited, but not required, to attend team meetings, and served as her key liaisons within their respective countries.

Another option for periodically involving persons who are key sources of expertise and information is to use them as "support groups" that the core team can seek out at various stages in the team's process and work. It is important, however, to recognize these individuals as "adjunct" team members and to not insist that they meet every time the core team meets or be included necessarily in all team decisions.

■ WHO PLAYS WHAT ROLE ON WORLD-CLASS TEAMS?

This section defines the basic attributes and "job responsibilities" for these key players on world-class teams: Sponsors, functional managers, Team Leaders, team members, and support functions or Associate team members.

➤ World-Class Team Sponsors

One or more team Sponsors should be publicly identified early in the setup process. The Sponsor may be an individual, such as an Area President, or a Steering Committee. In the Latin America example cited earlier in the chapter, the Steering Committee was made up of the Area President and his Business Development Director, Human Resources Director, and Medical Director for the Area.

Sponsors' responsibilities can include:

➤ Establishing the team's Charter and Boundaries.

➤ Selecting Team Leaders and members.

➤ Assigning a project to the team.

➤ Approving project priorities.

➤ Approving project plans and annual team objectives.

➤ Approving annual strategic/operating plans.

➤ Approving team resource allocation.

➤ Arbitrating team/stakeholder conflicts that need attention.

Sponsors may be drawn in to help address issues such as major deviations from the approved annual strategic/operating plan, conflicts related to project priorities that could not be resolved within the team, and boundary conflicts that could not be resolved with the stakeholders concerned. On the other hand, when we asked one executive-level world-class team in the publishing industry to describe what they wanted from their Sponsor, who was the president of the company, they said: "Nothing—unless asked. Just leave us alone and support our decisions."

In many teams, one individual is designated to be the Sponsor and acts as the day-to-day "operating boss." This individual usually serves as a member of the team's Steering Committee, which is typically a cross-functional senior management team whose functions are represented on the team. A word of caution: Don't fall into the trap of overlaying the team with another layer of management. The purpose in forming world-class teams is to empower the teams to make decisions and act on their own. The official designation of a Sponsor is geared toward ensuring top organizational support and linkages for the work of the team.

Gary Jortner, vice president of new product development for Pfizer Pharmaceuticals, expressed his view of his role as team Sponsor to one of his world-class Team Leaders in this way: "It's very simple. You take care of issues between you and your team members. If there are issues or other obstacles that you can't resolve, come to me and I'll work with you to figure out how to handle them." That may be an oversimplification, but, in his mind, he was empowering the Team Leader to act until she could not resolve border conflicts on her own, and acknowledging that, at that point, he would need to provide active support.

➤ Functional Managers

Functional managers are the department managers within the organization to whom the team members (particularly part-time team members) may report while also reporting to the Team Leader and performing team responsibilities. Functional managers assign individuals from their functional units to the teams and provide senior management linkage between the teams and the functional areas and/or countries (i.e., depending on whether the team is cross-functional, cross-cultural, or both). They may provide teams with resources as needed, support recommendations from the teams, and assist, as appropriate, in the implementation of functional area projects agreed on with the teams.

➤ World-Class Team Leaders

The Team Leader facilitates the establishment and accomplishment of the team's goals. He or she is responsible for ensuring that the team fulfills the team's Charter and operates within its stated Boundaries. The Team Leader is the team's point of contact with the Sponsor and other key stakeholder groups. The Team Leader coordinates the team's activities, clarifies the team's Boundaries, and helps to manage the team's borders. The Team Leader also may directly manage a specific function for the team, for example, its marketing activities. (See Chapter 9 for a more detailed description of selecting and developing Team Leaders.)

➤ World-Class Team Members

The composition of a team may vary during its life cycle. When determining who should be *core* team members, two primary considerations are: (1) the degree of the strategic contribution that a particular functional or country representative can bring to the team's performance; and (2) the need to keep the team size efficient and workable.

One Canadian company that formed regional product teams distinguished the core team membership for two stages of its products' life cycle, as illustrated in the following grid:

Functional Area	Filing/Prelaunch	Postlaunch
Team Leader	X	X
Product management	X	X
Medical communications	X	X
Regulatory	X	
Medical	X	X
Sales		X
Managed care		X

Each team member is accountable and responsible for identifying, securing, and directing the resources of his or her respective functional area. (See Chapter 7 for further detailed description of the roles and skills of team members.)

➤ Support Functions or Associate Team Members

Aside from the crucial functional or country/regional expertise that is represented through core team members, other organizations or functions may play important supporting roles in the team's success.

Individuals from these organizations or functions may be asked periodically to provide information or to respond to a team's request for their specific area of expertise. Because of the ad hoc nature of their contributions to the team, they are usually designated as Support or Associate team members.

It is important for a team to identify these roles and individuals as early as possible during the team's formation. As key stakeholders who will influence the team's success, they need to know their level and schedule of involvement so that they can effectively respond to the team's requirements and requests. It is equally important to review these team support roles periodically to ensure that individuals continue to be appropriately used. It may be helpful, depending on the nature of the team, to not even consider these resource and specialized people as team members. Instead, the team might think of them as providing specialized service support for the team and "contract" for the use of their services. (See Chapter 16 for some suggestions on contracting for team support services.)

Technical experts who provide consulting services to a team may go through periods of intense activity in supporting a world-class team. During such periods, they may attend several team meetings or spend much of their work effort on assisting with the team's projects. However, the core team should not expect them to attend all team meetings or functions.

■ SELECTING TEAM LEADERS AND TEAM MEMBERS

You know the exact Performance and Business Challenge your world-class team needs to meet. You've got the clearest of Charters, well-defined Boundaries, and the highest possible level of commitment from management. Even so, there's still no substitute for pulling together the right group of people to serve on a world-class team. In this section, we offer some guidance on selecting the most appropriate Team Leaders and team members as part of the Senior Executive Setup process. (Further details are provided in Chapters 7 through 10.)

➤ Team Leader Criteria

World-Class Team Leader responsibility carries with it both power and recognition, as well as visible accountability for the team's success. It is not a position that should necessarily go to the most senior person or even to the "expert" on the country or functional organizational charts. Although the Team Leader has high organizational visibility and accountability, to bolster the team's ultimate success the entire team must share in that visibility and accountability.

One group of senior executive Sponsors established the following set of competency criteria for selecting their world-class Team Leaders:

➤ Strategic perspective on business issues.

➤ Wide range of company knowledge and experience.

➤ Knowledge of the technical issues that the team will address.

➤ Team leadership skills.

➤ Project management skills.

➤ Change-agent skills.

➤ Problem-solving/Conflict resolution skills.

➤ Marketing/Selling skills.

➤ Political/Organizational sensitivity.

➤ Appropriate recognition by senior executives.

These criteria must be weighed against the context of the Performance and Business Challenge and the Charter of a particular team.

➤ Team Member Criteria

For teams to realize the full benefits of a team collaboration that combines individual expertise and knowledge from a variety of functions (and countries/cultures), those primary groups must be represented on the team, either through core membership or support group status. Team membership need not be restricted to company employees. Teams may select vendors, suppliers, customers, or other outside resources as core or "adjunct" team members.

In addition to their technical/functional expertise and experience, world-class team members should, in general, have the following competencies:

➤ Global orientation.

➤ Interpersonal skills.

➤ Multitask management skills.

➤ Team development skills (e.g., group decision making, conflict management).

➤ Planning and organizing.

➤ Initiative.

➤ Persistence.

➤ Customer orientation.

➤ Flexibility.

➤ Organizational sensitivity.

Again, the Performance and Business Challenge facing the team should drive the decisions about team member selection criteria.

Dr. Diana Bell, who has worldwide responsibility for one of Pfizer's global product development teams, offered this perspective on how team members are selected: "The requirements for team members are somewhat different in Asia, for example, than in Europe, beyond just the obvious cultural and language issues. In Asia we need a full-time medical person because of the need to expedite the registration process. We also need market research talent from people who understand the cultural attitudes about this product in the Asian marketplace."

An important caution in today's multiteam environment is *not* to overload your best "team players" by asking them to serve on too many teams. World-class team membership is an excellent strategy for developing less experienced employees and, if managed well, can enlarge the company's talent pool of people who can work effectively in a team environment. In fact, Pfizer believes that one of the primary benefits of forming global and area product teams is that it facilitates the development of an employee pool whose worldview encompasses both a functional and a cultural perspective, which in turn strengthens the company's goal to become a truly global organization.

Whatever the objectives served and the criteria used, senior executives need to communicate, to the team and the organization, the rationale for the decisions regarding selection of team members and leaders.

■ TEAM MEMBER TIME ALLOCATION

In planning and conducting their work, Team Leaders/members need to have clear expectations from senior executives regarding the time requirements for team participation. For example, a statement that "The Marketing Manager will devote 50 percent of his or her time to Team A" delivers a strong message that this team is important but assumes that the manager has responsibilities to other teams or functional activities, as opposed to someone who is expected to spend 100 percent on team responsibilities.

Our experience in reviewing the successes and frustrations of world-class teams over the years tells us that if there are part-time core team members, they should not commit less than 30 percent of their time to the team, and the optimum is an allocation of 50 percent or more time. Part-time team members should negotiate with their functional bosses to delegate some of their functional responsibilities to others, particularly if team time is allocated to be over 30 percent. If not, what often happens is that functional/country responsibilities and team responsibilities do not equal 100 percent but may, in fact, reach 120 to 150 percent!! Resentment, burnout, and low motivation may then develop among team members who are trying to meet the needs of "multiple masters," including their family and friends! We feel so strongly about the problems this issue creates, and about violations of "verbal agreements," that for long-term teams in particular, we suggest that some form of "contract" or "service agreement" be drawn up and signed by the team member, Team Leader, Sponsor, and functional manager.

A word of caution about part-time team members. When an individual works on multiple teams, several problems can result, such as:

➤ Conflicting priorities when multiple teams or multiple masters place requirements for resources, time, and so on, on the team member.

➤ Time management issues for the team member, who generally wants to meet all the demands placed on him or her.

➤ Justified or unjustified resentments of full-time team members who may see part-time team members as being not as fully committed.

These are natural tensions that arise in teams, and they should be anticipated and addressed early in each team's startup. As teams gain experience, they need to periodically review time management issues. Ideally, once team time allocations are agreed to, it is the responsibility of the team member—initially working with the Team Leader and his or her functional boss—to ensure that the allocation is appropriate and workable.

Other time-related issues that senior executives need to address include: relocation, travel time, and use of "virtual team" technology in relation to how and where the team will be working. Many of these operating decisions should be left up to the team, but if senior executives have clear expectations or assumptions, they should communicate them early on.

One world-class product team developed the following summary of some of its team membership decisions:

CORE TEAM MEMBERS

Core members will continue through product launch for all countries.

➤ For 1996, core member time allocation: 20–40 percent.

➤ For 1997, core member time allocation: 50 percent.

➤ Replace core team members, if necessary, in same functional skill.

All core team members attend every meeting.

ASSOCIATE TEAM MEMBERS

One Associate member per country.

➤ Can change as the team's needs change.

➤ 1996: 15–20 percent time allocation.

➤ 1997: 30 percent time allocation.

➤ Associates play key roles—they are individual countries' sources of team information, product champions, and places of local action.

Meeting attendance not always mandatory, but welcome.

■ DEVELOPING A TEAM LAUNCH DOCUMENT

Once a team's basic setup issues are resolved, we strongly suggest preparing a Team Launch Document that sets forth and formalizes the team's initial agreements. The document should be distributed to all team members, the team Sponsor(s), and key stakeholders, for their input and confirmation. Either in the document itself or in subsequent discussions, the Sponsor should be clear about which items are "non-negotiable" and the rationale for this position. For instance, to whom (and why) the team reports is sometimes a sensitive subject, particularly with virtual or matrixed teams that may have dual or multiple reporting relationships (e.g., to both the team and functional managers). Team members want to know where the "solid" and "dotted" reporting lines are.

A Team Launch Document is aimed at ensuring that everyone involved is operating from the same vantage point. It also can serve to raise new or overlooked issues, and may even point out certain disparities between team members' concerns and stakeholders' concerns that need to be addressed. For example, after a draft Team Launch Document was prepared and reviewed by a product team we worked with in Latin America, the team members put forth a series of questions that were clearly more operational in nature and focused on what team members *really* care about:

➤ Who will make the final decision to resolve conflicting priorities?

➤ Who will manage our budget?

➤ Who is responsible for the team's results—the team or the Team Leader?

➤ How will the support groups' responsibility to the team be measured and rewarded?

➤ How will team members be evaluated and rewarded?

The use of a Team Launch Document to communicate the decisions and agreements does not *guarantee* the success of world-class teams. But the document itself and the process of deliberation it inspires have proven to be highly effective means for reducing misunderstandings among the team and its Sponsors and stakeholders.

■ IDENTIFYING THE TEAM'S KEY STAKEHOLDERS' EXPECTATIONS

A world-class team's Charter is essentially to meet the needs/requirements of its key stakeholders. A *stakeholder* is an individual (or group) who is not a core member of the team itself, but who either directly or indirectly benefits from the work of the team, or is a critical contributor to the success of the team because of the expertise, resources, and/or organizational support the stakeholder can provide. Key stakeholder groups are usually defined as:

➤ *Sponsors/Champions/Steering committees.* The people who ultimately "own" accountability for the team's results and provide leadership and guidelines.

➤ *Support groups.* The people who provide information or expertise to the team.

➤ *Functional managers.* The organizational reporting relationships that team members maintain for functional work activities.

➤ *Customers/Clients.* Those people, internally or externally, who will directly benefit from the team's results.

Once a team's key stakeholders are identified, an essential step in the team's setup process is for the team and each of its stakeholder groups to define their mutual expectations. By openly sharing and discussing expectations, the team can establish mutually acceptable working guidelines with each of its stakeholder groups.

Teams have a variety of methodologies/approaches available for working with their stakeholder groups to define expectations. For some teams, a simple telephone call, an e-mail message, or a brief meeting with a stakeholder group may suffice. For others, the issues may be so complex that a major meeting of stakeholder group representatives may need to be held.

When we work with teams during these stakeholder meetings, we encourage explicit discussions between the team and stakeholder groups about their mutual expectations, and we suggest strategies for how to manage their respective "borders" (i.e., means of developing successful relationships with the stakeholders, defining their respective roles and responsibilities, determining the team's level of authority, establishing communications practices, and so forth).

(See Chapters 5 and 17 for a more detailed discussion and process for identifying and managing the team's borders with its key stakeholder groups.)

■ PROVIDING MANAGEMENT SUPPORT AND COMMITMENT

World-class teamwork requires real *work*. Teams face a variety of obstacles and pressures, such as time and budget limitations, changing expectations and objectives, and so forth. Although teams should have the major accountability for resolving such issues, they need to know that they can rely on the continuing support and commitment of their Champions/Sponsors.

Before the team starts its work, the senior executive Champions/Sponsors should determine their respective roles and responsibilities for supporting the team. In examining their roles, team Sponsors should ask their teams for feedback and should then decide what kind of leadership or process they will use to provide the team with:

➤ Visible organizational support for the team and its work.

➤ The resources (financial, time, human) that are required.

➤ The time the team will need with senior executives to review progress and discuss issues.

➤ Linkages to other resource/support groups.

➤ Individual and team recognition.

➤ A means for linking individual team members' contributions to compensation plans.

➤ Help in breaking down barriers and old paradigms.

➤ Opportunities to encourage shared learnings and "best practices" across world-class teams.

➤ A role model for "teamwork at the top."

One of the first actions of support, immediately following the team's setup phase, might be to allocate time for the team to attend a team development program to help the team to integrate senior executives' expectations for the team with their own, and to work through various team startup and team process issues. (See Chapter 7 for a discussion of team development options that are critical for world-class team success.)

One example of management support comes from a world-class team Sponsor who, approximately two months after the launch of three cross-functional/cross-cultural product teams in Europe, called for a meeting of the three Team Leaders to assess how well initial agreements were working and to resolve some of their "Open Issues." Among the issues discussed were:

➤ *Team objectives.* How will the corporate incentive compensation program be linked to team goals? How will the Team Leader work with local country management to ensure that team performance is included in team members' performance reviews?

➤ *Measures of success.* How will we know if the team concept is successful?

➤ *Team membership.* How will we resolve difficulties with getting countries to commit to providing team members? How will we work with country managers and functional managers to reconcile the work program for team members who have 25–50 percent time allocated to the team, but who are still spending 100 percent of their time on their current country/functional assignments? How can we ensure that team members will not be arbitrarily removed from the team by local country management (particularly without informing and involving the Team Leader!)?

➤ What should be the minimum length of the team assignment for both the Team Leaders and team members?

➤ How can we coordinate our work and roles with other organizational units so that our clients/customers do not perceive that we are duplicating efforts and wasting their time?

➤ What are some "creative" ways by which we can reward and recognize team members (i.e., beyond conventional incentives such as a promotion or raise)?

> How can the team make better use of technology and work process agreements to deal with remote site/distance management issues?

> What kind of *active* support and commitment do team members need, and what kind can they expect to get, from the Sponsor and senior management?

> What is the budget process? Will we be funded by corporate headquarters, by the Area, or by the countries?

> How do we get "buy-in" for the teams from the countries?

After the initial Team Leaders/Sponsor meeting, this group of Team Leaders met approximately four times throughout the year to share experiences and "best practices" and to mutually resolve issues that affected all three teams. These meetings were always attended by the team Sponsor, who was demonstrating, through these meetings, a true commitment to the team process and to its ultimate success.

On the flip side, we have seen teams that were launched without strong visible participation or support from the top senior executives, which naturally influenced the "buy-in" from other country or functional executives. For example, in one company, the president announced to his Management Committee that he wanted the organization to move forward toward creating world-class teams. He then proceeded to name as Team Leader, for one of the first teams, a woman who might have been the logical functional expert, but who openly voiced her opposition to teams and who did not attend the first team launch meeting. We later insisted that the president:

> Issue a memo announcing his rationale for and commitment to the teams.

> Either select a new Team Leader or meet with the present Team Leader to better understand and work through her resistance to the team concept.

> Attend the next team launch meeting himself, to further demonstrate his support.

Even if you choose not to prepare and distribute a full Team Launch Document, a comprehensive Team Announcement Memo can serve as an organizational announcement and a visible sign of senior-level commitment to the team structure.

Arguably, the best way for senior management to express commitment to teams is to be actively and visibly *involved*. Pedro Mata, a former senior vice president for W. R. Grace, has used cross-functional/cross-cultural teams successfully throughout his career. He makes the point that "support" from upper management feels like the proverbial lip service. "Senior management must *participate*," he says emphatically.

Team Sponsors and other senior managers also need feedback and recognition for their contributions and commitment to the team. After one world-class team's first meeting, the Team Leader sent her Sponsor the following note:

Charlie:

We all want to thank you for your active participation and support for the "startup" of our team.

As you know, it is critical, because of the complexity of this team's Charter, that the team know from the outset they have your personal commitment and support. Resulting from your presence and leadership, this team is convinced that their performance truly matters.

As we discussed in our meeting on Sunday, it is absolutely essential that you, I, and the Area President develop a strategy to communicate with and elicit the support of the regional/country managers for this team and its Charter. During our workshop, the team developed the framework and now they need the support from all of us to "sell it."

Again, thanks from all of us on the "V Team!"

Captain Christy

■ SHIFTING POWER TO WORLD-CLASS TEAMS

Paradoxically, senior managers who no longer want to use a traditional, hierarchical, and less authoritarian management style by moving toward empowered world-class teams must pay even closer attention to "authority issues." When they delegate authority to world-class teams, they may create, within other parts of the organization, a "power shift" that can destroy the very empowerment and participatory teamwork and collaboration they are hoping will be created with the teams.

This was the case, for example, with a major international bank that formed a cross-functional/cross-cultural team to examine the feasibility of developing a global technology platform. The team was made up of

worldwide representatives from information technology, private banking, commercial lending, human resources, and various other functions.
Soon after the team's launch, there were grumblings from senior managers within several of these functions who were not selected for the
team. They felt threatened and were anxious about the team's "authority." They worried that it would erode their own levels of control.

To avoid creating unproductive and dysfunctional teams, senior executives must, from the outset:

➤ Communicate to all stakeholders why the formation of a particular team is critical for addressing key business challenges.

➤ Create clear Charters and levels of authority and empowerment
(Boundaries).

➤ Help to manage the team's identity.

➤ Create effective task and political parameters to ensure productive work.

➤ Actively participate in the creation of the Team Launch Document.

➤ Encourage Team Leaders to attend Team Leader development
sessions.

(For a comprehensive checklist of "Questions to Ask" when you're
setting up world-class teams, see Toolkit 3.1.)

We started this chapter by imploring senior management to not take
lightly the need for their active involvement not only in setting up a
world-class team for success, but also in ensuring ongoing support. On
the other hand, we do not want to imply that the process of setting up
world-class teams is so complex and laborious that it begs the question:
"Are world-class teams worth the effort?"

There is nothing magical in why these teams succeed. It comes
down to establishing a strong foundation of basic building blocks and
skills that can be continually enhanced as the team develops.

For anyone who has played team sports or worked with a personal
coach, whether making $5 million a year playing for the NFL or just
staying in shape, success comes from learning the fundamentals and
paying relentless attention to them. We think nothing about investing
in coaches who set up a training schedule and a game plan and devot-
edly urge "Practice, practice, practice" before entering the game. The
same principles should apply to developing a world-class team. Investing in a formal setup process and training regimen goes a long way toward preparing a team of highly talented and compensated knowledge
workers for *their* game.

3.1   Questions to Ask

TEAM SETUP

- Who creates the team?
- Who is the team's Sponsor/Champion?
- Whom does the team report to?
- What Performance and Business Challenge is this team intended to address?
- How will the team relate to other organizational units? Will it eliminate some functional roles? Is the team in a matrix reporting relationship? With whom?
- Who assigns team members?
- Who selects the Team Leader?
- What are the roles and responsibilities of team members?
- Does the Team Leader (and do team members) have a full-time or part-time responsibility?
- What is the role and job description of a Team Leader?
- What are the selection criteria for a Team Leader and team members?
- What authority and responsibility are vested in the team and the Team Leader?
- How will individuals allocate their time to the team versus their other functional responsibilities?
- Who establishes the team Charter and Boundaries?
- Who measures overall team performance?
- Who allocates resources to the team? Does the team have its own budget?
- What is the relationship of the team to the functional areas? To other teams?
- What is the optimum size for this team?
- What determines core versus extended or ad hoc team membership? Does it change over time?
- What is the relationship between core and extended team members?
- Who establishes team priorities?
- Who arbitrates individual priorities for team members who serve on two or more teams?
- Who manages the team borders with other areas in the organization?
- How can limited company resources be shared effectively by multiple teams?

(Continued)

Toolkit 3.1 *(Continued)*

➤ What authority and responsibility are implied by a dotted-line reporting relationship?

➤ Does the team have continuous team members, or does the core membership change as the objectives change?

➤ Who are the key stakeholders and what are their expectations of the team? What does the team expect of them?

➤ How will cross-functional/cross-cultural conflicts and priorities be resolved?

TEAM CHARTER AND BOUNDARIES

➤ What is the team's Charter?

➤ What will this team uniquely contribute to the organization?

➤ What are the team's Boundaries? What are team members empowered to do? What is off-limits?

➤ What is the team name? Its identity?

TEAM PROCESSES

➤ What processes help teams improve productivity and effectiveness?

➤ How can the team improve internal and external communications?

➤ How often should teams meet, and which formats work particularly well for team meetings?

➤ Do the team members need to meet face-to-face? Can we use technology to facilitate team meetings?

➤ What written reports should teams produce?

➤ What processes encourage and support synergy within teams and between teams?

➤ How do teams manage allocated resources?

➤ What processes can be used to help teams evolve and continually improve?

➤ What are the team's Values?

➤ What is the team's budget? Is the team responsible for managing it?

TEAM PERFORMANCE MANAGEMENT

➤ How should team performance be motivated and team loyalty encouraged?

➤ How should outstanding performance by a team and by team members be recognized and rewarded?

Toolkit 3.1 *(Continued)*

➤ How should team results and individual team members' performance be measured?

➤ Who evaluates team member/Team Leader performance?

➤ How should an individual's team performance be linked to the company's compensation plan?

➤ What are the team's goals? What are its objectives? What are its key activities for the current year and for two to three years from now?

➤ Should all core team members' objectives be team-related objectives?

➤ How should the team celebrate its successes?

➤ By what process does the team evaluate its "internal" effectiveness (e.g., team member assessment, follow-up Team Leader development sessions, process observers)?

➤ How will the success of the team concept be measured?

TEAM TRAINING

➤ What skills are required for both team members and Team Leaders to perform on this team?

➤ What training programs are available to develop these skills?

➤ What would be a recommended training syllabus for the teams?

Chapter 4

World-Class Team Charter and Boundaries

We were called in by a senior executive who wanted to set up world-class teams. He indicated that he wanted to do some "training" for these teams before they got started. So we sat down and tried to better understand his request by asking him:

➤ Have you really thought about why you need these teams?

➤ Have you selected team members yet? How do you know they are the *right* team members for *these* teams?

➤ What are these teams supposed to *do?*

➤ Have you identified the key people who would have a vested interest in the team results? Have you sat down with these key stakeholders? Why would they support these teams? Do they even know about the teams?

After hearing our barrage of questions—and being able to answer only a few—he finally concluded: "Looks like we've got a lot of work to do to get everyone on the same page, don't we?" It was apparent that he hadn't thought through how complex team setup was going to be, but he wasn't daunted: "All right, then. Fix me up a proposal and let's get started."

As we noted in Chapter 3, forming a team seems to be the "*in* thing" to do these days when management is faced with a complex business issue. Unfortunately, too often, those individuals who are sent off to serve on teams are asking themselves, after several meetings: "Why were we formed, anyway?" "Who *really* cares about what we're doing?" "Just what *can* we do?" "How do I tell my boss the team wants me to attend *another* meeting?" And on and on. Such questions are symptomatic of cross-functional/cross-cultural teams that do not have a clear Charter and Boundaries. We have found that the first opportunity for success, among teams aspiring to be world-class, is the point at which they can clarify and gain consensus—among themselves and with their stakeholders—on their Charter and Boundaries.

■ THE TEAM CHARTER—ITS "RAISON D'ÊTRE"

The French have a wonderful phrase to describe why a world-class team has been formed: *raison d'être*—that is, its reason for existence. In organizational language, this is often referred to as a Mission Statement. From the outset, a world-class team, its Sponsor(s), and its key stakeholders need to be very clear and consensual about why *this* world-class team has been formed. Reaching a common understanding about what this team is intended to accomplish, distinct from any other organizational unit, is the first step in transforming a working group of individuals into a world-class team.

A team is a group of individuals who are committed to achieving a common goal. If the group of individuals who have been asked to serve on a team cannot agree on why the team exists, and for what they will be mutually accountable, it will be very difficult for them to work effectively and get successful results. Have you ever heard the adage: "Ask a team to draw an elephant, and you're bound to get a camel?" That's the kind of cynicism that can surface when a team lacks shared purpose and accountability.

We saw firsthand the power that comes from a process through which people decide to hold themselves mutually accountable. We were working with a newly formed team at their first team launch meeting. The team was made up of some people who had worked together loosely in the past and "strangers" (people unknown to each other before the meeting). They had been ordered from on high that they were now a *global team,* yet many of them saw no value in the team and, in fact, had protested openly about coming to the meeting.

We started the meeting by asking senior management to reintroduce *why* the team had been formed and what team members were expected to accomplish. The presentation clarified the team's structure and described how each person would be expected to contribute (and why each was valuable) to the team as a whole and to the corporation. For many, this was the first time they had heard *why* this team, which represented both different functions and different areas of the world, was important to the corporation. Their own functional/country bosses had not communicated the message.

Teams need a Performance and Business Challenge that focuses the value they will provide.

At the point in the meeting when it was time to create the team's Charter, we formed subgroups to provide input into the Charter content, within the parameters provided by senior management. We "co-opted" three or four of the most resistant team members and gave them important roles in the process. We selected the most vocally resistant team member to present the draft Charter statement to the entire group the next day. He read it with pride and proceeded to facilitate a productive discussion with the entire team about their mutual commitment to the goals. There was a lot of discussion about the *words* of the Charter—what they meant and whether the team wanted to unify under that banner. They examined its ramifications in the business and how they would have to go about integrating potentially conflicting interests (functional versus country managers) to achieve the Charter. Ultimately, it was that discussion that brought them together. The Charter was ratified by everyone, and all agreed that the experience had been team-building as well.

For some teams, the idea of spending time preparing a team Charter appears to be a tedious and seemingly meaningless process. They would rather get on with the "real" work of the team. However, a team's Charter is the touchstone that will help to keep the team focused and can serve as its "calling card" when it needs to cross its internal team borders and seek resources from outside the team.

In the video *Power of Vision,* Joel Barker talks about the importance of having a vision. He makes the point that countries, companies, and individuals alike flounder without a clear sense of purpose and direction because it is in our nature to want to make a difference. Instilling that element of "making a difference" into the team, collectively and individually, is precisely what the team Charter is intended to accomplish. By introducing direction, focus, and energy, it becomes clear that the team's performance matters.

A well-defined Charter and statement of Boundaries will:

➤ Clarify why the team exists and what it is expected to do.

➤ Build a shared commitment and purpose among the team members.

➤ Ensure organizational alignment within the team and with all the other organizational units with which it interfaces.

➤ Define the team's domain—the "playing field" on which it will conduct its business.

➤ Develop an explicit understanding of the role/responsibilities and authority or empowerment of the team, in order to provide energy and direction.

"No, I don't think our marriage would benefit from a mission statement."

➤ Provide a driving focus for team goal setting.

➤ Serve as a basis for measuring the team's success.

As suggested in Chapter 3, a broad outline of a team's Charter and Boundaries should be developed by the senior executives who are sponsoring the team. They should identify what the team is account- able for contributing to the organization that is unique and distinctive from the contribution of any other organizational unit. If they cannot, then there is a serious question as to whether the team should be formed in the first place.

An essential ingredient of the Charter is its identification of the dis- tinctive competency or competencies of the team (vis-à-vis other organi- zational units). A team's distinctiveness may be a function of the products or services offered, or of being a low-cost producer, or of providing supe- rior service. In the process of identifying its distinctive competencies, the organization can focus its energies and resources to move in a particular direction. The Charter also helps provide a rallying point for both Team Leaders and team members.

Think about your team in light of these questions: If I were your investment banker, why should I invest in you? What value and accomplishments do you contribute to the organization that are unique from those of any other unit? What is your overall purpose? Why do you exist? What types of products/services will you provide? What quality or attribute sets you apart from your internal or external competitors? How are you, or will you be, different from the rest of the pack? Who are the stakeholders you serve? What do they need/expect from you?

■ WORLD-CLASS TEAM CHARTER CRITERIA

Whether the world-class team has been given a broad mission statement by the people who created it, or its mission is left to the team to develop, the team Charter should meet certain criteria. It should:

➤ Be clear and understandable.

➤ Be brief enough to be memorable.

➤ Be specific about the business of the team, including:

—Who the team's primary customers or clients are.

—What customer/client needs the team is attempting to meet.

➤ Reflect the team's distinctive competency and the results or contributions that others expect from the team.

➤ Be aligned with the larger organization's mission, vision, values, and culture.

➤ Be broad enough to allow flexibility in implementation.

➤ Have primarily a single strategic focus that is attainable.

➤ Serve as a framework for making organizational decisions.

➤ Demonstrate the team's opportunity to provide added-value contributions.

➤ Serve as a template by which the team can make decisions.

➤ Be worded to serve as a source of energy and motivation for the team.

Does your team have a team Charter? If so, does it meet the team Charter criteria? If not, why don't you suggest that the team write one at its next meeting?

The Charter should be brief (typically, a hundred words or less) and should clearly identify the organization's basic business. The Charter, which should be well known and understood by all members of the team, answers the questions of what the organization does, for whom, and how. It also identifies the organization's major strategic driving force. By answering these questions for both internal and external use, the organization team can chart its course of action and provide a guide for making routine day-by-day decisions.

Here is an example of one team's Charter:

Our team's Charter is to recommend a new process for selecting research projects and priorities from site proposals around the world.

Notice that the reason that the team exists is to make a *recommendation* for the new process. It has not been formed for the purpose of *deciding upon* "research projects and priorities." Nor has it been formed (at this stage at least) to *implement a process for selecting* "research projects and priorities."

Here is another example:

The Product Assurance Team will be a focused executive decision-making team mandated to maintain product supply and integrity.

This example is from a team that wanted to make a very clear statement about its level of authority (decision making) in its Charter. This was done explicitly because the organization had a culture of upper management control and indecisiveness and cross-functional conflict. Team members wanted to communicate that the proverbial "cross-functional buck" stopped with them. Their Charter went on to delineate specific issues that the team would be responsible and accountable for managing.

How would you rewrite your team's Charter to better reflect the criteria for a team Charter?

A team Charter should be kept focused and concise, but it can encompass various ideas and aspects of the team's purpose. Here's a slightly longer example:

The worldwide Pharmaceuticals Development and Training Team provides consultative diagnostic and developmental resources to improve the Company's worldwide performance. We contribute to achieving our Company's goals by actively supporting the development of a culture based on accountability and empowerment. We will accomplish this by working in close

4.1 Sample World-Class Team Charters

Our team will pioneer—explore and introduce—new modes of working, across Europe, to prepare the best platform for the commercial success of the accelerated launch. It will form a collaborative partnership with *all* European countries and create the necessary conditions for a successful European alliance.

* * * * *

Our team is a proactive multicountry team formed for the purpose of ensuring the success of our product in Europe by working in close cooperation with headquarters, R&D, and the European countries. We provide:

➤ A European-based center of expertise/excellence for our product.

➤ Close support and guidance for countries for the product's medical/marketing initiatives.

➤ Synergies through cross-border working.

➤ A developmental model for high-performance cross-functional/cross-cultural teams.

* * * * *

Our team's challenge is to make our product number one in its product category in Latin America by 2001. We will initiate and facilitate additional and collaborative areawide projects of value to the product; cross-fertilize strategies, programs, and ideas for Latin American countries; and coordinate and focus Latin American input for corporate product planning.

---

partnership with our clients to develop solutions that address market needs and business objectives.

Other examples of world-class team Charters are given in Toolkit 4.1.

Although, as we mentioned in Chapter 3, senior managers should set the broad Charter for a world-class team, they also need to provide "Charter space." That is, even as they define the scope and boundaries of the team's effort in order to provide direction, they should allow enough flexibility for modifications by the team as part of its development and commitment-building process.

For example, in one area that was moving from a traditional hierarchical/functional organizational structure to an Area team-based structure, the Steering Committee, which formed the teams, established the following Charter:

To achieve and maintain a market leadership position for the assigned Therapeutic Team products.

One of the three Area teams took this parameter and created its own Charter, which read:

The Area team will guide the development, marketing, and support for each product to ensure that each achieves its maximum commercial potential and becomes a market leader in Mexico and Central America. The team will establish medical and marketing objectives and strategies in all support areas to ensure an increase in sales and product market share.

In another organization, a world-class team was formed because there were problems in providing and maintaining an adequate supply of quality product to the sales force. In the process of developing the team's Charter, we asked these questions, "Why would you want to create this team? What problems will it resolve? How will the organization be better or different in a year as a result of this team?" (The team's answers resulted in the Charter shown on p. 58 for the worldwide Pharmaceuticals Development and Training Team.)

Remember that Charters and Boundary Statements are not the Ten Commandments absolute and written in stone. A world-class team is established to address a particular organizational or marketplace challenge. As the team achieves its goals and the internal or external forces shift, the reason for the team's existence should be challenged and perhaps redefined. Over time, the Charter changes.

For example, one European product team was formed because, although the product had been successfully launched in the United Kingdom, two other major markets needed focused attention. After 18 months, having achieved the launch objectives in these new major markets, the Sponsor and Team Leader began to question the team's continued existence. As a result of this examination, it was determined that the team should continue to exist, but with fewer team members, and that the Team Leader could add another product to his portfolio, which led to a reworking of the original Charter.

■ WHAT ARE WORLD-CLASS TEAM BOUNDARIES?

A world-class team's Boundaries are the limits within which a team can conduct its business and accomplish its objectives. They define the team's roles and responsibilities, its level of empowerment or authority, the areas that can be addressed by the team, and any areas that are off limits. Just as we need clarity on what a team does for a living, we also need to be clear about those areas of responsibility that belong to others, or about issues and organizational boundaries that just won't get addressed by the team.

The definition of empowerment is to "invest with power, especially legal power or authority." An organization that encourages empowerment of its world-class teams creates an environment in which people are aligned with the business direction and understand their performance boundaries, thus enabling them to take responsibility and ownership for identifying the best course of action, and initiating the necessary steps to achieve their organizational results.

AUTHORITY in the "boundaryless" organization is not about control—it is about the containment of conflicts and anxieties that disrupt creativity and productivity.

As traditional organizational boundaries decrease, differences (and conflicts) of authority, talent, and perspective may, in fact, increase.

At a tactical level, you have to (1) get the structure in place for the team—that is, define the Charter and Boundaries—and (2) empower the team within its designated boundaries. In other words, define the playing field, then let the team go at it.

It is critical that your team answer the question: "What are we empowered to do?" Some teams may seek the answer to this question from those who have given the team its Charter. Other teams will assume full empowerment and test whether there are limits as they move forward with their work. Four significant types of Boundaries should be addressed:

1. The *Authority Boundary*.   What can we really *do?* Do we have the empowerment to make decisions? Implement?

2. The *Task Boundary*.   What exactly are we in charge of? Do any other teams think they are in charge of this task also? Which activities and decisions are "ours" versus "theirs" (i.e., other teams or work units)?

3. The *Identity Boundary*.   Who is "in" and who isn't? Who are core team members and who are Associates?

4. The *Political Boundary*.   Who are the stakeholders that matter? Whom must we serve? What's in it for them if they buy into our Charter?

You may also want to address any parameters or special conditions or constraints you must work within, such as budgets, time, or resources. When reviewing your Charter and Boundary statements, it is critical that you reflect on these questions, whether or not you specifically address them in your written documents.

Stakeholder Charter/Boundary Exercise

➤ Here's why we think we exist, and what we're accountable for and empowered to do.

➤ Here's why we think you exist and what you're accountable for and empowered to do.

➤ Here's what's off limits for us both.

Often, when global teams are made up of three to four key organizational units (i.e., functional or geographic), "subteams" within the larger team may not be clear about their Boundaries vis-à-vis the other subteams. This exercise can be used to clarify the fuzziness of roles/responsibilities among these units and avoid border skirmishes. It can also be used when forming a new team to assume roles that other units previously performed.

If a team has certain established and explicit constraints, it is important to identify those limits in advance so that they can be factored into the team's thinking and decision making. For example, one team's recommendations may have to be approved by all stakeholders who will be affected by the implementation, whereas another team's can be implemented by the team without higher approval. In each instance, Boundary differences must be understood.

At your next team meeting, test agreement among your team members about your "limits of authority." Ask whether you need to "test" these limits with your key stakeholders/Sponsor.

When setting Boundaries, a key step is to identify the minimal nonnegotiable framework within which the team must operate. Some people advise that a team (and its Sponsors and stakeholders) should avoid setting too many, or overly restrictive, Boundaries because that tightness may negatively impact the team's creativity or motivation. However, in our experience working with teams, we have never actually seen that happen. In fact, we find that looseness or lack of definition of the team's roles and responsibilities causes the problem. A team's creativity and resourcefulness can be unleashed once its boundaries are clearly defined.

Toolkit 4.2 shows some examples of team Boundaries (including some that are off-limits!).

Once the more formal process of establishing the team's Charter and Boundaries has been completed, some teams decide to add a "light touch" by establishing a "team identity" or "team slogan." This serves as a summary of its

4.2   Sample World-Class Team Boundary Statements

The following examples, which were developed by two different world-class product teams, illustrate some of the various areas that teams may focus on when identifying their particular set of Boundaries.

EUROPEAN PRODUCT TEAM

What is the team empowered to do? We can:

➤ Identify needs, and analyze and share valuable information across Europe.

➤ Initiate collaborative programs.

➤ Obtain clear commitments (including budget) from countries and headquarters product teams.

➤ Administer and budget projects across participating countries.

➤ Optimize team members' time management.

➤ Sell the benefits and successes of the team.

➤ Recommend to management ways to optimize the Euroteam concept.

➤ Learn from, and contribute to, other Euroteams.

What is "off limits" for the team? We cannot:

➤ Implement projects without country approval and support.

➤ Execute country-specific initiatives.

➤ Duplicate or substitute headquarters activities.

➤ Contravene country, European, or company guidelines or practices.

➤ Exert excessive team member effort on local country or Euroteam commitments.

*   *   *   *   *

AREA PRODUCT TEAM

What is the team empowered to do? We can:

➤ Identify and recommend Area opportunities for market development.

➤ Develop and recommend Area premarketing and marketing strategies and activities.

➤ Design, adapt, and implement market research plans.

➤ Determine, based on market research, the specific needs in the market, and develop appropriate strategies and programs to meet those needs.

➤ Develop product-sourcing strategies.

Toolkit 4.2 *(Continued)*

➤ Recommend customer-driven packaging preferences.

➤ Develop and recommend Area pricing strategies.

➤ Review and customize global marketing strategies for adaptation and implementation in the Area.

➤ Identify and alert corporate headquarters about Area problems and issues that have global commercial and public relations impact/implications.

➤ Create, advocate, and help implement the (realistic and optimistic) vision of the product's commercial success in the Area.

What is "off limits" for the team? We cannot:

➤ Plan and implement team activities outside of the Area.

➤ Engage in strategies or programs that are inconsistent with global product strategies without justification and approval from the Area vice president and headquarters.

➤ Finalize decisions on pricing, sourcing, packaging, and so on.

➤ Duplicate activities of headquarters or countries.

➤ Undertake activities in countries without notifying appropriate country personnel.

➤ Get involved in country operational management (e.g., set country sales targets, goals, objectives).

Charter and can be used as a motto for team members and as an internal marketing tool. The slogan is also an opportunity to incorporate some of the team's Values (see Chapter 6). Along with a slogan, a team might select a logo or even an animal "mascot," like sports teams do, as a visual representation.

After your team has developed its Charter and Boundaries, have them complete the following team identity exercise, either at the end of the Charter/Boundaries discussion or at the start of the next team meeting:

➤ Brainstorm ideas for a possible slogan for your team. Refer to your team Values. Do not criticize or evaluate any ideas at this point. Record all ideas on a flipchart.

➤ Review the list of ideas, eliminating any that are inconsistent with the Charter or not reflective of the team's Values. Then divide the group into pairs or trios and have them create a slogan (perhaps with a logo or other graphic) that best represents their Charter/Values and unique identity.

➤ Have each group present its ideas, and encourage a "like/dislike" analysis of each idea. Either have the team vote for a favorite, or draw from the best of each group's ideas to create another option.

■ READING FROM THE SAME PAGE

Earlier in this chapter, we mentioned how some team members just want to "get on with the work." Spending time attending to issues that provide for team structure—which we believe is essential for teams—seems inconsequential or irrelevant to them.

This reaction to structure and process was visibly and vividly demonstrated to us one day when we were facilitating a Scot, a Frenchman, and two Americans at a Team Setup Meeting. The Scot had bought into the idea of a team Charter and, in fact, provided the first draft. The Frenchman was tolerant of the process of developing a team Charter and Boundaries, but the thought of spending yet another day to work out Operating Agreements and goals presented him with too much structure. He was more comfortable operating in the "white spaces" of the organization. One of the Americans had participated in the session only because he didn't want to be left out of the loop. His reaction was like that of the Frenchman; another day spent on team processes was totally unacceptable.

So why bother? Organizational research tells us that when there are organizational and individual conflicts, nearly 35 percent of them revolve around misunderstandings about roles and responsibilities. If there is ambiguity about role expectations, people become confused, resentful, demotivated, and cynical. These are the potentially crippling forces that can invade your team unless roles and responsibilities are spelled out from the start and are continually reassessed over time.

As we move from the hierarchical and "smokestack" organizations, which have seemingly impenetrable walls between work units and functions, to more Boundary-less organizations, the issue of authority or empowerment needs to be more openly and explicitly discussed. The purpose in setting forth a team Charter and a set of Boundaries is not about *control*. These tools are intended to help contain the conflicts and anxieties that disrupt creativity and productivity. Their purpose is not to hinder, but to *help* "get on with the work" in a way that facilitates high performance, gratifying work experiences, and successful results.

Chapter

Aligning with World-Class Team Stakeholders

World-class teams do not exist in a vacuum. They are formed to address critical business issues and to fulfill specific Charters for their organizations. To do so, they must develop relationships and linkages with other units and individuals both internal and external to the team, and perhaps even outside the organization. These *stakeholders* are the people whose needs the team must meet and who can influence the outcomes of the team's work and, ultimately, its success.

Stakeholders come in all shapes and sizes. Some, like the Sponsor or Steering Committee who formed the team, have a high degree of interest in the team's projects. Others may be needed for resources or support, but will not be directly affected by the team's results and thus may have little vested interest in the team's activities. Team members themselves are stakeholders, but the roles we will examine in this chapter are those played by people outside the core team. To effectively manage the relationships with people in these roles, the team will cross several borders and may have to endure the inevitable border skirmishes and politics that nations and tribes have been dealing with for centuries.

■ WORLD-CLASS TEAM KEY STAKEHOLDER ROLES

Early in a world-class team's formation, the key stakeholders are identified by asking the question: *With whom do we need to work in order for our team to be successful?* We briefly described these potential stakeholders in Chapter 3. Listed below in more detail are the key roles that various stakeholders might play with the team. Although we are describing these stakeholder roles as discrete, some individuals may play more than one role in relation to a particular team.

➤ The Owners

These are the senior executives who take responsibility for forming the team and who ultimately are accountable for the team's performance. We often refer to an individual in this role as either a Sponsor or a Champion. If a group has the role, the members are often called a Steering Committee or Sponsor Group. At Virgin Atlantic Airlines, we determined that the Champion for the world-class teams was, in fact, Richard Branson, the company's well-known, highly publicized cheerleader. However, because Branson's widespread responsibilities precluded him from direct, active involvement with the teams, line managers from his Management Committee were selected as Sponsors.

The Owners provide the team with guidance, direction, and leadership. They have the authority to help the team remove roadblocks or detour around them. The Owners help network the team to resource people and will help build support for the team's existence and enhance its ability to achieve its Charter. Most Owners do not want to be involved in the day-to-day work and decisions of the team. They generally want to be contacted if questions arise regarding rules, regulations, and Boundaries, or if additional assistance or guidance is needed by the team.

➤ The Customers/Clients

These are the people, either internal or external to the organization, who will directly benefit from the team's accomplishing its Charter and Goals. They are the group to whom the team is ultimately accountable, although the team does not have formal reporting responsibility to them. As an example, for a regional pharmaceutical products team charged with maximizing the commercial success of products in their geographic markets, the ultimate customers are patients and doctors. But further up the "food chain" you find Opinion Leaders (external experts) and the company's internal sales force, both of whom could also be considered the team's customers.

➤ The Functional Managers

These are the department managers (and perhaps *their* bosses) to whom individual team members may continue to report while also working on team activities. The managers may reside in the country that "hosts" the team, or in a wide variety of countries. Whether the team assignment requires full-time or part-time participation, functional managers cannot be ignored. They provide linkage to ongoing functional or country activities, and they continue to influence individual team members' work priorities and compensation. Many team members would consider their functional bosses to be their single most important stakeholders and, as such, they would represent the most important border for the team members to manage.

➤ The Support Groups

These professional specialists provide expertise, information, or other resources, as required by the team. They are usually not permanent members of the team, but may be called on to perform specific tasks for the team or to attend some team meetings.

Let's look, for example, at the specific job titles of individuals who perform key stakeholder roles and functions for a world-class Regional Product Team that has responsibility for product marketing in Latin America:

Senior Management Owners

➤ Latin America Area President.

➤ Latin America Director of Business Development.

➤ Latin America Director of Medical Operations.

➤ Latin America Human Resources Director.

Customers/Clients

➤ Country Manager.

➤ Medical Director.

➤ Pharmaceutical Division Manager (Market Research, Marketing, Health Outcomes).

➤ Manufacturing Director.

➤ Regulatory Director.

➤ Product Champion.

Functional Managers

➤ Direct bosses of team members, representing various functions in team members' host/resident countries.

Support Groups

➤ Central Research Team.

➤ Global Product Team (NY).

➤ Manufacturing.

➤ Pricing.

➤ Public Affairs.

➤ Other Area teams (Asia, Europe, United States, etc.).

External Customers

➤ Opinion Leaders.

➤ Physicians.

➤ Patients.

As we learned in Chapter 3, once the key stakeholders are identified, it is critical that the team, working eventually with its key stakeholders, go through some kind of process to answer these questions:

➤ What are the critical needs/expectations that the stakeholder group has of us?

➤ Do the stakeholders agree on the team's Charter?

➤ Do we agree on the roles/responsibilities and goals of the team?

➤ What expectations do we have of the stakeholders?

➤ How can we arrive at mutually agreeable expectations/operating agreements?

➤ What help do we need (resources, support, expertise) from the stakeholders?

➤ What's in it for them (WIIFT) to work positively with our team?

➤ What obstacles might we face in working with the stakeholders?

➤ What strategies should we use to overcome obstacles and to deliver value to the stakeholders?

➤ Who should be the border manager for a particular stakeholder, i.e., the team member who can best develop a successful relationship with the stakeholder?

Again, it is extremely important that the sharing of expectations among key stakeholders and the team take place as early as possible in the team's formation. Although we have worked in several ways with teams and their stakeholders to clarify agreements, we believe that holding some type of Stakeholder Team Launch Meeting and creating a series of "contracts" between the team and its stakeholders provide a valuable model for this process.

Before engaging your stakeholders in the process of mutually establishing expectations, the team may find it interesting to create a graphic depiction—what the Europeans call an "organogram"—of the various stakeholder groups and each group's relationship to the team.

■ STAKEHOLDER TEAM LAUNCH MEETING

The purpose of any form of Stakeholder Team Launch Meeting is to bring out into the open, for all to examine, the expectations/needs of each of the groups that have a stake in the team's success. We have found that one of the major sets of issues that bogs down world-class team performance and productivity is that teams spend an inordinate amount of time working on the "politics"—clearing up misunderstandings and resolving conflicts between the team and one or more of its stakeholder groups. This type of forum will not eliminate these time-consuming and frustrating activities, but it should minimize them.

For example, at the first meeting of the Team Leaders for a Global Business Development Team (GBDT) of a major consumer products company and the European Area teams who would be the geographical extension of the global teams, we did a "core dump" of the issues that they had come to the meeting wanting to resolve. As we analyzed the issues, after the first day it became very clear that the two groups were anticipating and/or already experiencing turf wars or skirmishes that were directly related to how each group perceived the other's ideas. Some of the concerns they voiced were:

➤ How will the GBDT be kept in the communications link between Euroteams and the European countries?

➤ How do Euroteams get resources? Who controls those resources?

➤ How will the Euroteam leaders be evaluated? What input into the process will GBDT Leaders have?

➤ How will the countries know whether to call the Euroteam or the GBDT?

➤ Who will be responsible for establishing Euroteam goals?

These issues needed to see the light of day and be openly discussed. The groups were then able to negotiate operating agreements to help ward off potential conflicts down the road.

With some teams, the ultimate critical stakeholder(s), such as a key supplier and/or customers/clients, may reside outside of the organization. Even though they are not part of the formal organization, a Stakeholder Team Launch Meeting can be used with these groups to initiate an early dialogue and build a strong working relationship. For example, one small consumer products company entered into a licensing agreement with a larger company to distribute the smaller company's products. In this case, they were both core product teams and stakeholders of each other. Because the working relationships between product team members in both organizations were so critical for the success of the product in the marketplace, we suggested considering them stakeholders of each other and convened a Stakeholder Team Launch Meeting. It was the first time that the product team members from each organization had come together specifically to clarify their respective roles and operating agreements.

Depending on the nature of the relationship, we generally recommend that internal and external stakeholders (particularly if they are customers of the team) not be involved in the same Stakeholder Team Launch Meeting. The primary reason is that internal stakeholders tend to focus more on the internal operations and processes of the team. External stakeholders are more concerned with the team's results that have direct value and impact on them. Both agendas are important, but they should be addressed in separate meetings.

■ STAKEHOLDER MEETING OBJECTIVES

The specific objectives for a Stakeholder Team Launch Meeting are to:

➤ Develop a shared understanding of the team's structure (vis-à-vis other organizational units).

➤ Review and agree on the Team Launch Document.

➤ Identify the team's stakeholders' expectations and develop key Operating Agreements.

➤ Identify how each stakeholder will measure the team's success.

➤ Resolve any "anticipated" issues.

➤ Who Should Attend?

Ideally, all of the team's key stakeholders (or representatives of stakeholder groups) and all of the team members should be present at the Stakeholder Team Launch Meeting. At the very least, the Team Leader, the team Sponsor, and any other key stakeholders who are available should attend. It may be necessary to repeat all or parts of the meeting with key stakeholders who cannot attend, although this should be avoided.

Over the years, we have heard our clients initially balk at the suggestion that people fly in from all over the world to spend one to two days participating in either a team setup or a Stakeholder Team Launch Meeting. Arguably, face-to-face meetings such as these are expensive and could be replaced by using various forms of technology, such as a videoconference. (See Chapter 17 for the advantages and limitations of this approach.)

Invariably, however, the same individuals who balked at the suggestion have, after attending such meetings, walked away with (1) a stronger commitment to the team's success; (2) a deeper understanding of the role they will play in the team's success; and (3) clarification/resolution of the issues the team faces as it begins its launch.

➤ What Is the Agenda?

Prior to the meeting, a draft of the Team Launch Document should be prepared. (See Chapter 3 for a description of how to prepare a Team Launch Document.) If this has not been reviewed previously with the stakeholder groups, it then becomes a very important early part of the agenda. Each stakeholder group should be given the opportunity to review the Team Launch Document, ask clarifying questions, and, with the Sponsor and team/Team Leader, work out any issues regarding the basic operating structure of the team, including its Charter, Boundaries, team member time allocation, reporting relationships, and so forth. Before this discussion takes place, however, it is important that the Sponsor clearly specify which portions of the Team Launch Document are nonnegotiable.

For example, with one team we launched in Latin America, from the beginning the team's (and Team Leader's) reporting structure was a controversial issue. Much preliminary discussion took place among the Sponsor and key stakeholders and, by the time the Team Launch Document was prepared, the Sponsor had made a final decision. It would have been useless to have discussed the issue during the meeting. Instead, he explained the decision, announced it was nonnegotiable, and encouraged discussion of the various "open" issues instead.

The major portion of this meeting should be centered on each of the stakeholders' expressing what he or she expects and needs from the team and, conversely, what the team can expect from the stakeholders. It is equally important that the team have the opportunity to tell each of the stakeholder groups what the team expects and needs. Because different stakeholder groups will have different expectations, the process must accommodate each group's spending time with the team in order to arrive at some mutually acceptable working agreements.

Another agenda item that may be included in this type of meeting is to provide each of the stakeholder groups with the opportunity to tell the Sponsor and Team Leader how they will be measuring the success of the team. Often, when teams are formed, there is much skepticism about what value they will bring to the organization. This forum allows each stakeholder group to tell the team what will bring value to them—from their unique perspective. The input from this session can be used by the team to structure goals and projects (see Chapter 11) and "manage the

5.1   Sample Agenda for Stakeholder
          Team Launch Meeting

OBJECTIVES

➤ Identify mutual team and key stakeholder expectations/needs for this team to become world-class.

➤ Review Team Launch Document and arrive at consensus agreement.

➤ Develop team/key stakeholder Operating Agreements.

PARTICIPANTS

➤ Team Sponsors.

➤ Key stakeholders.

➤ Team Leaders (and team members, if appropriate).

➤ World-class team facilitators.

MEETING AGENDA

➤ Review meeting agenda/expectations.

➤ Review team's history.

➤ Introduce team structure and stakeholder roles.

➤ Review Team Launch Document: issues and agreements.

➤ Identify and exchange team and stakeholder expectations.

➤ Develop team/stakeholder Operating Agreements.

➤ Identify team's measures of success.

➤ Identify next steps—plan of action.

---

border" (see Chapter 17) with that particular stakeholder. Toolkit 5.1 provides a sample agenda for a Stakeholder Team Launch Meeting.

■ EXCHANGING STAKEHOLDER EXPECTATIONS

The process of having each stakeholder group express what it wants from the team in an open forum can be enlightening and empowering. Stakeholders often go into such a meeting assuming "the worst"—that is, that the team is being empowered to have it their way and that the stakeholders will not really have a voice.

For example, in one organization, the international headquarters-based project teams were used to having direct interaction with their country organizations. When geographically based Area Project Teams were formed, there was very real concern that control and communications would shift away from the headquarters teams to the Area Project Teams and that they would be prevented from interacting with countries. As it turned out, however, the Area Project Teams wanted to share country interactions with the headquarters teams because very specific project expertise would then be combined with local "cultural" knowledge.

Listed below are some examples of "expectation exchanges" we have facilitated over the years with various types of stakeholder groups.

Team Expectations of Country (Regional) Management

➤ Support, support, support.

➤ Respect our "right to exist."

➤ Identify "high potential" people for the team.

➤ Approve and support allocation of team members' time.

➤ Provide local budget for country-specific initiatives.

➤ Be a public supporter of the regional team concept.

➤ Provide fast decisions on team actions.

➤ Be clear about your role versus the team role versus headquarters' role.

Country (Regional) Management Expectations of the Team

➤ Meet your team's Charter and Performance and Business Objectives.

➤ Move key priorities forward.

➤ Act as product/project Champions.

➤ Keep us informed of key decisions, and seek input.

➤ Develop the skills of team members.

➤ Provide more timely product planning to countries.

➤ Share "best practices" across the region and around the globe.

Team Expectations of Headquarters

➤ Have open communications; no hidden agendas.

➤ Provide appropriate levels of attention and understanding of regional needs, and give quick response.

➤ Make regional visits.

➤ Include our region in product/project decisions.

➤ Respect each others' goals and objectives.

Headquarters' Expectations of the Team

➤ Have open lines of communication; no hidden agendas.

➤ Provide quick feedback on key issues and questions.

➤ Plan visits for important meetings.

➤ Plan and budget for regional and local activities.

➤ Respect each other's goals and objectives.

Out of these expectations exchanges can come even more tactical stakeholder Operating Agreements. For example, one product team issued the following "contract" to address some key stakeholder issues:

We, the team, will:

➤ Hold quarterly planning meetings with headquarters.

➤ Have weekly telephone contact with our Sponsor.

➤ Attend senior regional management meeting.

➤ Use technology and not travel for stakeholder meetings whenever possible.

➤ Speak with "one voice" (headquarters *and* regional team) to the countries.

➤ Send all "functional communications" to the "functional reps" in the countries.

➤ Manage the borders with our own functional bosses.

➤ Manage the border with Sponsor and regional management, through our Team Leader.

The mutual sharing of expectations can also provide the team with benchmarks for measuring success. Team members could return to their stakeholder groups at a designated point—say, after six months to one year—and ask expectations-related questions to determine how well they are doing from their stakeholders' point of view. For example: Have we met your expectations to:

➤ Move key priorities forward?

➤ Provide earlier product knowledge and planning?

➤ Keep you informed?

➤ Share best practices?

■ TARGETING THE TEAM TOWARD SUCCESS

Getting clarity *up front* on what stakeholders expect and need puts the team in a better position to meet those expectations. Besides being able to establish benchmarks by which to gauge the team's effectiveness, developing agreements between the team and the stakeholders on how they will plan and communicate with each other, and how often they will check in to assess their progress and working relationships, goes a long way toward preventing the conflicts and political infighting that would ultimately sap the energy of the team.

The importance of building strong stakeholder relationships was emphasized by Susan Silberman, former European Team Leader for a pharmaceutical product team, when she reflected on both the successes and failures of her tenure as a world-class Team Leader. The good news, she concluded, was that her team had accomplished significant results that exceeded senior European management's expectations. The bad news was that, in her task-focused approach, she had neglected to communicate or develop relationships with the functional bosses to whom her team members also reported for 50 percent of their job. Consequently, she experienced significant turnover at critical junctures of the team's work. The results were: demoralized team members, an overworked Team Leader, and less than enthusiastic support from country/functional management in the region.

You also can't count on the "No news is good news" theory. During a Team Development Follow-Up Meeting with a product team in Asia, we conducted a team assessment that essentially provided the team with feedback that the border management with key stakeholders was the least effective area of their overall performance. The team had invited two key stakeholders to the meeting to solicit firsthand feedback. Although the direct feedback was generally positive, both stakeholders concluded, "You haven't managed your borders with us as well as you could."

It was clear that, like most teams, this team had spent the first year getting organized and achieving the team goals—all of which was great news. But they had not spent sufficient time on border management (such as practicing open communications, ensuring no surprises, involving stakeholders in questions of value versus investment). As the Team Leader said, "I made presentations periodically throughout the year and didn't hear any negative feedback, so I just assumed everyone was pleased."

As we told this team, you must get very clear, early in your team's formation, what your key stakeholders expect, and then manage to those expectations. These are the people who keep your team "in business." (See Chapter 16 for more about the "how to's" of border management.)

Much of what we are recommending in the setup process for world-class teams should be obvious—but it's not. World-class teams are implicitly or explicitly measured on the added value they bring to the organization as perceived by a set of stakeholders, whether they be senior management or customers further out in the food chain. Simply put, how can a team add value if team members don't know what their stakeholders perceive to be valuable? By taking the time to define stakeholders' needs and expectations at the onset of the team's formation, and then benchmarking progress against those needs and expectations over time, teams can avoid shooting in the dark in terms of producing meaningful results.

STRATEGY

2

Developing World-Class Teams

Chapter

World-Class Team Values and Operating Agreements

Some people have referred to the team's processes as its brain, its work outputs as its hands and feet, and its core Values as its heart. Faced with the challenges, complexities, and pace at which teams need to function, it is easy to forget how critical the heart is to a fully functioning life form. In the human body, the heart functions as a critical life-support mechanism and also represents the source of human spiritual dimension and passion. Similarly, a team's Values—if committed to—can sustain, inspire, and vitalize the team.

A world-class team's Values are the beliefs and the moral and ethical principles that guide the team's behaviors. They reflect what the individual team members believe to be the specific code of conduct under which they personally and collectively prefer to operate. These values determine team norms, which usually develop implicitly for teams. Though many teams come to explicit agreement on their Charter and Goals, they may not perform optimally because there is no similarly explicit consensus among team members about their team Values and their day-to-day operating principles, which we call Operating Agreements.

The glue that holds teams together, particularly during the rough moments, is trust. How does a team develop trust among its members? One way is for each team member to consistently act within the boundaries of the team's collective thinking on how team members should *behave.* Not all teams will have the same beliefs and principles, therefore all will not behave in the same way. What is most critical, however, is that each team discusses and agrees on its *unique* Values and subsequent Operating Agreements. These Values serve as the primary mindmap/filter through which the team evaluates others' behavior and which drives your own behavior in the team.

■ BUILDING SHARED TEAM VALUES: HOW DO YOU BEGIN?

Deciding on your team's Values should not be taken lightly. Although these may appear to be the "softest" elements of a world-class team's effectiveness, they may, in fact, be the primary determinant of whether a world-class team achieves its highest levels of performance. If there is not a set of Values or guiding principles that all team members have agreed to and operate under, or if there is disparity between what team members express and how they actually behave, what develops is a "trust gap."

Chris Argyris, a professor of business and education at Harvard Business School, describes the gap between what a person values, and how he or she lives those values, as the difference between a person's "espoused theories" and "theories in use." The more commonly used description is: "The walk doesn't match the talk." This trust gap, if it exists for any team member, prevents that individual from wanting to fully commit and contribute to the team's efforts. Conversely, if team members have consensus on their Values, the team's work activities are likely to be well-coordinated and their relationships can be expected to be characterized as cooperative.

A team's agreed-on Values establish a set of expectations that, if not fulfilled, can seriously affect team trust. For example, if a team establishes that they have a Value of "Full Team Participation," yet one of the team members is consistently late to team meetings or does not fulfill team assignments, his or her commitment to the team may legitimately be called into question.

What is your team's "true North"? Without the compass of your defined Values, what instrument do you have to guide yourself and others?

Our Values are deeply held views of what we think is "right." They come from many sources: our parents, teachers, religious philosophies, peers, role models, heroes/heroines. Some are developed very early in life. In *The Book of Virtues,* William Bennett states: "For children to take morality seriously they must be in the presence of adults who take morality seriously." Children learn the "rules and precepts—the do's and don't's of life" by watching and developing the good habits of others. Bennett makes the point that we can begin to teach Values to even very young children through "moral education," using stories and tales that teach life's lessons.[1]

World-class team members have traveled through their own worlds of values and norms by the time they come together as a team. Just as their childhood experiences introduced them to "the do's and don't's of life," their prior experiences working in teams—both positive and negative—have taught them lessons and informed their sense of what's "right." Those perspectives come into play when teams begin to develop their Values Statements.

To get teams thinking about what critical beliefs and principles should guide their behavior, we have found it helpful to first engage team members in what we call the Dream Team Exercise.

Reflect back over your career, or perhaps go as far back as your school days, and think of a team that you were part of—one that, for you, would earn the title "Dream Team." This team was one you cared about and were proud to be a member of. It might have been a sports team, a team that came together to put on a play, or a task force that did a community project. Perhaps it was a team that you worked on in a previous company, or a team that you worked on earlier at your current company. Go back in time and consider some of the particulars about that team. Who was on it besides you? What were you doing? Where were you doing it? What role were you playing? What were you achieving? How well were you working with others on the team and with your "coach"?

Now think about the wonderful experience you had as a member of the Dream Team. Why did this experience stand out in your mind? What made this such a Dream Team? From the list of Dream Team Values below, select the ten factors that are most important to you as guides for how your Dream Team behaved and for how you want the team you are on today to behave. Feel free to add any Dream Team Values that you do not see on the list.

If you want to go to the next step—prioritizing your values—ask yourself: Is #_____ more important than #_____, etc.?

Are you surprised by the results? You will always move in the direction of your number one value and away from anything that threatens that value. This happens from the heart, often without your even knowing it.

Dream Team Values

1. ____ Coordination	14. ____ Making the most of
2. ____ Working hard	limited resources
3. ____ Having fun	15. ____ Clear ambitious goals
4. ____ Recognition	16. ____ Time pressure
5. ____ Trust	17. ____ Success; accomplishments
6. ____ Added value	18. ____ Mutual development of
7. ____ Enthusiasm	mission/vision
8. ____ Complementary skills	19. ____ Agreed-on priorities
9. ____ Common goals	20. ____ Each person empowered
10. ____ Productivity	to do tasks
11. ____ Creativity	21. ____ *"Arbeitsfreude"* (joy of
12. ____ Helping each other;	work)
cooperation	22. ____ Measurable results
13. ____ Building of friendships	23. ____ Well-trained people

(Continued)

24. _____ Celebration of success
25. _____ Positive attitude
26. _____ Sharing expertise and experience
27. _____ Focused discipline
28. _____ Good communication
29. _____ Commitment
30. _____ Positive stress
31. _____ Good planning
32. _____ Continuous improvement
33. _____ Striving for excellence
34. _____ Being open-minded
35. _____ Demonstrating empathy and support
36. _____ Setting clear expectations
37. _____ Role clarity
38. _____ Balanced task and process focus
39. _____ Balanced workload among members
40. _____ Tolerance of diversity
41. _____ Valuing diversity
42. _____ Flexibility
43. _____ Open and candid feedback
44. _____ Coaching
45. _____ Respect
46. _____ Accountability
47. _____ Honesty
48. _____ Team rewards
49. _____ Fairness
50. _____ Courage

Developing Team Values Statements

After individual team members have selected and perhaps prioritized their top ten team Values, it is time to begin to develop a set of team Values Statements to which each team member contributes and eventually, by consensus, gives support. It is important to support and nurture the highest Values in team members. This form of intrinsic motivation will engender more commitment than any other form of reward.

The following exercise can be used to help the team arrive at a list of five to six key Values that they can agree to support and live by. We say again that it is critical to arrive at consensus. If team members walk away from this exercise believing that *every* team member has agreed to these Values, you have created a set of very important mutual expectations and boosted your odds of success.

Tell the team that you want to create a Dream Team set of Values for *this* team. Create the scenario by saying: "It is one year from now and this team is achieving its results and performance goals. Imagine you are telling someone how proud you are to be on this team because it really lives its Values. What are those beliefs and principles that bind you together?"

➤ Create a group list by asking each team member to read out his or her list of top ten Values. Make sure to note any that were added, rather than taken from the model list.

➤ Did any Values receive a unanimous vote? If so, they are your first "wins."

➤ Circle the Values that received the highest number of votes.

➤ Work through this list, asking if there could be unanimous or consensus agreement on any of these Values.

➤ Discuss areas of strong disagreement. Look for areas of compromise.

➤ Continue to test for unanimity or consensus.

➤ As a final "test," ask if anyone could imagine any circumstance that would cause him or her to *not* be able to put a Value into action.

You might want to remind team members that some Values are "deal breakers"— that is, a particular team member could not live with or without the Value being included on the list. These are the most difficult but significant ones to resolve. It is much better to understand the Value biases of your team and work them out in the beginning than to experience conflict, frustration, and perhaps disappointment down the road.

Many teams are not satisfied with just one-word or single-phrase Values Statements. They take a core Value (such as "trust" or "continuous improvement") and expand on it to "personalize" it for their team. Listed below are examples of team Values that we have collected from world-class teams over the years. We have noticed that, when it comes to selecting Values, there are few to no cultural differences among teams from around the world, whether the teams are in Argentina, Canada, or Hong Kong. People know what makes teams "dreamlike."

➤ We value learning—that is, encouraging risk taking and examining mistakes—as well as successes.

➤ We will speak directly to each other about issues and not "sandbag" other team members behind their backs.

➤ We will focus our energies only on those matters that we can control or influence.

➤ All team members and their contributions are equally important.

➤ We will focus our team's efforts on the larger good of the organization, not on our particular team or team members' agendas.

➤ We will balance the needs of the team with the needs of individual team members.

➤ We will actively listen to and respect others' opinions.

➤ We will stay committed to our task and our team.

➤ We are honest, open, and trustworthy.

➤ We are focused on results.

➤ We value projects of excellence.

➤ Each team member's contribution is valued.

➤ We value personal growth.

➤ We have fun in doing what we do.

6.1 Hopes and Fears of Teams

HOPES

➤ We will have agreement about mission, goals, and projects among stakeholders and the team.
➤ We achieve self-development from the team experience.
➤ We have clear Boundaries and border agreements with key stakeholders.
➤ We are accepted and valued by the key stakeholders.
➤ We achieve breakthrough results.
➤ We have key stakeholders who share accountability for our success.
➤ We learn how to compromise and negotiate priorities/resources.
➤ We are a "model" for high-performing teams.
➤ We continue to articulate our "fears" and to resolve issues.
➤ We gain cross-functional/cross-cultural skills.
➤ We are so successful that people will want to join the team.
➤ We become a *team*, not just a working group.

FEARS

➤ We will experience difficulties with empowerment and decision making.
➤ We won't have enough resources (in particular, time and money) to achieve results.
➤ Our team members will be diverted by other functional/country requirements.
➤ We will duplicate or do wasteful work.
➤ We will not meet stakeholders' expectations.
➤ Our team members will feel isolated.
➤ We won't get enough feedback or coaching from stakeholders.
➤ We won't get enough recognition.
➤ We won't have senior management support.
➤ Our team members will experience "burnout" from trying to meet multiple masters' expectations.
➤ We will have misunderstandings about our roles.
➤ We will run up against traditional, bureaucratic thinkers.
➤ Our stakeholders' expectations will be too high.

We do another exercise with new teams in which they describe their "hopes and fears" about being a part of this team and about the work ahead of them. By identifying their expectations and areas of concerns, their responses can help to inform and shape the team's Values. We learn what really matters to team members. (See Toolkit 6.1 for the "Hopes and Fears" one team listed at the team launch meeting.)

■ WORLD-CLASS TEAM OPERATING AGREEMENTS

During the early phase of forming your world-class team, your team needs to establish and agree on guidelines—what we call Operating Agreements—for how it will conduct its team business. Operating Agreements should be the "best practices" that reflect the team's Values. They should clarify actions and roles, and lessen confusion and mixed expectations, all of which can be sources of conflict for teams. They provide a solid practical foundation for the teamwork that is required if the team is to accomplish its goals.

Among the issues on which you should obtain agreement are:

Meetings

- ➤ How frequently and where will we meet?
- ➤ How will we manage our meeting time?
- ➤ Who will manage our meeting time?
- ➤ What is our meeting attendance policy?

Communications

- ➤ How will we ensure that individual opinions and concerns are expressed and discussed?
- ➤ How will we communicate within the team and between team meetings?
- ➤ How will we communicate with the Sponsor/Steering Committee and other key stakeholders?
- ➤ How will we handle confidentiality issues?

Decision Making

- ➤ Who will make decisions?
- ➤ How will we make decisions?
- ➤ Who will resolve differences or conflicts?

Stakeholder Relationships

> ➤ Who are the key influencers and what are their expectations of the team?

> ➤ How can we build relationships and support from them?

> ➤ Who from the team should be "border managers"?

Work Processes

> ➤ How will we divide up our tasks?

> ➤ How will we integrate our outputs?

Results and Metrics

> ➤ How will we measure our team's task and process results?

> ➤ How will we change things that are getting in the way of our producing results?

Recognition

> ➤ How will we periodically celebrate the team's efforts/accomplishments?

> ➤ How will we recognize and reward individual contributions?

> ➤ How will we communicate our results to others outside of the team?

We observed firsthand the importance and power of Operating Agreements, and the effect they can have on a team's morale, when we were working with a team of people from throughout the Asian Pacific region. The team began to examine the effect of culture on their operating style. The Team Leader, an expatriate from the United States, wanted the team to have an open and participatory style. Several team members, however, expressed concern because their cultures do not consider it appropriate to publicly disagree with colleagues, let alone their bosses—in this instance, the Team Leader.

After much discussion, the team agreed that this was an important team Value. To address it, they developed an Operating Agreement whereby individuals would signal with a Koosh® ball (a squiggly rubber toy) and call "Time out" when they wanted to say something that might be in disagreement or conflict. Throughout a two-day meeting, they practiced the use of this strategy and were pleased to find that the techniques had not only served to raise issues on a timely and open basis, but also had done so in a "fun" manner that facilitated individuals' moving beyond their cultural norms toward the team's Values.

On the other hand, disregarding or thwarting a team's Operating Agreement can have the opposite effect—it can demoralize a team. This proved to be the case with one Latin American team we worked with. During the setup phase, we worked the team through a process of setting mutual expectations with key stakeholder groups (see Chapters 3 and 5 for further descriptions of this process). The good news was that after the two-day session, the team had written Operating Agreements delineating what the team was empowered to do, and the agreements were signed off by both the team Sponsors and the key functional managers of the team members. The bad news was that, five months later, the functional managers were violating several of the agreements—for instance, removing team members without notice and not allowing team members to attend team meetings. Consequently, the Team Leader and team members were quite skeptical about the ability of their team to succeed under the "current reality" and did not trust that senior management truly supported the team concept.

As the two examples above illustrate, Operating Agreements can have a powerful effect in either a positive or negative direction, depending on the level of compliance among team members, Sponsors, key stakeholders, and other individuals/groups associated with the team. Operating Agreements are powerful in their effect, but they are fragile in the sense that their tenets can be easily violated and impaired. It is important to assess, over time, both the level of compliance and the viability of the Operating Agreements themselves. During their formation, teams should spend time establishing Operating Agreements and should then take them to heart without considering them to be "cast in stone." Teams need to review their Operating Agreements periodically to determine whether they are still workable.

In Toolkit 6.2, we offer an example of a world-class team's Operating Agreement.

To show that stakeholder meetings, Operating Agreements, and Team Launch Documents do not *guarantee* smooth sailing for world-class teams, we offer this list of issues that a newly formed project team identified as major stress points, even though, at a formal meeting of the team and its key stakeholders, these issues had been agreed to:

➤ Stakeholders are continuing to communicate around our team and to conduct activities without our knowledge.

➤ Team membership is not complete—departments are reneging on their agreements to provide team members.

6.2 World-Class Team Operating Agreement

WE WILL

➤ Heed the maxim: "If you're uncomfortable with something, don't leave the meeting with it."

➤ Require full participation and allow no domination.

➤ Operate, in general, as a decision-making body, and request explanation of any reversals of our decisions by more senior management groups.

➤ Model what we preach.

➤ Establish and maintain a "buddy system" with the expanded core group.

MEETINGS/COMMUNICATIONS

➤ Develop a premeeting agenda and circulate for review.

➤ Designate a local team member to coordinate the meeting.

➤ Start meetings with update of "context."

➤ Make sure we build in "brainstorming" time.

➤ Record/Publish meeting minutes/notes in timely fashion (draft in five business days) and in a standard format.

➤ Provide a personal touch: the Team Leader will call Associate/core members to inform them about meeting topics/issues if they did not attend the meeting.

➤ Appoint team roles for team meetings (e.g., scribe, timekeeper).

➤ Provide stakeholders with appropriate update of the team's accomplishments and Plans of Action.

➤ Communicate, to appropriate people, information on any issues concerning the team.

➤ Circulate work of subcommittees in advance.

➤ Be familiar with local progress on team issues.

➤ Schedule meetings as often as required—early on, hold them at least once per month.

➤ Include a "social" time as part of each meeting.

➤ Rotate meeting locations from country to country.

➤ Propose to the team in advance the decision-making method that should be used for particular issues.

➤ Wear what's comfortable for each individual team member.

➤ Ask "why" if some decision is not clear.

Toolkit 6.2   *(Continued)*

➤ Self-assess our own individual performance.

➤ Allow no substitution of core team members at team meetings.

CULTURAL ISSUES

➤ Respect each "integrated person," including cultural/language differences.

➤ Forgive unintentional "misbehavior" that is due to a lack of awareness or of cultural sensitivity.

INTERPERSONAL RELATIONS

➤ Speak "our own individual minds" with respect.

➤ Be sensitive to and supportive of each other's needs.

➤ Harbor no hidden agendas.

➤ Have fun.

➤ Celebrate accomplishments and successes.

➤ Speak up if we don't agree—silence is not golden.

➤ Challenge with respect.

➤ Let go of grudges/complaints.

➤ Enable anyone, besides the Team Leader, to "go into the helicopter" and help to balance team processes, tasks, and individual needs.

➤ Listen actively, and without interruption, to the contributions of others.

TEAM DEVELOPMENT AND TRAINING

➤ Schedule ongoing team training to develop team skills/technical knowledge.

➤ Appreciate each other's liabilities and help each other improve through our own individual expertise.

➤ Practice time management.

➤ Treat team members as our "most potential asset."

MISCELLANEOUS

➤ Periodically assess and give feedback, to the team and individuals, regarding effectiveness.

➤ Be fully committed to the team.

➤ Attend all meetings; core members must have 100 percent attendance.

➤ Follow-up on all action items in timely fashion.

➤ Come prepared to meetings; have assignments completed.

(Continued)

Toolkit 6.2   *(Continued)*

➤ Be advocates for the team within and outside of the team.

➤ Contribute creative ideas.

➤ Actively participate in meetings.

➤ Always keep the team's goals in mind.

➤ Look for ways to link and synergize differing points of view.

➤ Ask the team for help in resolving an individual team member's conflicts between functional and team responsibilities/priorities.

➤   The headquarters organization is providing short turnaround times for key decisions and is going directly to departments, rather than to the team, for input.

Besides being a violation of the Operating Agreement, this list indicates a failure to remember that the new team was put into place to coordinate all project-related activities. What would you do if you were a member of this team?

■ LIVING THE VALUES

World-class teams believe that values must be preached, but, even more important, they must also be practiced. Team surveys reveal that the leading cause of cynicism and distrust toward teams is team members' belief that other team members, Team Leaders, team sponsors, or team stakeholders are not "walking their talk."

World-class teams can help ensure that they are practicing what they preach by checking in periodically, with themselves and their key stakeholders, to see whether they are, in fact, consistently operating in accordance with their espoused Values. A typical mechanism for doing this is a Values Assessment—a kind of EKG exam. Essentially, it is a methodology for the team to answer this question: "To what degree do our stated team Values differ from the actual behavior in our team?"

Toolkit 6.3 is a basic assessment form created by a team six months after its formation and distributed to team members prior to a team meeting. The purpose was to determine (1) the degree to which team members thought they were individually aligned with the team's Values and (2) how well they thought the team as a whole was performing. Upon completion of the assessment, which was compiled by a facilitator, they discussed those areas in which they were not living their Values.

6.3 Team Values Assessment

Team Values	My Individual Performance							Our Team Performance						
	Lo						Hi	Lo						Hi
Trust and respect	1	2	3	4	5	6	7	1	2	3	4	5	6	7
Open communications on a regular basis on all levels	1	2	3	4	5	6	7	1	2	3	4	5	6	7
A mutual appreciation of work and time constraints	1	2	3	4	5	6	7	1	2	3	4	5	6	7
Being allies and supporters of each other for better or worse	1	2	3	4	5	6	7	1	2	3	4	5	6	7
Maintaining a balance of work and fun	1	2	3	4	5	6	7	1	2	3	4	5	6	7
Providing feedback to each other, including addressing criticism directly	1	2	3	4	5	6	7	1	2	3	4	5	6	7
Effective collaboration on team projects	1	2	3	4	5	6	7	1	2	3	4	5	6	7
Making sure our customers perceive us as "one" team	1	2	3	4	5	6	7	1	2	3	4	5	6	7
Honesty and openness	1	2	3	4	5	6	7	1	2	3	4	5	6	7
Joint annual planning by team members	1	2	3	4	5	6	7	1	2	3	4	5	6	7

"Effective Collaboration on Team Projects" received a very low evaluation by the team. After some discussion, we found that the lead person on several of the team's projects usually went through the motions of asking other team members for their ideas, but then proceeded to do the projects as if he were an individual contributor rather than a *team* member. The discussion was not easy, but the exchange raised important issues. The lead person had not realized he was being noncollaborative, while the other team members became aware that they had never given him direct feedback.

Although we recommend a "formal" periodic team Values Assessment, there may be times when you, as a team member, begin to observe a trust/Values gap with one of your team members. What should you do if you think you need to take some action? Here are some guidelines:

➤ Don't ignore the team member's behavior that is causing you concern. A small irritant can become a major impediment for you if it's allowed to fester.

➤ Talk to the team member; give feedback and attempt to resolve the issue with the team member directly.

➤ If you're not sure how to approach the team member, ask the Team Leader or another "personal coach" for some insight and advice.

➤ Refer to the team's Values Statements and Operating Agreement as the bases on which you are confronting the situation.

➤ If you are unable to resolve the issue, ask the team member to go with you to discuss the situation with the Team Leader.

Conversely, if someone approaches you with examples of your behavior that seem to be outside of the team's code of conduct, be willing to listen and work on the issue. If you hear that others are complaining about your behavior, don't collude in what we call "triangling." Go to the source and take a proactive and positive approach to resolving the issue.

Remember—nicely laminated slogans are not enough. The hard work of developing Values is for naught if it is not backed by actions that consistently reflect those beliefs and principles. Both Values Statements and Operating Agreements are key steps that a team can take to "operationalize" its Values and establish parameters by which members can periodically assess how well they are living their Values or "walking their talk."

Our work with teams from around the world has convinced us that a team's Values lie at the heart of all of the team's actions and decisions. Unfortunately, these Values are usually implicit and can only be seen indirectly by examining the team's actions and decisions. We strongly advocate using a formal process to examine actions and decisions so that the team's Values can be made more explicit and seen more directly.

These guiding principles have too much power and impact on the team to be ignored. World-class team members need to recognize when they are acting congruently within—or, more problematic, violating—their Values and Operating Agreement so that their driving behaviors can be, respectively, continued and fostered, or corrected and prevented.

Chapter 7

World-Class Team
Roles and Skills

World-class team members come in all shapes and sizes, and they can represent as much diversity of thinking and cultural styles as you could possibly imagine. They are, in essence, the raw materials of teams. Accordingly, if you select the wrong materials and then don't shape them into a cohesive unit or give them each a "special feature" or function to perform, how will they themselves create the quality work products that we expect from world-class teams?

As we described in Chapter 3, a world-class team has several other elements in the mix—including Sponsors, stakeholders, Team Leaders, and support groups. In this chapter, we turn our focus specifically toward team members to answer the following questions:

- ➤ How do you choose team members?
- ➤ What roles do they play on a team?
- ➤ What competencies do they need at the outset?
- ➤ What competencies can be developed?

These questions, as with all the other aspects of developing world-class teams, need systematic attention.

■ SELECTING TEAM MEMBERS

Team members may hail from any part of the world, from any division or functional business unit of the organization, and possibly even from outside the organization. They may serve the team on either a part-time or a full-time basis. They may be integral to the team from the earliest days of its formation, or may help shape its destiny by coming aboard at particular stages of the team's journey. World-class teams selectively merge a variety of functions and countries/cultures. The greater the diversity, the greater the potential for creative collaboration.

In general, a *team member* is responsible, either individually or in collaboration with others, for implementing the programs, projects, and activities that will enable the team to meet its goals. On a world-class team, team members are expected to play the following roles:

➤ Technical specialist.

➤ Functional department representative.

➤ Cross-functional/cross-cultural proponent.

➤ Country or cultural delegate.

➤ Company advocate.

The guiding principle for team membership is the degree to which an individual, representing a particular area of expertise or perspective, is strategically required for the team to fulfill its Charter. At the same time, it is insufficient for the team member selection criteria to be based *solely* on a person's functional or technical expertise relating to the team's Charter. Team members need to bring to the table many competencies (knowledge, skills, and abilities) at a baseline level of effectiveness in order to perform their role on a world-class team. We've seen time and again that a team will only be as strong as its weakest link.

What precisely is a competency? David McClelland, Professor Emeritus of Harvard, defined the term as referring to the characteristics and behaviors of people who do a particular job well. The basic team competencies listed in Toolkit 7.1 can be observed as the people you are considering as team members perform their work, or even outside the context of working on a team. They are examples of the "raw materials" a team member can contribute to a team, in addition to his or her technical or functional expertise. The list in Toolkit 7.1 gives a set of criteria for selecting team members (after you prioritize the importance of specific team competencies against the backdrop of the particular team for which you are recruiting).

Who should be involved in selecting team members? Minimally, team Sponsors, Team Leaders, and key stakeholders from the functional and country units from which the team members will be selected should have a say in the selection process. To make the process as objective as possible, you should first establish a list of specific criteria—in order of priority—that can be used to assess and interview the various candidates. (Toolkit 7.1 offers a partial list of criteria from which you can structure your own list.)

Remember: Context, context, context. Every team is different and has different needs, not only as compared to other teams but even at different

7.1 Selection Criteria/Team Member Competencies (excerpted from 20/20 Team Player©)

CATEGORY: PERSONAL LEADERSHIP

➤ Demonstrates high standards of ethical conduct.

➤ Follows through and delivers on promises.

➤ Takes initiative—does what needs to be done without being asked to do so.

CATEGORY: TEAM COHESION

➤ Abides by team norms and standards.

➤ Puts team goals before individual goals.

➤ Represents the team effectively to the rest of the organization.

CATEGORY: TEAMWORK

➤ Helps others learn important skills and knowledge.

➤ Takes on a fair share of the workload.

➤ Coordinates own work with work of others.

CATEGORY: EFFECTIVE MEETINGS

➤ Makes an effort to attend all meetings and to arrive on time.

➤ Arrives at team meetings prepared to contribute.

➤ In meetings, stays focused on agenda topics.

CATEGORY: INNOVATIVE PROBLEM SOLVING

➤ Informs others about new knowledge, methods, technologies, and other developments.

➤ Encourages others to question the status quo.

➤ Affirms the positive aspects of a person's suggestion before stating concerns.

CATEGORY: INTERACTIVE LISTENING

➤ Listens to others without interrupting.

➤ When listening, asks questions to check understanding.

➤ When listening, checks the meaning of the speaker's tone of voice, gestures, and facial expressions.

(Continued)

Toolkit 7.1   *(Continued)*

CATEGORY: FEEDBACK

➤ Gives praise or recognition to others who have performed well.

➤ When giving constructive feedback, describes specific undesirable actions in a nonjudgmental way.

➤ Receives constructive feedback without reacting defensively.

CATEGORY: DIALOGUE

➤ Communicates without ridicule, threats, or emotional outbursts.

➤ Explains the reasoning behind own opinions.

➤ Demonstrates a willingness to change an opinion.

CATEGORY: CONFLICT RESOLUTION

➤ Speaks up when in disagreement with others.

➤ Uses consideration and tact when voicing disagreement.

➤ When in conflict with a coworker, discusses possible areas of agreement.

Source: 20/20 Team Player, copyright © 1995 by Performance Support Systems, Inc.

stages in its own life cycle. Select those team members who can help your team succeed *now.* Don't just take whoever is available. The work of world-class teams is too important not to select the right raw materials.

■ DEFINING TEAM MEMBERS' ROLES

To achieve high levels of team performance, world-class team members must know what their roles and responsibilities will be. (See Chapter 11 for a process of defining these roles and responsibilities in more detail as they relate specifically to the team's goals.)

Using a definition provided by Dr. Udai Pareek, a management training advisor for USAID/Health in Jakarta, Indonesia, a world-class team member's role can be viewed as "the set of functions an individual performs in response to the expectations of the significant members of the social system [team] and his or her own expectations about the position he or she occupies in the social system [team]."[1] Within a certain team member role, the individual performs specific functions—for example, project manager—as well as specific tasks, which are the smallest units of work. Each team member takes on discrete responsibilities and tasks appropriate to his or her skill sets. Each also shares with other team members various roles and responsibilities for completing team assignments.

Within a world-class team structure, it becomes absolutely essential for team members to define their respective roles because there is a high potential for "role conflict," given the other roles they are expected to play, such as their functional department roles or roles on other teams. Part-time team members in particular are bound to have multiple roles, and each role may have a different set of expectations and time demands to be met. When team members' roles are not clearly defined (and agreed to by both team members and stakeholders), even those with the best intent to do the right thing may wind up engaging in border skirmishes, stepping on toes, or failing to meet others' expectations.

In stressing the importance of this concept, Pareek coins the phrase "role efficacy." He explains that a person's effectiveness in an organization is the result of (1) the person's having the requisite "knowledge, technical competence and skills" to perform particular roles *and* (2) being assigned to roles that allow the use of those traits. This perspective has direct implications regarding participation on world-class teams. First, it suggests that the core competencies for the team need to be defined and then team members are selected because they either have or will be provided sufficient opportunities to develop these competencies. Second, it strongly supports the idea that if people are placed on world-class teams, they need to have *real work* and to be empowered to do work that matches their competencies; otherwise, they will become frustrated and ultimately less effective to the organization.

Paraphrasing from Pareek's work and translating it into the context of world-class teams, we recommend that team Sponsors and Team Leaders heed the following advice when structuring the roles of their team members so as to increase their "role efficacy":

➤ Give team members roles that capitalize on and allow them to use their unique strengths.

➤ Allow team members to initiate either changing or expanding their roles.

➤ Allow flexibility for creativity in how team members perform their functions in a role.

➤ Encourage team members to confront the team when they are dissatisfied with their role or are in role conflict.

➤ If a team member's role is a peripheral one, then explicitly put that person on the periphery and don't insist on core participation.

➤ Allow the team members to use the influence of their roles; empower them.

➤ Provide ongoing personal growth opportunities to team members.

➤ Encourage team members to link with others to perform their roles.

➤ Facilitate team members, if required, in receiving help from others to perform their roles.

➤ Continue to ensure alignment between a team member's role/responsibilities and the team's Charter/goals. People who feel that their contributions make a real difference are ultimately more satisfied and productive.

Whenever you start up a team or are at a point where you determine through some form of diagnosis that there is a need for role clarification or adjustment among team members, consider doing the following exercise.

First, explain that there are four aspects of a team member's role:

1. Role expectation—what others think the person is responsible for and how he or she should do it.

2. Role conception—what the person thinks his or her job is, and how he or she has been "taught" to do it.

3. Role acceptance—what the person is willing to do.

4. Role behavior—what the person actually does.

Second, ask the team members to make notes about their own jobs in terms of the four aspects of role discussed. (Allow twenty minutes, or assign as prework for the session.)

Third, ask for a volunteer who wants to clarify his or her role within the team while the other team members make notes on their understanding of this person's activities. (Allow ten minutes.)

The volunteer states what he or she sees as the other members' "role expectations" of his or her role, and lists the key points for all to see. (Only questions of clarification are allowed from other team members.)

The volunteer then questions the other team members and lists their actual expectations. A discussion of the confirmed and misperceived expectations should follow.

The volunteer next discusses his or her own "role conception," while making notes. (Again, only questions of clarification are accepted.)

Fourth, conduct a renegotiation session in which the volunteer makes a new contract with the other team members. The above steps now can be repeated with other volunteers. (You may want to use a facilitator in this process.)[2]

■ ANALYZING YOUR TEAM ROLES

In Chapter 11, we describe a process of looking at the specific goals for your team, and we help you to examine the *team task* roles and responsibilities that each team member will take on to accomplish these goals. In this section, we provide you with insights on how team members function within a team in terms of the various *team process* roles that individuals characteristically play.

The team process roles that an individual performs when working on a team consist of demonstrated behaviors, perspectives, and skills that either help or hinder the team's achieving its results. It is important to look also at how well the team is balanced in terms of the team process roles being performed. Are all of the roles that need to be played on this team covered by one or more individuals on the team?

Here's a closer look at what we know about team roles:

➤ *Teams need a variety of roles to be filled in order to most effectively accomplish their goals.* "Variety" is the operative word. Research shows that putting together teams of people who are very similar in terms of expertise and how they approach work—even if they are highly talented—results in poorer outcomes than staffing teams with people who have more heterogeneous expertise and roles. Managing the mixture and taking advantage of the differences becomes, then, a critical part of the team's process.

➤ *Some people have a natural inclination to slide into certain roles successfully.* For example, extroverts tend to migrate to roles that involve interpersonal skills, and people who are prone to be analytical often take on roles that require attention to task details.

➤ *Each role that a person plays serves a certain purpose and can help a team achieve its goals.* However, there may be times when a role is not necessary or is used to an extreme that may actually be dysfunctional for the team. For example, at times, teams do need someone to act like a "General"—leading a charge up a hill and keeping the team focused on its tasks and deadlines. But that role might not be useful at other times, such as at the beginning of a team's work or when issues are still being analyzed. Alternatively, it could have a detrimental effect if a team member plays the General role extremely and consistently, exhibiting such behavior as not listening, running roughshod over people, or caring only about getting work done, regardless of the quality.

➤ *Some roles are particularly important at certain stages of a team's development.* For example, in the early stages of a team's development, as the team is forming its Charter and deciding on goals, it can be especially useful to have someone on the team who is a strategic thinker, another who can help the team get organized, and another who uses his or her facilitating skills to make sure all team members are contributing.

➤ *Both assets and liabilities are associated with the roles team members assume.* The trick is to use the assets of the role at the appropriate time in a team's process, and to monitor the potential downside of using that role so that you don't inhibit the team's functioning. Each role contains the seed of its own limitations; great soldiers are not necessarily great politicians, and great strategists sometimes can't get things done.

➤ *If you do not characteristically use or play certain roles on a team, you can develop the necessary skills and behaviors and learn how to use them for that role.* The decisions you make about developing your role repertoire should be based on your own desire to round out your skills, your opportunity to practice, and the team's need for having more people capable of performing the role.

In our work with world-class teams, we use an assessment process called the *Team Role Analysis*™ to provide individual team members and the team itself with a process for understanding team members' various roles on the team, and the assets and liabilities associated with those roles. The Team Role Analysis, which was developed by the Management Research Group in Portland, Maine, can be used either as a self-evaluation tool or for 360-degree feedback. Along with providing valuable information about how team members are currently performing the various team roles, it also facilitates the development of strategies either for "smoothing out" the potential liabilities (if the role is being overperformed) or for nurturing the assets associated with the roles you tend not to use. Similarly, it enables the team itself to identify its strengths and perhaps recognize areas that need further development, within the context of its Charter, Boundaries, goals, and border management requirements.

As a framework for the assessment process, the Team Role Analysis breaks down the work that teams perform into these five major functions:

1. Evaluating issues.
2. Making decisions.
3. Getting things done.
4. Following through.
5. Building the group.

In the course of carrying out these team functions, team members may play a number of different roles. More specifically, the Team Role Analysis describes 23 different roles and associates each role with a particular major function that the team performs. For example, when a team is performing the function of "Getting Things Done," one or more team members may play such roles as The Organizer, The Magician, and The Producer. (Toolkit 7.2 lists all the roles, grouped under the functions with which they are associated. A comprehensive description of each specific role can be found in the Appendix.)

When we work with new teams, we use the Team Role Analysis only for self-evaluation (versus 360-degree feedback), given that the team members do not yet know each other *as a team,* even if certain individuals have previously met or worked with each other in a different context. Before coming together, the new team members are asked to respond to a survey in which they indicate how they typically behave in a team of peers.

When they arrive at the first team meeting, we provide them with the results indicating the roles they typically do and do not perform. Concurrently, we review the composite of the team's results, which shows both

7.2   Team Role Analysis™: Major Functions and Roles

EVALUATING ISSUES

➤ The Strategist

➤ The Visionary

➤ The Data Doctor

➤ The Traditionalist

FOLLOWING THROUGH

➤ The Enforcer

➤ The Bottom-Liner

➤ The Troubleshooter

➤ The Teacher

MAKING DECISIONS

➤ The Facilitator

➤ The General

➤ The Promoter

➤ The Contrarian

➤ The Democrat

BUILDING THE GROUP

➤ The Cheerleader

➤ The Team Player

➤ The Therapist

➤ The Politician

➤ The Comedian

GETTING THINGS DONE

➤ The Organizer

➤ The Craftsperson

➤ The Magician

➤ The Producer

➤ The Delegator

Source: Team Role Analysis™, from Management Research Group, Inc.

the distribution of the team's scores and the median. This will indicate the "tendencies of the team" as well as the degree of balance on the team—at least in terms of how they perceive themselves.

Before analyzing the team's strengths and weaknesses in detail, however, we ask the team to select five or six roles that they believe are absolutely critical for their team to focus on over the next year, once the team has developed a Charter, Boundaries, goals, stakeholder expectations, and so forth. One team we worked with selected the following roles to work on over the year:

➤ *The Strategist.* We need to think about the "big picture" and not just our tasks.

➤ *The Facilitator.* We need to learn how to make effective team decisions when we come together infrequently during the year.

➤ *The Promoter.* This team concept is new; we will need to sell the idea that these teams are important.

➤ *The Producer.* We need to get results.

➤ *The Cheerleader.* We're a new team, and we need to keep ourselves motivated.

➤ *The Politician.* We need to build bridges and negotiate work compromises with our stakeholders.

A team's strategic requirements can change over time. For example, at the next team development session a year later, this team decided to drop The Cheerleader because they felt they were such a close team. They added The Bottom-Liner because it was becoming increasingly important that they deliver work products in very short time frames.

We ask individual team members to select certain roles that they want to cultivate to increase their effectiveness within the team. Using a Developmental Action Planning process, we help them determine the following:

➤ What are your strongest team roles?

➤ In assuming these roles, how does your behavior affect your team? Are there any rough edges that need to be smoothed? If so, what are they?

➤ What are your weakest roles? Do you feel you are actively avoiding or rejecting these roles? If so, why?

➤ How does your avoiding these roles affect your team? Would your team be strengthened if you instead built up these roles? How?

➤ Based on the strategic requirements of your team, is there a role that you would be a good prospect to fill?

➤ Do you want to play that role? Would the various skills associated with the role be helpful to you in reaching your own career goals?

Although you probably do not have the results of a Team Role Analysis in front of you, look over the list in Toolkit 7.2 and ask yourself the questions provided above.

Based on your assessment, you may want to develop some specific strategies for strengthening one or more team roles. There are specific actions you can take for developing the skills required to perform certain team roles. For example, if you want to become more effective as The Promoter, you could take a presentations skills program that focuses on how to sell your ideas. Or, you could think about a project or issue for which you want to be the champion, and develop a strategic campaign for convincing others to support it. (Refer to the Appendix for more detailed descriptions of these roles.)

We often combine a "Nickname" exercise with the process of having team members choose a role from the Team Role Analysis assessment that they want to work at developing. Here is one team's list of nicknames/roles:

Speedy Susan (The Democrat).

Captain Christy (The Strategist).

Perfect Peter (The Visionary).

Crazy Catherine (The Contrarian).

Fantastic Fidela (The Visionary).

Another team developed a specific Plan of Action (POA) regarding their individual Team Role Analysis results. Their objective was to catch each other "doing something right" regarding the roles each planned to work at developing, and then to follow up on each other's progress at their next team meeting. They all received a reminder in the team's minutes:

We will each work on our own strategies to develop our team roles [as follows]:

➤ Ian will be practicing his Facilitating and Organizing on the team—give him feedback!

➤ Trond will be thinking of the "Big Picture" and doing some Strategic reading.

➤ Fanny will volunteer for Strategic task groups and try to think of the long-term implications of what she does and count to ten before doing!

➤ Caroline will be getting more involved in team projects and will be looking for a specific team project to organize.

➤ Mary will be visioning beyond the job description.

➤ Carlo will be cheerleading by engaging with people and doing his "Stop, Listen, Relax" routine to smooth our politics!

Can team members really change and develop their roles? Certainly. In fact, we can cite a specific example. One Team Leader had recently been named to head up his world-class team. We observed his behavior in several team activities during the first day, before providing him with his Team Role Analysis results. He scored very low as The General and The Organizer. We also observed that, during the team activities, his team had seemed to struggle with finding a focus and moving forward with decisions. Although The General may appear to be a role inappropriate for leading teams, he came back the next day and announced that this was, in fact, the role he wanted to strengthen. There was little chance that he would "overdo" the role because it was not in his "nature." The next day, he became more assertive and provided more structure for his team in the team activities, and they were more productive and less frustrated during those activities.

Believing it is vital for teams to know the competencies of their team members, we suggest that, early in their formation, they create a Team Competencies Inventory that goes beyond the team member roles/competencies described in Toolkits 7.1 and 7.2. This inventory of the specific knowledge, skills, and abilities (KSAs) of each team member, along with some particular experiences and accomplishments, provides the team with a comprehensive personal "data bank" of whom to go to for specific information, knowledge, and relationships.

To help create this inventory, we initially do a "Wanted Poster" exercise. When a team first meets, each team member is asked to prepare a flipchart that completes the statement: "I am wanted for:

➤ Having *these* unique KSAs and experiences . . . .

➤ Having produced *these* significant accomplishments . . . .

➤ Living by *this* personal slogan . . . ."

The Wanted Posters created through this exercise provide a brief introduction and overview of the rich diversity that typically exists on a team, and offer a glimpse at the key Values of individual team members, as revealed in their slogans. The exercise is also a precursor to developing a more detailed Team Competencies Inventory later in the team's development process.

■ DEVELOPING TEAM MEMBER COMPETENCIES

When we ask a newly formed team to identify, based on their past experience, what constitutes a Dream Team for them, we are trying to identify the *core competencies* for that team. As we saw in Chapter 6, this exercise is designed to get teams to specify their Values and then develop Operating Agreements that will help them create their own Dream Team.

Similarly, when we ask team members to describe an ideal team member for their team, we are trying to ascertain not only the skills and knowledge that are necessary for top performance, but also the personal attributes and behaviors that will predict high levels of consistent performance over a long period of time.

Remember that an assessment of a team's core competencies should consider the context of that particular team. A team must spend time clarifying the team's Charter and Boundaries as well as the roles that team members will need to fulfill in working toward achieving the goals within this context. Here again, it is helpful to view what research has shown to be the general competencies of effective team members. The list in Toolkit 7.1 can be used not only toward the initial selection of team members, but also for the following purposes:

> ➤ As a model for "ideal" team behavior and Operating Agreements.
> ➤ As a methodology for doing team peer or 360-degree assessments.
> ➤ To develop competency-based team development programs.

After you have identified your team's core competencies, how do you help team members develop them? There is no one best answer. The only truly compelling lesson learned is that while organizations are investing a lot of resources assigning people to teams and asking them to participate in team-related activities, they are on the whole spending precious little time on team competency development. In survey after survey, those involved in setting up or serving on teams agree that team competency development can make or break the success of team implementation. Yet, ironically, team competency development is one of the first things that is sacrificed because of time or money constraints.

Our experience tells us that another significant difficulty in team competency development is the sheer variety of methodologies available for doing team development. For instance, there are numerous external team development programs to which Team Leaders or team members individually are sent to "learn something and bring it back to the rest of us." There are also what Nolan Brawley refers to as "tree-hugging" experiences—going to a forest for two days of activities that bear no relationship to the team's work, processes, or relationships. And there are highly structured team meetings (with team members and/or with their Sponsors and stakeholders) that focus on building core team competencies while the team is engaged in performing its real work. From these options and any number of variations on these themes, how do you choose the best development strategy for your team?

Having participated in and facilitated a broad range of team development programs, the authors have developed their own set of biases about what should guide the selection of team development strategies.

1. Do not set the team up to receive its own internal team competency development/training program until you have engaged in the steps we set forth in Chapters 3 through 6. Without the proper team setup, all the training/development time focused on team leaders and team members will only reduce the return on your investment.

2. Team Leaders and team members should not receive initial team development separately or individually. Teams need to start learning together as they work together. At some point, you may want to single out Team Leaders for specific development because of their role, or suggest particular skill/knowledge development strategies for individual team members, but that move should be based on a diagnostic assessment of an individual's effectiveness, and the development strategies should be tailored to his or her specific needs.

3. Because time is a precious commodity for teams, we strongly urge that, in the first team development session, you combine a team competency focus with time spent on helping the team get some real work done. For example, in our "Crossing the Borders" program—or *Cruzado las Fronteras* as it is called in Latin America (see the Appendix for a detailed description)—we focus on the team competencies of listening and decision making. However, by the time the team leaves this two- to three-day program, they have also developed a Charter and Boundaries for their team; a set of Values and an Operating Agreement; a Plan of Action (POA) for further team and individual development of team roles/skills; and a framework for establishing their team goals. Instead of

Team Building Blocks

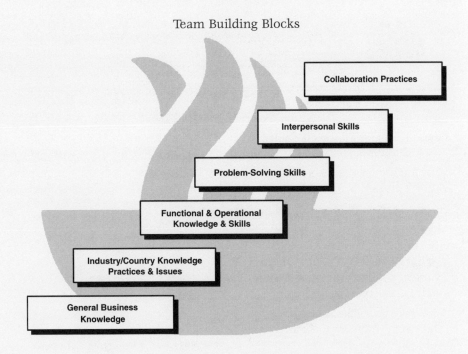

investing their time to learn skills outside of their team context, they are learning such team skills as listening and decision making while they are creating real work.

4. Team development should be programmed and conducted over a period of time. At the end of each of our "Crossing the Borders" sessions, we insist that the team establish a POA for their development (see Toolkit 7.3 for an example developed by one team). A POA helps the team to continue to focus on team development and process issues after they leave the initial session. It is usually a challenge for them to continue to do so, given that, with most teams, once the task pressure mounts, the team process and team competency development issues can get pushed to the background.

■ A COMMITMENT TO TEAM DEVELOPMENT

Teams and team members should commit to conducting periodic competency checks to help them pinpoint their developmental needs. For example, we regularly use a survey such as the Team Effectiveness

7.3   What Is Next? A Sample Plan of Action (POA)

What	When	Who
Charter/Goals wall charts—type up/cc:mail	July 26	LS
Reward/Recognition wall charts— type up/cc:mail	July 23	NB/LM
Stakeholder Expectations wall charts—type up/cc:mail	July 23	NB/LM
Hopes/Fears wall charts and Lessons Learned wall charts—type up/cc:mail	July 26	CS
How to Help Countries [see "WIIFT" (What's In It For Them)], Team Values, and POA (Plan of Action) wall chart—type up/cc:mail	July 24	DV
Team role analysis: Integrate individual roles with "strategic role requirements"	Next team meeting	Team
Facilitator skills: Do's/Don'ts	NB/LM	
Facilitator guidelines to ALL team members; rotate Facilitator role at team meetings		Team

Assessment (see Chapter 14 for an excerpt from this survey), which can help a team evaluate its overall effectiveness, or how team members are performing, in the following areas:

➤ Team Charter/vision.
➤ Stakeholders/border management.
➤ Team roles.
➤ Team Values/process.
➤ Team Operating Agreements.

Depending on how team members, and perhaps their key stakeholders, assess their performance, this can lead to suggested topics/developmental experiences for the team. For example, one team we worked with wanted to focus a second session on goal setting and collaboration;

another team decided that work on interpersonal and decision-making skills was needed.

You may want to have the Team Leader or all team members receive 360-degree feedback on how they are performing. For example, Toolkit 7.1 has been excerpted from a computer-based 360-degree feedback survey developed by Performance Support Systems, Inc. The survey can provide team members with focused feedback on how they are perceived as performing their team competencies, accompanied by a developmental planning process.

■ BRINGING NEW TEAM MEMBERS ON BOARD

Last but not least, keep in mind the possibility of a team's composition changing over time. If new members come aboard at different stages of the team's progress and evolution, their particular KSAs need to be integrated into the team and their roles on the team must be defined. Here are some ways to help new team members make the transition:

➤ Provide them with the minutes of past meetings, handout materials, progress/status reports, and any other historically significant team data.

➤ Familiarize them with the team's Charter, Boundaries, goals, and stakeholder expectations.

➤ Define the team's Values and Operating Agreement.

➤ Have current team members introduce themselves and give a brief "bio," and have new team members do the same.

➤ Do an information dissemination, including a review of current assignments and key team activities.

➤ Involve new members in team-building exercises the team has gone through, such as the "Nickname" or "Wanted Poster" exercises described earlier.

➤ Assign a current team member to serve as a mentor or "buddy."

➤ Encourage new team members to participate; ask for their input and reactions to key pieces of the team's work.

➤ Arrange a special activity/event to spend time interacting socially.

As you will learn in Chapter 10, when new team members join a world-class team, it has considerable impact on the team's dynamics. The more attention given to helping the new team members' transition, the sooner they can become productive team members.

Chapter **8**

Valuing Cultural Diversity

World-class teams will gain competitive advantage from having strategies to deal with the cultural differences they will encounter, whether the differences are regional, as when the French work with Germans in Europe, or intercontinental, as when Latin Americans work with Asians.

The behavior of people from different cultures is not something that can be treated lightly. Distinctive traditions and differences can be anticipated and managed. A working knowledge of other cultures, as well as an awareness of one's own cultural attributes, will help to minimize embarrassing situations and encourage successful interactions with people from all over the world. In this chapter, we will introduce some generalizations about different cultures, particularly as they relate to the aspects of teamwork: decision making, communication, leadership, and meeting participation styles.

■ WHAT IS CULTURE?

Culture provides us with a way of identifying with others. It informs the rules, values, ethics, and behaviors of a group—the ties that bind. Anthropologist Margaret Mead, who spent years exploring and explaining the importance of culture in shaping our lives, defines culture as "a principal element in the development of the individual that will result in [his or her] having a structure, a type of functioning, and a pattern of behavior different in kind from that of individuals who have been socialized within another culture."[1]

Values are one of the most important elements of culture. Some of the distinctive values in American culture have been "rugged individualism," the right to personal beliefs and independence, the practice of free-market enterprise, and the ability of a law-abiding and hardworking person to achieve the "American Dream." These espoused cultural values may well be reflected in the individual values of a person who has been socialized in the American culture. At the same time, some individual Americans will still expect the government to take care of them and will believe they are entitled to welfare benefits without working.

In the realm of developing world-class teams, it is important to understand how the predominant values of a team member's culture can influence his or her individual values and behavior. Yet, each team member is a unique individual and may not agree with the predominant values of his or her culture. Culture can help explain the background of team members, but each person must be evaluated individually as a singular human being. You do team members a disservice if you stereotype them in any way. To best understand their values—what they personally cherish and hold dear—you need to learn about and/or consider not only their particular cultural heritage, but also how they have been influenced by other forces such as age, birth order, education, socioeconomic class, and travel opportunities, among myriad others.

We have found, over the years, that a company's culture, or perhaps the functional or professional culture, often has a stronger influence than a country's culture. This is especially true if the company has a history of moving people frequently to "foreign" assignments, or typically mixes people of different nationalities and functions on committees that meet at various places worldwide. For example, throughout its long history as a multinational company, Pfizer has moved people at the executive level to positions in different countries, or has placed them on multidisciplinary and multinational committees or councils. As a result, at least at the senior and middle management levels, people know each other, share personal stories, and are bound by a competitive Vision and work ethic that appear to cut across cultures.

A major requirement for building world-class teams that are culturally diverse relates to the concept of "social tolerance." Sometimes we mistake our cultural values for "universal values" and judge behavior negatively if it does not conform to our own standards. For example, one night in China we were waiting for an elevator with a group of Chinese businessmen. When the doors opened, Lynda, who was closest to the doors (and holding a baby) was shoved aside by the group of men. Her first reaction was anger, not at their lack of chivalry, but at the open *rudeness* of their actions. Later in the week, she observed that it was common to "fight to be first" into the elevator, as if the space were a limited commodity. Initially, however, Lynda had judged the behavior "wrong," based on her own cultural experience of politeness among people entering elevators.

The lesson learned is that how one enters an elevator is not based on some universal code of conduct. (Nor is it unique to one particular culture. Anyone who has lived in New York and experienced the rush-hour "fight" to board a subway car would equate the two sets of behaviors!) When cultures meet, there is a possibility for conflict because each cultural representative believes he or she knows the "right" way to live. When team members are unwilling to accept people and ideas other than

their own—even ideas presented by someone from their own country—
this intolerance will prevent the team from achieving high performance.

The least you can do is learn how to say "Good Morning":
　　Guten Morgen (German).
　　Günadyin (Turkish).
　　Bonjour (French).
　　Buon giorno (Italian).
　　Buenos días (Spanish).

■ WHAT ARE YOUR CULTURAL STEREOTYPES?

Stereotyping is the process by which we attribute certain traits or characteristics to individuals based on a group (or groups) to which they belong. One of the most common forms of stereotyping that occurs literally around the world is gender stereotyping—for instance, the notion that, by nature, all women are passive and all men are aggressive.

Individuals also hold certain cultural stereotypes about themselves and people from other countries. To get a glimpse of this stereotyping, we asked a group of Americans who have done no business and little personal travel outside of the United States to identify the traits they associate with certain cultures. Here are some of the responses we received:

➤ Germans: scientific; intelligent; methodical; structured.

➤ English: conservative; closed-minded; reserved.

➤ French: passionate; arrogant; *"laissez-faire."*

➤ Japanese: slow to trust; consensus builders; reticent with feedback.

➤ Italians: impulsive; emotional; argumentative.

➤ Latin Americans: lazy/procrastinating; casual; friendly.

➤ Australians: selfish; not very direct.

➤ Thais: shy; nonconfrontative; reserved in public settings.

On our first visit to Argentina, we confronted some of our own stereotyping. Having had no time to pick up a *Fodor's Guide* in advance, we were ill-prepared to see how "un-Latin" the people looked who were standing in the Residents Immigration Line at the airport. We thought the plane had been diverted to Europe. After working and socializing in Buenos Aires for five days, we learned that Argentina, particularly Buenos Aires, had in its history been a popular immigration spot for

Europeans. Without that experience, we might have assumed that Argentines, like Chileans or Peruvians or Mexicans, all have more racially darkened skin and—in keeping with another stereotype—are always late for meetings. While discussing these traits over lunch with Latin colleagues, we were informed that Argentines and Peruvians tend to be true to their Latin stereotype and typically *are* late for meetings; however, most Chileans, because of the strong influence of their German immigrants, are generally punctual.

In sorting out the cultural nuances and sensitivities of world-class teams, the following exercise may be helpful. The Team Leader or a facilitator could direct the activities. (This is not an icebreaker. Do it after a team has done some work together.)

Write down a specific stereotypical behavior of each of your team members' cultures that you believe *could* be a source of annoyance or an irritant to you. Share this with each team member, confirm or disconfirm the stereotypes, and then develop a working agreement about the behavior.

A related exercise would be to propose one of your own behaviors that you believe could be annoying to others on the team. This is a disclosure as well as a feedback exercise.

One team we worked with did a modified version of the exercise above. Here are a few of their responses about how their own cultures were playing out in their teamwork:

➤ *Carolyn/French.* "We are more individualistic and challenge authority."

➤ *Ian/British.* "We are reserved. It's difficult to open up and let you share in my world."

➤ *Trüng/Norwegian.* "We are very informal."

➤ *Fanni/Italian.* "It is difficult for us to follow rules—we try to escape the rules."

As a result of this sharing, they began to not only understand each other better, but also to good-naturedly tease each other when an acknowledged behavior manifested itself.

■ CATEGORIES OF CULTURES

In *When Cultures Collide: Managing Successfully Across Cultures,* author Richard Lewis provides a framework for understanding different cultural "types." He indicates that "the several hundred national and regional cultures of the world can be roughly classified into three groups: task-oriented, highly organized planners (linear-active); people-oriented, loquacious interrelators (multi-active); and introverted, respect-oriented listeners (reactive)."[2]

Linear-actives are generally analytical and have a tendency to break projects into small tasks that are undertaken one at a time. They like to have a high degree of structure and conformity. For example, the German country manager of one of our clients, upon formation of a team structure throughout Europe, wanted to have a "rule book for teams," in which every operational aspect of the teams could be spelled out as a standard operating procedure.

Multi-actives rely more on human interaction, rather than policies and procedures, to get things done. They do not have time for memos, but will talk over an issue for hours. They move from one project to another and try to use their influence skills to get work done. This cultural characteristic was much in evidence when we were asked by the division manager of one of our Italian clients to come to Rome and help her convince her colleagues to reorganize into cross-functional teams. We went to Rome for two days to conduct a team diagnostic session (see Chapter 15). At the end of the session, we suggested a Plan of Action to "push for a decision" (true to our American style) and they, including the division manager, resisted our process suggestion. When we were back in the United States, we inquired regularly about their progress and wondered when they would finally decide. Almost a year later, we learned that they would be moving to a team structure and would probably want our help with the implementation. Typical "unhurried" Italians dealing with typical "impatient" Americans, right?

Reactives are among the best listeners in the world. They are intent on understanding the points made by others before offering their own points of view. So they practice what we call "active listening," which is intended to both register and demonstrate understanding. They will rarely interrupt, and they avoid confrontation. They are thoughtful and may be perceived by their multi-active counterparts as "painfully slow" at arriving at a decision. Lewis cites Finns and Japanese as examples of those who exhibit these listening habits—a "culture-oriented silence"—during negotiating processes: "The American habit of 'thinking aloud,' the French stage performance, the Italian baring of the soul in intimate chatter, the rhetoric of the Arabs—all these are communicative gambits designed to gain the confidence of the listener, to share ideas which can then be discussed and modified. The Finn and the Japanese listen with a kind of horror, for in their countries a statement is a sort of commitment to stand by, not to change, twist or contradict in the very next breath."[3]

Toolkit 8.1 lists some examples of those cultures, based on Lewis's research, that fall into these three categories.

8.1 Categories of Cultures

LINEAR-ACTIVES

Germans, Swiss.
Americans (White Anglo-Saxon Protestant).
Scandinavians, Austrians.
British, Canadians, New Zealanders.
Australians, South Africans.
Chileans.

MULTI-ACTIVES

Russians, other Slavs.
Portuguese.
Polynesians.
Spanish, Southern Italians, Mediterranean peoples.
Indians, Pakistanis, etc.
Latin Americans, Arabs, Africans.

REACTIVES

Japanese.
Chinese.
Taiwanese.
Singaporeans, Hong Kong residents.*
Finns.*
Koreans.
Turks.†
Malaysians, Indonesians.†

---

* Linear-active tendencies when reacting.
† Multi-active tendencies when reacting.
Source: Adapted from *When Cultures Collide: Managing Successfully Across Cultures* by Richard D. Lewis.

■ ORGANIZATIONAL STRUCTURE AND LEADERSHIP

When working with people from different cultures—either to examine the desirability and viability of establishing a team-based structure, or to identify how to develop high-performing teams—you should examine the larger "cultural issues" (of the company and/or the countries involved) that will exert a strong influence on your success and strategies.

Traditionally, we refer to company cultures with such terms as "entrepreneurial," "hierarchical/command and control," or "team-oriented/

consensus-driven." Countries, too, have distinct preferences for how they organize their societies, governments, work, and family units. The research compiled by Richard Lewis, for example, shows "autocratic" as the preferred organizational structure and leadership culture for the French; "consensus rule" for Asians; and "hierarchy and consensus" for Germans.

Let's take the latter example a bit further and apply it to world-class teams. The Germans value technical qualifications, prefer working within their functional silos (cross-functional communication is discouraged), and respond well to the authority of their bosses. This could prove to be important knowledge if you are seeking to put a German on your world-class team. We had one client who succeeded in getting a highly qualified German expert in a field of specialized marketing on his team, but unfortunately had difficulty accessing this valued addition for team endeavors. Though working on the pan-European team was seen as important, the German team member's first loyalty was to his functional boss and to his work back in his country's department, which consistently prevented him from attending team meetings.

On Toolkit 8.2, put a checkmark (√) next to the adjectives that best describe you. Add up the checkmarks in each of the columns. Column A is a list of adjectives for Linear-active cultures, Column B is for Multi-active cultures, and Column C is for Reactive cultures. Your behavior (according to your self-perception) is best reflective of the column in which you checked the most items. Compare your results to the research outlined in Toolkit 8.1. Does your behavior conform to your cultural "stereotype"? If so, in what way? If not, why not?

■ DEVELOPING INTERCULTURAL SENSITIVITY

As we've noted earlier, there are national and sometimes regional "norms" of Values and behaviors, but we must be careful not to assume that all the French are arrogant or that all Japanese value consensual decision making. Human beings the world over have basic needs and personal traits that may override their cultural traditions. Although you do not want to engage in stereotyping by assuming similarities in all Italians or all Latin Americans, research has shown that people who share a national origin have certain core beliefs and values that influence how they think and act.

World-class Team Leaders require a great deal of knowledge of different cultures to manage their team members and work toward successful outcomes. The challenge increases exponentially when each team member is from a different function and nation. Once values (both cultural and personal) are formed, they do not change easily. "Culture

8.2 What's My "Culture"

Column A	Column B	Column C
Introvert	Extrovert	Introvert
Patient	Impatient	Patient
Quiet	Talkative	Silent
Minds own business	Inquisitive	Respectful
Likes privacy	Gregarious	Good listener
Plans ahead methodically	Plans grand outline only	Looks at general principles
Does one thing at a time	Does several things at once	Reacts
Works fixed hours	Works any hours	Works flexible hours
Punctual	Unpunctual	Punctual
Dominated by timetables and schedules	Timetable unpredictable	Reacts to partner's timetable
Compartmentalizes projects	Lets one project influence another	Sees whole picture
Sticks to plans	Changes plans	Makes slight changes
Sticks to facts	Juggles facts	Statements are promises
Gets information from statistics, reference books, database	Gets firsthand (oral) information	
Job-oriented	People-oriented	People-oriented
Unemotional	Emotional	Quietly caring
Works within department	Gets round all departments	
Follows correct procedures	Pulls strings	Inscrutable, calm
Accepts favors reluctantly	Seeks favors	Protects face of other
Delegates to competent colleagues	Delegates to relationships	Delegates to reliable people
Completes action chains	Completes human transactions	Reacts to partner
Likes fixed agendas	Interrelates everything	Thoughtful
Brief on telephone	Talks for hours	Summarizes well
Uses memoranda	Rarely writes memos	Plans slowly
Respects officialdom	Seeks out (top) key person	Ultrahonest
Dislikes losing face	Has ready excuses	Must not lose face
Confronts with logic	Confronts emotionally	Avoids confrontation
Uses minimal body language, if any	Uses unrestricted body language	Uses subtle body language
Rarely interrupts	Interrupts frequently	Doesn't interrupt
Separates social/professional	Interweaves social/professional	Connects social and professional

clashes" are inevitable, and successful team leaders need to learn how to bridge the cultural gaps between team members.

Some strategies that people use for dealing with cultural diversity have been put forth by Nancy Adler, a pioneer in international research, in her article "Cultural Synergy: Managing the Impact of Cultural Diversity."[4] These strategies are:

> ➤ *Ethnocentric and parochial strategies,* where people view differences as problems; their main approach is to minimize the diversity by ignoring it or deeming it inferior.

> ➤ *Cultural synergy strategies,* where people assume that myriad perspectives on a situation, if equally considered, will yield better outcomes.

When you are trying to find the glue for your culturally diverse team, we strongly believe that the *wrong* strategy is to adopt an ethnocentric approach or, alternately, to try and get a team member to adopt or change a value. Instead, look for common or shared values and develop agreed-on operating behaviors that the team can share. The sequence is: first acknowledge the differences and then look for areas of similarity and agreement.

Cultural Diversity Ground Rules

1. Understand yourself. What are your explicit values? Do you act in accordance with those values or are they just "espoused" values? Be a role model for behavior that is inclusive and not prejudicial, curious and not alienating.

2. Try to relate to each team member as an individual and not as a stereotype of his or her national culture. Leave stereotypes and right/wrong judgments behind; bring along an appreciation for cultural—and individual—diversity instead.

3. Think of yourself as a "translator" of your particular culture. Engage with other team members in openly comparing different cultural Values, behaviors, communication styles, and attitudes toward work, both for the purpose of learning and to find common ground.

4. Err on the side of more rather than less team structure and communication. Don't assume that people will automatically know the "ground rules" for teams.

5. Explicitly ask each team member how he or she would like to be addressed and treated, and work out some Operating Agreements to guide the team's interaction.

6. Do not assume that a certain unacceptable or disagreeable behavior is intentional. Clarify potential misunderstandings, especially around cultural values. Be tactful and discreet if you are not sure about areas or issues that may be particularly sensitive, given a team member's cultural and/or individual values.

7. Lighten up and tease each other about—and maybe even make use of—cultural stereotypes that apparently hold true for an individual. For example, if someone from Australia is quite blunt, and you suspect the team is in conflict and not "owning up" to it, ask (if you even need to) for "the outspoken Australian's" perspective on the issue.

8. Hold your team meetings at different locations. Ask each host-country team member to include some form of cultural learning during the team's visit. Show an interest in national and local sources of pride.

9. Be aware of other team members' time zones and working hours. Don't expect unreasonable availability for conference calls.

10. Be aware of local customs (thou-shalts and thou-shalt-nots). Ask team members about special holidays or celebrations in their respective countries, and be sensitive to these dates in preparing the team's work and meeting schedule.

11. Master the correct pronunciation and spelling of every team member's name!

12. Learn at least the basic phrases of each team member's language, such as *hello, good-bye, thank you,* and *please.*

13. Seek to discover the "unique glue" that holds together the diversity represented in your team.

14. Rely on your own self-esteem and self-confidence. People who trust themselves are more poised in unfamiliar surroundings and are willing to consider perspectives different from their own.

■ CROSS-CULTURAL COMMUNICATIONS

When working in Asia with a cross-cultural team of information systems specialists from China, Korea, Southeast Asia, and Australia, we asked at the beginning of the first team meeting: "What cultural issues do we need to be aware of that might influence this team's process and success?" Team members from Malaysia and Thailand suggested that their lack of openness and their unwillingness to criticize ideas in public might affect the team. That prompted a contrary remark from an Australian team member, who noted that his bluntness might put his team members off. By the week's end, the Australian was stopping himself before he spoke, and the Asians were more forthright (to the point that they expressed concern about carrying this new open style of behavior back home!).

One of the traditional hallmarks of a successful team, as defined by Western culture, is "open and honest communications." We talk about the ideal team member as someone who is candid and truthful about his or her thoughts and feelings. However, the concept of *truth* varies in different cultures. To Germans, truth tends to be Truth (capital T)—absolute and direct even if it is harsh or possibly hurtful. The British, on the other hand, may avoid telling the truth for fear of "rocking the boat." The French, Americans, Italians, and Latinos tend to be less open with their true thoughts and feelings because they value smooth social relationships. Among the Chinese, Japanese, and other Asians, truth is commonly perceived as a "relative concept" and may be withheld to avoid "losing face."

Another core team concept is maximum involvement and participation of team members during meetings and in between-meetings communications. However, different cultures react to and use silence or nonparticipation differently. Americans, Italians, and the French not only tend to communicate frequently, but are also prone to interrupt when others are speaking. Conversely, the Japanese and Chinese often use silence as a strategic tool. An old Chinese proverb says: "Those who know do not speak; those who speak do not know." In the Asian cultures, silence indicates a willingness to listen and learn and demonstrates a respect for the other person. Talking too much may be perceived as boastful and selfish.

The communication process of Americans (among others) is generally *dialogue*. They are known for "thinking out loud," and brainstorming is a common team tool for them. The prevalent communication style of Asians is *monologue*. Interestingly, if team members could learn to use both types of behaviors—alternating talkative involvement with listening/learning silence, as appropriate—they would be very effective.

Bhinneka Tunggal Ika (Unity through Diversity)

—National motto of Indonesia

It cannot be overemphasized that there is no good/bad or right/wrong in terms of cultural perspectives on "what makes a good team." An important aspect of aligning a world-class team is to ensure that different cultural values are allowed expression. We noted a striking example of this concern following a teambuilding session with another team we worked with in Asia. It came in the form of this e-mail from one of the team members:

I guess the fact that the dynamics changed somewhat as the meeting progressed is more evidence that people are the same the world over, but with one striking difference—in most parts of Asia, the expression of that sameness is often muted by cultural mores. Thankfully, the teambuilding seemed to have begun to work as the meeting progressed. But I am left wondering whether we're possibly force-fitting our desires to see team behaviors expressed in a Western way and, out of their desire to please, they simply caught on to what we wanted, and the behaviors followed. In other words, I am wondering whether we haven't led them down the same old Western concepts of what we see as team behavior when, in fact, some Asian cultures have a quite different concept of what a team is and what is "good team" behavior.

■ CROSS-CULTURAL INTERACTION IN BUSINESS MEETINGS

Sharon, an American, had been given her first international assignment, working with a cross-cultural team of marketing specialists based in Chile. From her perspective, all was not well. She approached us with frustrations about not being able to make things happen as fast or as completely as she'd like, noting in particular that not all of the team members were attending meetings and that people were not being responsive to her information requests.

Sharon attributed the problems to her own lack of skills and abilities. We turned the discussion toward the Latin culture, talking to her about the value Latinos generally place on building relationships and how, compared to her own cultural norms, her team may tend to take a more conciliatory and "laid-back" approach to getting work done. Through this discussion, Sharon began to see that because her *context* had changed, she needed to adapt her leadership strategies, which were primarily task-focused, to meet the needs/expectations of team members from more relationship-oriented cultures. Did she need to drop her task orientation? No; she just needed to balance it and use it competently within her new context.

This story points to one of the main advantages of heightening your level of cultural awareness when you start working with cross-cultural teams. If you're headed to a new country or region and/or will be working with people of various nationalities, learning about the cultural/social norms can help you to anticipate in advance what *might* happen so that you can adjust or be ready to adjust your behavior accordingly.

You can get a "Culturgram" for a specific country (a map, briefings on culture, lifestyle, travel, and so forth) by calling Kennedy Center Publications, part of the David M. Kennedy Center for International Studies at Brigham Young University, at 1-800-528-6279 (Provo, Utah).

From our own travels and work with culturally diverse teams, we have seen much evidence that, on an emotional level, people tend to be driven by many of the same fundamental needs and concerns; yet, how they express or act on those needs and concerns can be quite different, depending on their cultural backgrounds. The observations that follow focus on cross-cultural interaction in business meetings and are gleaned from our personal experiences working around the globe—from which we have indeed learned to adapt our leadership styles to the context! A word of caution: as we've said repeatedly, we are offering these as generalizations and not guideposts.

➤ Humor

Americans are known for their sarcasm and use of jokes in business meetings, particularly at the expense of a common enemy, such as "management." American author Scott Adams has become a self-made millionaire from his Dilbert© cartoons that depict the foibles and stupidity of managers. Reproductions of his cartoons are used as handouts and slides at many American team meetings. He even makes fun of the overuse of teams, deeming it a strategy for calling more meetings to avoid real work.

The British tend to use humor as a distraction tool during meetings. Australians frequently use it, along with their harsh honesty, to be provocative and perhaps argumentative. The Japanese and Germans, however, generally avoid joking in business situations. They consider it inappropriate behavior for the serious context of a business meeting. In social situations, they are quite willing to share some laughs—as long as they are not poking fun at any one person.

Whatever the context, a good rule of thumb with regard to jokes and storytelling is to remember that what is funny to you may be offensive— or totally incomprehensible—to others, depending on their cultural upbringing. Not only the subject matter, but also the use of expressions or slang words may be literally "foreign" to a team member.

➤ Time Management

If Germans or Asians are in attendance, you can almost guarantee that they will arrive on time and will expect a smoothly running agenda and a specific Plan of Action with responsibilities and deadlines assigned.

Americans are typically results-oriented. Their punctuality is more often a function of their company's culture, although they are more prone to having meetings start and end on schedule.

The Spanish, Italians, Latin Americans, and other Latinos tend to place less importance on punctuality or deadlines—although, as noted earlier, the opposite tendency among Chileans points to the need to be careful about making across-the-board assumptions.

➤ Decision Making

Americans are, on the whole, results- and decision-oriented, but they will modify their opinions after being "sold." The French tend to like talking about possibilities and will delay decisions if an action does not seem logical from their perspective.

The Japanese are well known for using consensual decision making. What is perhaps less well known is that this strategy is used by individuals to avoid making decisions independently. Decisions are talked about with several partners over a long period of time during which the decision becomes a fait accompli.

Latinos typically look to authority figures to make decisions. The Arabs, Chinese, and Japanese often use interactions outside of formal meetings, or "go-betweens," to help facilitate decision making.

■ THE USES OF DIVERSITY

Kelly O'Dea, president of worldwide client services for Ogilvy & Mather Advertising, believes that "people, just like brands, must be 'globalized' if they're to compete successfully in rapidly changing international markets." In other words, you must develop a global perspective on your products and projects, and to do that, you need to know how business is done in other parts of the world.

International teams are here to stay, and we must invest the time necessary to educate team members about each other's cultures and languages (which influences thought and working/social patterns) if teams are to be harmonious and integrated. The investment will be primarily in time, not in money, and the task certainly becomes more difficult on world-class teams comprised of multiple cultures and languages.

Nancy Adler notes that, in numerous studies she has conducted, "Neither managers nor academics generally think of culture as affecting an organization's day-to-day operations. Very often, good managers perceive themselves as beyond passport and good organizations as beyond nationality."[5]

Generally, our experiences suggest *people are people* no matter where they reside in the global community, but there can be no dispute that cultural heritage (norms, values, customs, and so on) influences how a person thinks and behaves. For example, in the Thai language, there is no concept of assertiveness and no vocabulary to support the idea of "selling yourself." In fact, the idea is not only "foreign" in Thai culture; it is considered "wrong." Most Americans, on the other hand, think nothing of selling themselves as "Me, Inc."

Evaluating such cultural differences—that is, deeming them inherently good or bad—leads to undesirable ethnocentric attitudes and behaviors. At the other end of the extreme, failing to recognize or acknowledge cultural differences is highly unproductive. When we ignore or downplay the impact of cultural diversity, we limit our ability to minimize the problems it can spark and, conversely, to maximize its potential advantages.

Often, simultaneously, people neither "see" nor "want to see" differences. Why is that? Our guess is that differences create dissonance and discomfort; they stir up "problems" that must be dealt with. So, the reasoning goes: Ignore them and they will go away. That, of course, is a naive and ineffective mind-set.

We can never truly understand a culture that is "foreign" to our own upbringing, language, traditions, mores, and historic/landmark events, but world-class teams can aim to appreciate and learn as much as possible in order to facilitate productive work and complementary and respectful relationships. As we mentioned earlier, the best world-class teams we have observed have been those that had respect for—and actually sought out—balance and diversity in perspectives and skills. These are the teams that achieve breakthrough results.

For all the particular difficulties world-class teams may face with regard to communications and decision making, they gain overwhelming advantages in being able to draw from the broad, multiple perspectives of their team members' knowledge of the prevailing political, social, and economic forces in different countries/markets.

At the same time, it is important to remember that world-class teams need to create their own "culture," that is, a set of Values and Operating Agreements that will accommodate and bring out the best in each of their team members. Every successful team is held together by its own unique "glue"—those attributes and proficiencies that transcend cultural differences and characterize and unite the team as a whole. If you can express cultural curiosity and empathy, and then add some careful listening, sensitivity, patience, and politeness, you will be seen as a valuable international team member anywhere in the world.

STRATEGY

3

Leading
World-Class Teams

Chapter

Selecting and Developing World-Class Team Leaders

HELP WANTED: WORLD-CLASS TEAM LEADER. Will ensure that our company maximizes and leverages the intellectual capital of our knowledge workers, who will work under your leadership in cross-functional/cross-cultural networked teams from remote locations. Compensation will be directly linked to your team's ability to add substantial value to the company's profitability and market share. Will consider candidates with related job experience, which may include orchestra conductor, emergency room triage coordinator, improvisational jazz ensemble player, and/or sports team coach.

Up to this point in our book, you must be thinking that the job of a world-class Team Leader is pretty important and difficult. Indeed, some who have held that distinguished position have told us that "can walk on water" should be the sole criterion for selection. They believe that the responsibility for leading cross-functional/cross-cultural teams is so complex that it defies specification. Then how can you go about choosing the right person? And who would even want a job with this kind of pressure?

Admittedly, the job isn't for everyone. But there are more than a few good women and men who are capable of leading world-class teams, and several parameters can be used to figure out what these leaders actually *do* and, thus, what requirements to look for. To succeed, much care and attention must be directed toward both the selection and the development of individuals to fulfill this role. Whether you're the candidate yourself or you're trying to single someone out, you first need to appreciate how complex—and how exhilarating—the ride can be.

■ "MIRROR, MIRROR, ON THE WALL . . ."

Who is the best Team Leader of them all? If we knew the definitive answer to our version of the Wicked Queen's question, we would have the task of finding a Team Leader half done—that is, we would know what skills, knowledge, and competencies are required. The second half of the task is harder: finding and selecting those candidates that best fit the profile.

Unfortunately, many Sponsors, when seeking to fill their world-class Team Leader positions, don't spend a significant amount of time analyzing both the team's requirements and the Team Leader's job description before looking at candidates. For example, one Sponsor we worked with had spent months looking for a new Team Leader for a product team. Over a lovely dinner in London, he told us about his dilemma: "At first I had no candidates for this job, but now I have three, and I just can't choose which one I like best. I have an American who's an expert on the product. A British expert working in the United States who wants to come back to Europe to lead. And a Brit who's dying to get on a European team. How do I decide?"

When asked if he had thought through, systematically, the requirements for the job, he replied, "Well, not really." (His tone implied, "What's that got to do with anything?") He happens to be a highly intuitive manager, but as we talked about the relative skills of his other Team Leaders, he realized that he had possibly made some selection errors in his previous choices. He decided that this time around he might want to go through a more systematic selection process.

As we noted in Chapter 3, the world-class Team Leader is vested with a considerable level of diverse responsibilities for the management of a substantial amount of human and financial resources. The model in Toolkit 9.1 illustrates the various dimensions that a Team Leader must keep in his or her spotlight (or on a computer screen!) at all times. Like a helicopter pilot scanning the landscape, the world-class Team Leader must maintain a balanced focus on the key elements that will help his or her team achieve the Vision (the team's Charter and Boundaries) and the Results (the team's goals) expected by the stakeholders (customers, owners, suppliers, and support groups). These elements are:

➤ Team Performance: *What* are we doing to achieve our Vision and Results?

➤ Team Process: *How* are we working to achieve our Vision and Results?

➤ Team Members: *Who,* with what individual needs and accomplishments, is working for this team?

➤ Border Management: *Who* are our key stakeholders, and how are we managing their needs and expectations?

Toolkit 9.2 lists the specific job functions that Team Leaders must perform in each of those "spotlight areas" of focus.

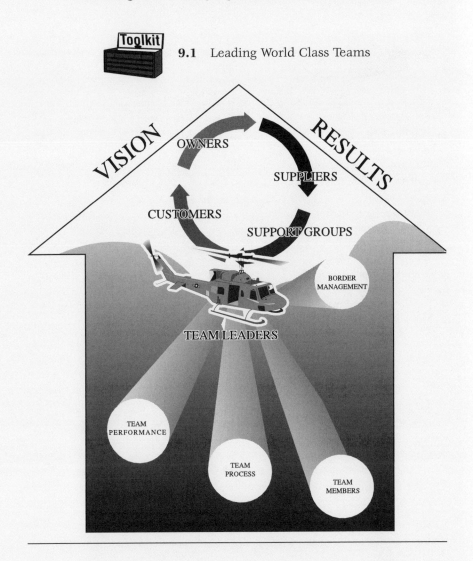

Toolkit 9.1 Leading World Class Teams

■ WORLD-CLASS TEAM LEADER ROLES

As we learned in Chapter 7, performing these job functions requires the Team Leader to assume different *roles*. (See Chapter 7 for a description of the Team Role Analysis™ process.) For example, when fulfilling the Team Performance function, the Team Leader will likely be engaged as The Strategist. Or, when performing the Coaching function, he or she may need to be The Enforcer, The Teacher, or The Cheerleader.

9.2   What Do World-Class Team Leaders Do?

Team Leaders manage four distinct areas of focus (to some degree, the areas overlap):

1. *Team Performance*
   Strategic Planning and Goal Setting
   Performance Management
   Project Management

2. *Team Process*
   Team Decision Making
   Managing Change
   Communications
   Facilitating Meetings
   Creative Problem Solving

3. *Team Members*
   Delegation and Empowerment
   Motivation and Coaching
   Constructive Conflict Management
   Handling Problem Team Members
   Building Trust and Collaboration
   Team and Individual Recognition

4. *Border Management*
   Stakeholder Analysis
   Stakeholder Strategies
   Stakeholder Relationships

World-class Team Leaders need to select the job functions and roles that are *strategically required* for a particular team, as we'll discuss later in this chapter.

Beyond the major job functions listed in Toolkit 9.2, what does a Team Leader specifically do for a living? For example, in one Team Launch Document, the Team Leader's task-related job functions were broadly defined to include:

➤ Coordinates team meetings, including setting team meeting agendas.

➤ Clarifies the team's Charter.

➤ Keeps the team focused on achieving team objectives.

Although we have attempted to provide you with a framework for what world-class Team Leaders do, why not create your own job description?

Invite your team members, Sponsor, and any key stakeholders to a meeting (or try the process electronically) to help you develop a job description so that you and they are clear about what they can expect from you. Ask each participant to respond individually—either on index cards (if you're in the same room) or by making a list of bulleted points (if you're on e-mail)—to this question:

"In my role as Team Leader, what do you expect of me?" (Please write out your expectations beginning with an infinitive, e.g.: "*To monitor* Team Performance through a focus on Team Objectives.")

As Team Leader, you should prepare your own set of expectations for your role.

After you have received all of your requested inputs and opinions, try to consolidate the various statements into six to ten categories. For example, some specific items may fit into a category called *Communications* (e.g., "To develop and conduct key presentations with senior-level project stakeholders"); others may fall under *Project Management* (e.g., "To conduct quarterly project review meetings/videoconferences").

When you have completed a first draft, send it back out to those who participated in the initial process (and any others who might be appropriate) for their review. When you receive their feedback, prepare a final document titled: Team Leader Job Description/Expectations. It will serve as a "contract" among you, your team, and your stakeholders.

■ WORLD-CLASS TEAM LEADER COMPETENCIES

When you have the "what"—clear job expectations—in place, you can define and align the "how"—the competencies necessary to meet the expectations. By defining and aligning competencies with job expectations, you will be able to create a "job profile," as well as a training and development plan that is focused and aligned. (More on that in a later section of this chapter.)

Competency was described in Chapter 7 as the "characteristics and behaviors of people who do a particular job well," based on a definition provided by Harvard Professor Emeritus David McClelland. For Team

Leaders in particular, we have defined their competencies as broadly falling into these six categories:

1. Managing Team Performance.
2. Managing Team Process.
3. Building the Team (team focus).
4. Developing Team Members (individual focus).
5. Providing Personal Leadership.
6. Global Management.

These competencies are directly related to the four major spotlight areas described in Toolkits 9.1 and 9.2. They represent, in fact, the means by which Team Leaders keep their spotlights focused!

Other subcategories of competencies appear in various competency-based leadership assessment tools, such as the 20/20 Team Player© assessment from Performance Support Systems, Inc. They include:

1. Managing Team Performance:
   ➤ Planning.
   ➤ Team problem solving.
   ➤ Team decision making.
   ➤ Organizational alignment.
   ➤ Client/customer focus.
   ➤ Project management.
   ➤ Strategic perspective.
2. Managing Team Process:
   ➤ Leading meetings.
   ➤ Time management.
   ➤ Communication (interactive listening and dialogue).
   ➤ Encouraging innovation.
   ➤ Process observation.
   ➤ Organizing and controlling.
   ➤ Use of team technology.
3. Building the Team (team focus):
   ➤ Collaborating.
   ➤ Resolving conflicts.

4. Developing Team Members (individual focus):
   ➤ Delegation/empowerment.
   ➤ Coaching.
   ➤ Appraising performance.
5. Providing Personal Leadership:
   ➤ Influence.
   ➤ Developing followership.
   ➤ Interpersonal skills.
   ➤ Stress and ambiguity management.
   ➤ Technical, industry, and business expertise.
6. Global Management:
   ➤ Managing individual and cultural diversity.
   ➤ Remote management.
   ➤ Language.

On world-class teams, it is difficult for the Team Leader to keep the spotlights balanced and focused when team members work in remote locations, have different functional and cultural backgrounds, and may report to multiple bosses. In her article on "Global Work Teams," Sylvia Odenwald talks about the unique competencies of those global Team Leaders who must be able to coordinate across time, distance, and culture.[1] In some cases, they manage team members who speak different languages, use different technologies, and have different beliefs about authority, time, and decision making. Often, the team members have never met face-to-face.

Accordingly, we believe that Team Leaders also must display competencies related to the category of "global" management, which would include:

➤ Intercultural proficiency.

➤ Collaborative orientation.

➤ Ability to prioritize and respond to demands coming from multiple sources.

➤ Capacity to develop a broad organizational perspective.

➤ Ability to maintain flexibility and deal with the stress of ambiguity.

➤ Aptitude for influencing others without having the authority of positional power.

(Refer to Chapter 8 for strategies related to valuing cultural diversity.)

■ TEAM LEADERSHIP STYLES AND STAGES OF TEAM DEVELOPMENT

In Chapter 7, we advised you to remember "Context, context, context" when assembling a world-class team. The same advice holds when selecting a person to *lead* that team. Before interviewing a candidate for a Team Leader position, you must give careful thought to the context within which he or she will be leading. You must address issues such as:

➤ Is this a new team or one he or she is inheriting?

➤ How comfortable is the organization with teams and/or with this team specifically? Will this Team Leader be breaking new ground or stepping into familiar territory?

➤ How complex and visible is the work of this team?

➤ Beyond team leadership skills, is there a critical requirement for particular technical or functional expertise?

➤ What border management issues will need to be resolved?

A team's organizational context raises major considerations regarding team leadership, not the least of which has to do with the team's stage of development. Over the years, several models of group and team development have been designed to explain the stages of growth that teams go through from their inception until their completion. The model that works best for us is presented graphically in Toolkit 9.3 and described more specifically in Toolkit 9.4. Although the source is unknown, it likely is a refinement of the "Forming, Storming, Norming" theory of team development coined by Bruce Tuckerman in the mid-1960s.

Here are a few principles to keep in mind when analyzing your team's stage of team development:

➤ Work can get done at any stage, but it can be extremely difficult if you haven't at least explored issues in the "Why We're Here" stage.

➤ A team evolves naturally through these stages and may, in fact, be in more than one stage at a time.

➤ Just when you think you have one set of issues (e.g., goals) resolved and can get to the "real" work, another set of issues (e.g., Who *really* makes decisions on this team?) emerges.

➤ Team members' behaviors unwittingly may change to match the stage of team development. You may be surprised to see a team member who seemed very polite, respectful, and engaged start to get into conflicts or appear to passively drop out as issues about "who's doing what" begin to surface.

Toolkit

9.3   Stages of Team Development

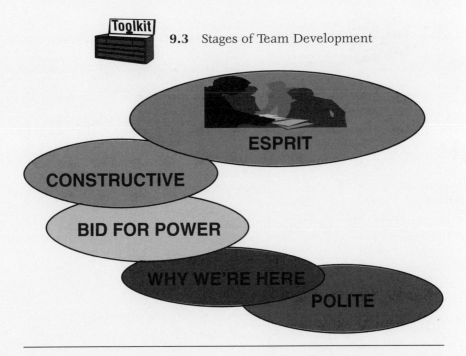

ESPRIT

CONSTRUCTIVE

BID FOR POWER

WHY WE'RE HERE

POLITE

➤   As frustrations and nonproductive behavior appear on the scene, don't try to submerge or avoid them. They are inevitable manifestations of growth (just like a two-year-old's temper tantrums).

As Team Leader, you should be well versed in these developmental stages and help your team move through them and toward the "Constructive" and "Esprit" stages.

What Team Leader style is appropriate at each stage of the team's development? After responding with the typical consultant caveat—"It depends"—we would note that we have made use of several comprehensive and complex leadership models to assess and coach Team Leaders over the years. We have extended Ken Blanchard and Paul Hersey's "Situational Leadership Theory" to stages of team development, with practical results. Essentially, this theory, as it applies to teams, suggests that, in the first stages of a team's development (the "Polite" and "Why We're Here" stages), commitment or motivation of team members is probably tentative because people are unsure of the team's Charter and Boundaries and of their individual respective roles and responsibilities. In addition, their individual technical expertise and functional knowledge may be high, but their abilities to serve in the roles of a cross-functional team

9.4   Stages of Team Development Description

tStage	Purpose	Activities/Behavior	Facilitative Actions
Polite	Get acquainted	Active participation Ideas kept simple Agreement Clique forming Need for approval strong Avoid: Conflict 　　　　Serious topics 　　　　Self-disclosure	• • • •
Why We're Here	Set goals, objectives	Agenda setting Cliques influence activities Hidden agendas emerge Disagreements Risk taking Commitment/Structure Look for outside help	• • • •
Bid for Power	Establish norms and rules	Competition Rational influence attempts Power plays Leadership struggle Attempts to resolve by voting, 　compromise, seeking help Cliques used to wield power/ 　influence Roles emerge: 　　　　The Groupbuilder 　　　　The Harmonizer 　　　　The Gatekeeper 　　　　The Follower	• • • •
Constructive	Work to achieve goals, solve problems	Active listening Willingness to change Cliques begin to dissolve Group identity begins Use resources Manage conflict Shared leadership Creativity Reject new members & external 　influence	• • • •
Esprit	High-perform-ance group	High morale Intense group loyalty Empathic relations No cliques High creativity Create identity symbol Group strongly "closed"	• • • •

member and company advocate (that is, to provide a strategic industry and company perspective) are probably low.

In that stage of development, our experience with teams has shown a need for what Blanchard and Hersey would refer to as a high task/low relationship Team Leader style. When we help new teams to launch, we recommend that some time (but not a lot) be spent doing relationship-building exercises, and relatively more time be put toward providing the team with structure—developing a team Charter and Boundaries, explicitly outlining Operating Agreements, establishing team goals, and so forth.

Remember, experience tells us that teamwork does not come naturally, and team members generally have low competence in addressing team process/teamwork issues. Alternately, a more highly supportive (relationship) style with less direction is more appreciated by team members who have struggled through the issues of "Who are we?" and "What do we do?" These particular team members need more help in managing their resources and processes, their borders, and team members' individual needs.

How does this relate to Team Leader competencies? Early in a team's formation, you probably should select leaders who have both high task competencies (e.g., technical and project management: The Organizer role) and high relationship competencies (e.g., consensus building, interpersonal relationship: The Cheerleader role). As the team develops through to the "Constructive" stage, the Team Leader needs less technical/functional knowledge, continues with relationship competencies (consensus building, border management: The Politician role), and becomes more empowering (e.g., coaching: The Delegator or The Teacher role) in his or her style.

Throughout these stages of team development, the Team Leader must maintain a balance among all four spotlight areas of focus by:

➤ Keeping a strong focus on the team's Charter and the accomplishment of short- and long-term goals by reviewing and celebrating goal accomplishments.

➤ Reviewing, adapting, and creating new team processes that will continuously improve the quality, speed, and efficiency of the team's work products.

➤ Continuing to build the competencies and confidence of team members by shifting team assignments and roles.

➤ Continuously reviewing the border management issues and developing creative strategies for strengthening relationships with key stakeholders.

■ DEVELOPING WORLD-CLASS TEAM LEADERS

Are Team Leaders *born* or *made?* This age-old question has sparked many a debate about leadership development through the years. We are in the business of *development,* which clearly means we believe that individuals and organizations can change. Our experience provides us with example after example of people who believed they "had it" (and they didn't) or others who believed they "didn't" (but just hadn't labeled their competent behavior as "leadership"). However, as much as we believe people *can* develop leadership competencies and grow in the leadership role, we also believe that won't happen without an internal level of motivation—a certain quality we like to call *commitment.* If you're going to take a job as a world-class Team Leader, you had better be committed because a lot of people will be counting on you.

Even those Team Leaders who have been "perfectly" matched to the context and job profile relative to their new team will need some form of leadership development. How, you may wonder, can we make a statement implying that, universally, Team Leaders require development? Mostly, because the team context is always changing—goals change, projects change, team members change, stakeholders and their expectations change—and in the spirit of continuous improvement we all must continue to learn and grow to keep up with the pace of change.

In conducting a field study of 100 project team leaders in large Fortune 500 technology-based corporations (which historically have had more experience in multidisciplinary project team management), and 65 percent of whom managed teams with part-time members (matrix structure), here is what two researchers found:

> ➤ The major frustrations of the Team Leaders were in the areas of:
>
> —Apathy and lack of commitment among team members, which made the Team Leaders feel "helpless and powerless."
>
> —Not being empowered to secure important resources, e.g., information (to the team), budget, external cooperation.
>
> —Inability to arrive at team consensus because of diversity of views (and functional loyalties).
>
> ➤ Of the Team Leaders surveyed, 92 percent had received no formal training in group process or team building.[2]

This does not necessarily imply that had they received some form of training, their problems would simply go away. But we have learned that helping Team Leaders to anticipate problems, and providing them with ideas or access to other colleagues' experiences, can be of enormous value. Bill Waite points out two particular areas in which Team Leaders have benefited from training initiatives: "In conducting team leadership training in approximately 31 countries over the past four years, we have found that the two most prominent team leader weaknesses/developmental needs are 'Communications'—defined as setting clear performance expectations and consistently delivering clear messages about those expectations—and 'Feedback'—letting people know whether and to what degree team members are meeting your performance expectations."

The developmental strategies for Team Leaders (or team members) should be based on the specific competencies of individuals and the performance gap, if any, that exists between these competencies and what is required for a particular team. As we pointed out in Chapter 7, a wide variety of options are available to develop the competencies of world-class team members—including, of course, Team Leaders. Beyond the prospect of jumping into the job and learning as they go, Team Leaders could choose to attend an external development program. These range from inexpensive one-day U.S.-based Career Track™ seminars (such as "How to Lead a Team") to longer and more costly programs available through organizations such as the Center for Creative Leadership (such as "Leadership and High-Performance Teams") or the Management Centre in Brussels (such as "Remote Teams: Managing across Distance, Culture, Time and Technology"). (See Toolkit 9.5 for an example of one development program.)

Our own strong bias is to provide development to Team Leaders within the context of their own teams—at least initially. Later on, as a result of a Team Leader's own developmental assessment (or that of the Sponsor or other key stakeholders), he or she may decide to pursue other developmental options in addition to any further "on-the-job" team competency development activities. Laurie Smith, a European Product Team Leader, worked with his team in our two-day "Crossing the Borders Workshop" for new world-class teams, which provides ample opportunity for a Team Leader not only to exercise that role, but also to be observed and receive feedback from the team and the facilitators. A few months later, Laurie decided to attend the Management Centre's development program for leading "remote teams." Because his Team Leader experience, while broad, had never included leading a team of people who would be residing in different countries, he thought the program could provide him with some valuable information from outside experts as well as from people in other companies who would be in attendance.

Just after appointing eight new product teams, one company we worked with had each of their teams (including Team Leaders) attend our "Crossing the Borders" program. (See Chapter 7 and the Appendix, for further description of this program.) Then they followed our suggestion that

9.5 Team Leader Development Workshop

Purpose: To develop knowledge and skill in preparing for and leading world-class teams.

Objectives: At the end of this workshop, Team Leaders should be able to:

➤ Set objectives for and develop a plan to lead cross-functional teams.

➤ Establish an appropriate climate for individual and team effectiveness.

➤ Design team meetings, record progress, and conduct stakeholder briefings.

➤ Demonstrate facilitation and team leadership techniques (such as leading group discussions, asking questions, giving and receiving feedback, and working with team technologies).

➤ Critique their own and others' facilitation and team membership skills.

➤ Identify situations that arise during team meetings, and develop alternative strategies for handling them.

➤ Know how to assess team effectiveness, to provide feedback to the team, and to move teams to a higher level of effectiveness.

Content Topics: ➤ Crossing "The Borders."

➤ World-Class Team Defined.

➤ World-Class Team Startup.

➤ Selecting Team Leaders/Membership (Leadership 360 degrees).

➤ Facilitating Team Startup Issues.

➤ Defining Team Agreements/Ground Rules.

➤ Structuring a Meeting.

➤ Key Team Leader Activities.

➤ Facilitating the Team's Work.

➤ Conflict Management.

➤ Problem Solving and Decision Making.

➤ Keeping the Team and Stakeholders Informed.

➤ Evaluating Your Team and Yourself as a Team Leader.

the eight Team Leaders and their Sponsor attend a "Leading for Results" program together, six to eight months after all the teams were launched. This particular program focuses on their roles as *leaders* and is designed to provide participants with:

> ➤ Leadership 360-degree feedback on how they are performing their team leadership roles, individually and collectively.

> ➤ The opportunity to share their team leadership learnings and best practices.

> ➤ Customized skill development experiences (such as consensus building and facilitating) based on their 360-degree feedback.

This program is especially powerful because it is based largely on feedback that the Team Leader receives from his or her Sponsor, team members, and peers/colleagues/customers (thus, the term "360-degree").

We have also built into our World-Class Team Performance System a two-day Team Development Session, which we use with all new teams we launch. The session is held 10 to 12 months after the teams have been formed. As mentioned in Chapter 7, the agenda for this session is driven largely by three inputs:

1. The Team Leader (in consultation with team members) asks the team to reflect on areas they believe require further development.

2. The results of the Team Effectiveness Assessment (see Chapter 7) are distributed and analyzed in advance.

3. As prework for this session, we administer a 360-degree feedback assessment of the Team Leader. He or she asks each team member, the Sponsor, and any appropriate cross-team peers or stakeholders to complete the survey. (See Toolkit 9.6 for sample questions from this survey.)

Tips from World-Class Team Leaders

> ➤ Prioritize: Put first things first.
> ➤ Be sensitive to team members' workload.
> ➤ Make opportunities to build relationships with and between team members.
> ➤ Ensure clear communication (remember: English isn't everyone's first language).
> ➤ Look for synergies, and support interdependence.
> ➤ Look for win (team)/win (functions/countries) outcomes.

9.6   Excerpts: Team Leader Skills Survey

	Almost Never	Seldom	Sometimes	Usually	Almost Always
BUILDING THE TEAM					
➤ Facilitates communications with and among team members between team meetings.	1	2	3	4	5
➤ Respects and leverages the team's cross-functional roles and cross-cultural diversity.	1	2	3	4	5
DEVELOPING PEOPLE					
➤ Provides feedback/coaching to individual team members on their performance.	1	2	3	4	5
➤ Recognizes and rewards individual contributions to team performance.	1	2	3	4	5
TEAM PROBLEM SOLVING/DECISION MAKING					
➤ Encourages creative and "out of the box" thinking.	1	2	3	4	5
➤ Uses the appropriate decision-making style for specific issues.	1	2	3	4	5
STAKEHOLDER RELATIONS					
➤ Continues to clarify stakeholder needs/ expectations.	1	2	3	4	5
➤ Facilitates and encourages border management with the team's key stakeholders.	1	2	3	4	5

Toolkit 9.6 *(Continued)*

	Almost Never	Seldom	Sometimes	Usually	Almost Always
TEAM PERFORMANCE					
➤ Keeps team members' responsibilities and activities focused within the team's Charter and Boundaries.	1	2	3	4	5
➤ Ensures that the team meets Plan of Action and Operating Agreement team commitments.	1	2	3	4	5
TEAM PROCESS					
➤ Organizes and runs effective and productive team meetings.	1	2	3	4	5
➤ Brings *team* issues and problems to the team's attention and focuses on constructive problem solving.	1	2	3	4	5
PROVIDING PERSONAL LEADERSHIP					
➤ Demonstrates integrity and personal commitment.	1	2	3	4	5
➤ Has excellent persuasive and influence skills.	1	2	3	4	5
➤ Provides a clear vision and direction for the team.	1	2	3	4	5

This person's greatest strengths as a Team Leader are: _____

_____

_____

This person's opportunities to develop as a Team Leader are: _____

_____

_____

➤ Take time to recognize the unique contributions of team members.

➤ Learn team members' personalities and preferred work/thinking styles.

➤ Show regular interest, in a coaching way, in the progress of projects.

➤ Set stretch goals, but be sensitive to what is achievable by a remotely operating team.

➤ Manage stakeholder borders.

➤ Promote the team's projects/assignments inside and outside the organization.

■ MAKING THE TRANSITION TO TEAM LEADER

In her book *Caught in the Middle: How to Survive and Thrive in Today's Management Squeeze,* Lynda McDermott described how organizations were moving toward creating the role of "Center Leader" for middle managers. In the early 1990s, she saw this as an emerging role and addressed the need for managers to begin to see themselves—if not by job title, then at least in attitude—as a professional operating from "the center of a web of critical relationships, much like the brain center of a network, that function with mutual interdependence. . . . Being a Center Leader implies no specific structure or hierarchy; your job is to influence and mobilize others toward achieving results."[3]

With the prevalence today of world-class teams, that Center Leader role has been formalized into a position called world-class Team Leader. And it is a *pivotal* role: "As Center Leader, you'll need to coach, empower your people, act as a facilitator, learn how to elicit participation. . . . At the hub of many wheels, you'll be ensuring that information and resources are being deployed quickly to critical projects and tasks, thus increasing the ultimate value of your contribution and the recognition you gain." The team, McDermott adds, is the vehicle for the role of Center Leader—a.k.a. *Team Leader*—and this role is absolutely essential for world-class team success.[4]

"Every team needs a leader who gets people excited about achieving the goal. Team members will then come together around that goal," says Microsoft's Jeff McHenry. "We find that effective team leaders are very good at helping people set goals and make plans, giving feedback on performance, following up, and creating a strong sense of teamwork. Those teams tend to be more productive, and the team members stay with us longer." McHenry goes on to note that, in singling out potential team leaders, Microsoft looks first for "technical competence" and then for "people who are good at leading their peers . . . and are respected by others."[5]

Whether you are going from being an individual contributor on the team to being Team Leader, or from Team Leader of one team to another, here are some "transition tips":

➤ Focus on *who:*

—Team members.

—Sponsor.

—Stakeholders.

➤ Focus on *what:*

—Goals—results (projects/tasks) (team performance).

—Stakeholder relations (border management).

—Team members' needs.

—Team process issues.

Specific Tasks:

➤ Meet with each team member individually to review positive and negative perceptions of team experience, accomplishments, and concerns.

➤ Meet with your Sponsor or key stakeholders to review team performance and expectations.

➤ Take the Team Role Analysis™ (Chapter 7) and share your scores with the team.

➤ If the team has engaged in a symbolic identity exercise (e.g., each team member receives a nickname), then go through the same "rite of passage."

➤ Meet with functional bosses of team members to review team member performance and career issues.

Primary Responsibilities:

➤ Organizing the team to meet its goals.

➤ Developing the team.

➤ Managing the interface between the team and the organization.

➤ Bringing a structured approach and good planning ability to the team.

➤ Measuring team effectiveness and giving feedback.

➤ Demonstrating self-confidence and resilience.

➤ Demonstrating leadership (initially, explanation and supervision; later, less supervision) and flexibility.

➤ Piloting the helicopter!

The focus of this chapter is on the individual who has officially been selected for the world-class Team Leader position, but we firmly believe in *expanding* and *not isolating* the role of Team Leader. The complex tasks and processes facing world-class teams as they work at meeting their performance challenge are sufficiently daunting that there must be *shared leadership.* In fact, we often use Toolkit 9.1 to remind teams that while the Team Leader is the official pilot in this helicopter, it is one of those *large* models that accommodates several copilot seats. In other words, if another team member notices something out of alignment (or, conversely, something going right!) in any of the spotlight areas, he or she should feel free to "jump into the helicopter" and share the leadership role with the Team Leader.

We have two great examples of that response. Interestingly, both are from Australians with whom we have worked. Peter Brown, upon seeing that his Team Leader had taken some "poetic license" in rewriting the team's Charter and name, sent her a cc:mail that read:

Subject: Heading Skywards

Author: Peter Brown

Captain Christy,
    From my position on the ground, I have made an observation that impels me to take a seat next to you in the helicopter. The incidence in question is the use of "poetic license"! You may ask, what incidence(?) and rightfully so.
    Captain (CC), it relates to the massaging of the team name, a name selected by the same democratic processes that you and I (and many others) have employed when electing our chosen leaders, i.e., Dole, Reagan, Keating, etc. Democracy is fundamental to our existence and should never, never be tampered with!
    Our elected name was "The V Team," the massaged version "The Asian V Team." Alas, alack, I and you are not Asian. Perhaps a compromise:

In Asia—"The V Team"

or

"The V Team"
Asia

Hope you're enjoying your break,

Perfect (well, nearly) Peter.

What we like about this example is that, by using the helicopter metaphor, Peter was "asking permission" to give his Team Leader, Captain

Christy, some feedback about what, for him, was a critical issue—the team's name—and was expressing concern that the process used by the team ("democratic") appeared to have been ignored ("poetic license").

However, even when you, as a team member, initially climb into the helicopter, you don't always have the "big picture." Captain Christy Fleurat, one of Pfizer's high-performing Team Leaders, had received a different set of feedback when she presented the "V Team" name to the Sponsors. They had suggested she add "Asian" to the name to reinforce the region's identity to accurately reflect Pfizer's organizational structure, and not necessarily the individual members' nationality.

This example also serves to reinforce, once again, that Team Leaders often find themselves "caught in the middle" and need to continuously explain and integrate the needs of all their stakeholders. When Christy explained this to Peter, he commented, "That's fair" and the team became known throughout Pfizer as the Asian "V" Team.

The other example comes from Ken Smith, who alerted his Team Leader (along with other core team members) that the second full team meeting was going to occur in two months and he was concerned that several Plan of Action (POA) items from the last meeting had not been addressed. His helicopter alert was heeded by one core team member, who recapped that several actions had, in fact, been accomplished. One effect this had was to raise the issue of how to communicate achievements and occurrences *between* team meetings. Ken was to be applauded for sharing the team leadership role and helping the Team Leader avoid potential embarrassment in the event that any POA items actually had dropped through the cracks. (His action also reinforced the importance of establishing a POA at the end of every meeting as a follow-up tool. See Chapter 10 for more on that subject.)

We think that it is essential for team members to nurture and help to develop effective Team Leaders. Without them, teams can fall prey to:

➤ Team member recruiting and turnover problems—"No one wants to work for him."

➤ Team floundering—"I knew we couldn't do this 'by committee.'"

➤ Low team productivity—"We have no direction. Nothing's really getting done."

■ THE FAIREST OF THEM ALL

Anyone charged with the important responsibility of selecting a world-class Team Leader should keep these parting "words of wisdom" in mind:

➤ Contrary to popular belief, neither expediency nor comfort zone is the operative term here. Speed of selection and past history should not be the driving factors. Just because you have to get the team started, or just because, traditionally, certain departments have supplied the Team Leaders, there is no reason to rush the decision or acquiesce to "the way it's always been done around here." Challenge past thinking and select Team Leaders based on context and criteria. On the other hand, don't belabor or overanalyze the selection process. There are a lot of people with a wide variety of skill sets who can develop into the role.

➤ Do not assume that once you've selected a leader your job is done. All good Team Leaders need continuous development.

➤ Do not, under any circumstances, select someone as Team Leader who is not committed to either the team concept or the Team Leader role. World-class teams are like African violets: they are very fragile to touch. Teams can wilt or drown from too little or too much attention.

Finally, a word to those who accept the role. Along with demonstrating a solid commitment, world-class Team Leaders must maintain an unwavering "Can do/the cup is half full" attitude. In fact, this could be viewed as the competency that enables all others to develop. The job of World-Class Team Leader is *not* easy and the moment you fall prey to thinking it's impossible and unworkable, you will have lost the valuable perspective of a "Center Leader."

Chapter

Leading and Aligning World-Class Teams for High Performance

Building a team's high-performance alignment is about enhancing its capacity to evaluate information, make decisions, and get things done in an innovative and synergistic way while building its capacity for collaboration and loyalty.

This chapter, which addresses how to lead two spotlight areas, team process and team members (see Chapter 9, Toolkit 9.1), has been included with some reluctance because: (1) we don't want our readers to have the impression that leading world-class teams can be oversimplified and reduced to these team leadership functions; and (2) we don't believe a Team Leader (or team member) can best learn the competencies to perform these functions by reading about them in a book. On the contrary, we believe they are best learned in the context of his or her own team where the Team Leader can use (and practice) leadership skills, receive feedback on his or her effectiveness, and continue to fine-tune the art of world-class team leadership.

Having made this preemptive disclaimer, suffice it to say that our rationale for this chapter rests on the fact that we constantly are asked by Team Leaders, "Do you have anything I could read on . . . ?" Accordingly, we have included in this chapter (and in others, as outlined below) those Team Leader/team member processes that are asked about most frequently.

◼ THE TOP TEN TEAMWORK QUESTIONS

1. How do I manage relationships with key stakeholders? (Chapters 5 and 16)
2. How do I help my team establish its mission and goals? (Chapters 4 and 11)

3. How should team members be rewarded? (Chapter 14)

4. How do I help our team and individual team members better manage their resources (e.g., time)? (Chapter 11)

5. How do I manage team members who have very different interpersonal styles (let alone cultural differences!)? (Chapter 8)

6. How do I become a better meeting facilitator? (Chapter 10)

7. How do I encourage *and* manage conflict on my team? (Chapter 10)

8. How do I manage team decision making? (Chapter 10)

9. How can my team manage projects and communications across functional and national borders? (Chapter 10)

10. How do I motivate (create buy-in from) my team? (Chapters 10 and 11)

The first five questions are covered in other chapters. The last five are almost entirely covered in this chapter on leading and developing world-class team performance. We have provided you with plenty of tips and several Toolkits for quick reference should certain situations or needs arise where they will be helpful. Again, we caution that leading team processes and team members is much more complex in "real time." This chapter only scratches the surface.

■ PRODUCTIVE MEETING MANAGEMENT

Although most world-class teams meet infrequently (and some don't meet face-to-face at all), meeting management is worth a section in this book because of the number of team meetings that we—and team members—have found to be unproductive.

Unfortunately, much of what we learn about running meetings is through osmosis. We watch how others run meetings and we learn a few techniques, but rarely do we learn how to systematically structure and facilitate meetings to maximize their results. World-class teams in particular, however, need to have structure. Because they tend to meet infrequently, they have to be even more disciplined when they *do* meet because they have less practice and experience interacting with each other.

The tips we provide in this section are written for the context of a face-to-face team meeting, but some of them can be tailored to videoconferences and online meetings. In fact, we encourage world-class teams to have fewer in-person meetings and to make use of ever-changing technologies to accomplish their team tasks (see Chapter 17).

➤ Why Are We Meeting Anyway?

Because meetings of world-class teams usually result in considerable expense and travel time, everyone should be clear beforehand about *why* the meeting is being held, what is to be accomplished, and who are the critical participants. Teams may meet for a variety of purposes:

➤ Review goals and objectives.

➤ Create strategies.

➤ Develop plans.

➤ Exchange information (such as project reports, schedules and assignments, research articles) and ideas/points of view.

➤ Reach agreements.

➤ Identify action items.

➤ Identify next steps.

➤ Solve problems/resolve conflicts/make decisions.

➤ Provide feedback/coaching.

Whoever calls the meeting should ask these questions before sending out a team meeting announcement:

➤ What is the purpose of this meeting?

➤ What are the expected outcomes?

➤ Who are the key people who should attend this meeting, and what are their roles (e.g., decision makers, information/idea/expertise providers, facilitators, observers)?

➤ What is the specific agenda for the meeting?

➤ What types of work/discussion/decisions should occur during the meeting? What could/should occur outside the meeting?

➤ What equipment/facilities will accommodate the team's work (e.g., table setup, flipcharts, electronic meeting technology)?

➤ Are there materials that should be read or prepared in advance?

➤ Who should receive the agenda/notice of the meeting?

Before the meeting, the agenda should be circulated, and participants should be asked to review it and suggest any necessary revisions. Each topic on the agenda should include the following:

1. Estimated allotment of time for addressing the topic.
2. Who will lead discussion of the topic.

3. Whether a topic is "FYI," "Discussion: Input Requested," or "Decision to be Made." (If the latter, clearly state the issue to be resolved.)

As part of the agenda, if at all possible, include an activity that allows for social interaction either before or during the meeting. Throughout this book, we have emphasized the importance of building trust across borders. The process is more critical and difficult with world-class teams. Invariably, we have heard team members complain that they travel long distances for 12-hour-day meetings and have little time to really get to know their team members.

➤ Starting the Meeting

Depending on the size of the team and whether everyone present knows everyone else, you may want to start the meeting by introducing participants and explaining why they are there, particularly if any participants are not team members. In conjunction with the introductions, it sets a good tone to announce any team or individual successes that the team as a whole may not know about. Often, because world-class teams meet so infrequently, the tendency is to jump right into "the task" and ignore the interpersonal/social needs of the team.

Along with reviewing the overall objectives of the meeting, remind the team of any meeting ground rules that they may have agreed to as part of an Operating Agreement (see Chapter 6). For example, one team started every meeting by assigning a timekeeper and a scribe and reminding people about team process issues, such as rules for consensus. This is a good habit to build into team meetings.

➤ Facilitating the Agenda

Certain key roles should be assigned to people in team meetings. Besides the roles of Team Leader, team members, and perhaps invited guests and/or support group members, attendees should be assigned the roles of facilitator, recorder, and timekeeper. These roles can be fulfilled by any member of the team, and we strongly suggest that the roles be rotated among team members to help build everyone's competencies.

There are single books and training programs devoted to teaching facilitation skills. Our own observations of teams, including executive teams, is that, for *most* people, facilitation does not come naturally. It is a learned skill. (We recommend the book *Faultless Facilitation* by Lois Hart as a "primer" for basic facilitation skills. The text is both comprehensive and user-friendly.[1])

10.1 Facilitator Tips

Do	*Don't*
➤ Start the meeting with a "social" warm-up.	➤ Kill ideas.
➤ Review past progress and accomplishments.	➤ Dominate the conversation or thought processes of others.
➤ Clarify and manage the purpose, agenda, and ground rules of the meeting.	➤ Let anyone monopolize discussion.
➤ Identify team roles (e.g., recorder, timekeeper).	➤ Allow the group to waste time guessing about information or making decisions based on assumptions.
➤ Ask the group how they want to make decisions (e.g., majority rule, consensus).	➤ Start meetings late or run over, unless the group agrees.
➤ Use brainstorming rules when first exploring issues.	➤ Let the group wander off the agenda topic onto unproductive discussions.
➤ Use a flipchart to record ideas, whenever possible.	➤ Ask leading questions. Say "What would happen if . . . ?" or "What has been your experience . . ." instead of "Don't you think . . ."
➤ Encourage participation by everyone present.	➤ Argue, ridicule, take sides, or lecture.
➤ Discourage side conversations, interruptions, and other nonlistening behaviors.	➤ Set yourself up as an authority or expert.
➤ Model active listening (e.g., paraphrase, keep eye contact).	
➤ Bring discussions to closure with summarized conclusions, recommendations, or plans of action.	
➤ Periodically ask the group to look at its "process."	
➤ Celebrate progress and success!	

Facilitation skills, like those described in Toolkit 10.1, may seem easy to understand (for example, how difficult can it be to "Ask the group how they want to make decisions"?). However, as we point out later in this chapter, diagnosing a group/team's process (who's communicating with whom, how decisions are made, who's dominating, who's not participating) and knowing how to act on what you observe may require advanced team-building "technology." To improve your skills, we suggest you enroll in a development program where you can actively practice using facilitation skills and will receive coaching and feedback.

A facilitator of a meeting helps to balance and manage both the *what* of the meeting (the agenda: problems, goals, ideals, subjects needing discussion) and the *how* (group dynamics, communications, interactions, nonverbal reactions). Most teams want to spend their time on the *what*. The facilitator, being in charge of the *what* and the *how,* must keep the meeting productive. Survey respondents indicate that 75 percent of meetings are unproductive, frustrating, and a waste of time!

The Team Leader is not necessarily the only person who should facilitate a team meeting. Often, the best team is the team that operates under the concept of "shared leadership." We recommend that teams either rotate the role of facilitator from meeting to meeting, or ask different team members to facilitate particular agenda topics. You also may want to ask someone who is not part of the team to observe and comment on the team's approach to its work.

As you begin each agenda topic, remind the team about the allotted amount of time and the expected outcome at the end of discussion of the topic. You may need to remind the team of these two critical items periodically. As you work through the agenda, remember these points:

➤ Meetings should start and finish on time, unless deviations are agreed to by participants.

➤ A Plan of Action (POA) should be created at the end of each meeting to guide between-meeting activities, and then reviewed at the next meeting. Toolkit 10.2 is a sample of a Plan of Action.

➤ Meeting minutes should be circulated within two days of the meeting and should include the POA. (Increasingly, we are using on-site meeting transcribers so that participants leave for their planes with the meeting minutes in hand.)

➤ A 20-minute review of the meeting's effectiveness should be held before the close of the meeting.

➤ In any meeting that lasts longer than one day, periodically review "team process issues"—issues involving how the team is working. (See the checklist in Toolkit 10.3.)

10.2 Sample Meeting Plan of Action

What	Who	When
Define communications issues/processes (e.g., reports, meetings, etc.), formal/informal	Task Group	6/20
More clearly define team structure, core team + "support"	Team Leader	
Continue process of role clarification	Team Leader	6/13
Team rewards/recognition	HR Staff	6/9
Develop goal-setting process	HR Staff	6/9

10.3 How Productive Are Your Meetings?

_____ 1. We ask that only those whose expertise/opinion is required attend our meetings.

_____ 2. Meeting announcements make clear where, when, and how long the meeting will be.

_____ 3. The meeting agenda is circulated ahead of time so everyone knows why the meeting has been called.

_____ 4. Meetings are not interrupted for anything that is not absolutely critical.

_____ 5. All meeting notes are recorded visibly, so all can see them.

_____ 6. The leader helps all discussions to stay on track and to deal with the subject at hand.

_____ 7. We wrap up each agenda item before moving on to the next one.

_____ 8. Everyone is given full opportunity to ask questions, make comments, and contribute ideas, including opposite points of view.

_____ 9. Whenever we can, we decide important issues by consensus after full group discussion.

_____ 10. When attendees leave the meeting, they know exactly what their responsibilities are.

_____ 11. After the meeting, minutes are distributed to those people who need them (inside or outside the core team).

_____ 12. At the end of each meeting, we discuss how the meeting was conducted and consider ways to improve our meetings.

_____ 13. We provide sufficient follow-up to encourage and remind people to carry out their assignments from the meeting.

We know of one world-class team that carried on its work for one year without ever meeting face-to-face. As more world-class teams are formed, simultaneous multisite meetings will become the norm. We must translate the best current practices and create new ones to ensure that remote meetings are productive.

Why Meetings Fail

➤ No goals or agenda.

➤ Too long.

➤ No actions/decisions.

➤ Lack of control and focus.

➤ Starting late, ending late.

➤ Individuals dominate discussion.

➤ Interruptions.

➤ Rambling or digressive discussions.

➤ Wrong people in attendance, right people absent.

➤ Diagnosing Team Process during Meetings

It's one thing to manage the agenda of a meeting, and developing the skills of facilitating is usually the next step. Team Leaders who reach an advanced stage of proficiency are able to diagnose a team's process, even when the process may appear to be invisible for remote teams.

During our "Crossing the Borders" sessions (see Chapter 7), we engage the team in several collaborative activities. Team members must work together to make decisions and take actions, either in case study simulations or in discussions of actual team issues. At the end of each session, we ask the team, including the Team Leader: "How did we do in terms of our team's *process*?" (Toolkit 10.4 indicates what to look for in evaluating your team's process.) After such a meeting, one team listed its "Lessons Learned" and kept the list posted as a reminder of the team's strengths and of areas that required ongoing attention (see Toolkit 10.5).

Team Leaders should also be on the lookout for these team process issues:

➤ Interpersonal conflicts between team members.

➤ Interpreting all conflict as unhealthy.

➤ Assumed or untested consensus because of lack of argument.

➤ Team members' hidden or conflicting agendas.

10.4 Team Process Questions

➤ What were the results we wanted to achieve? Did we achieve them?

➤ What did we do well as a team?

➤ What could we have done more effectively?

➤ What process did we use to make decisions?

— Did we effectively separate facts from assumptions?

— Did we analyze consequences and benefits of each alternative?

— Did we keep focused on our objectives?

— Did we use consensus, majority rule, or another form of decision making?

➤ How well did we:

— Listen to each other?

— Encourage full participation?

— Resolve disagreements?

— Build on each other's ideas?

You may choose not to intervene when you observe issues that should be addressed, but be aware that rarely does a team's dysfunction, even if it seems to be minor or insignificant, take care of itself "naturally." As more team members are brought together remotely, an "out of sight, out of mind" attitude may begin to blanket team issues. In our experience, when team members meet infrequently and must then tackle heavy agendas, they find it easier to keep pushing dysfunctional team issues to the back burner rather than deal with them. We strongly urge you to keep a task *and* process focus and to continually work to develop your own and your team members' team process skills. We also strongly urge you (see Chapter 7) to have one- or two-day sessions devoted only to team development (skill development process) every 6 to 12 months.

■ CONFLICT MANAGEMENT

Team Leaders, particularly those who are inexperienced, are usually fearful of conflict. However, what they must come to realize is that conflict among team members can be good; without it, you will wonder whether you have true harmony and agreement among team members,

10.5 Our Team Process: Lessons Learned

Positive	Negative
➤ We set a process and a Plan of Action (strategic).	➤ We didn't have objectives and we had no agenda.
➤ We managed out time.	➤ We didn't do process (facilitator) assignments or were not clear about assignments.
➤ We stayed focused on important issues.	
➤ We collected all current information.	➤ We didn't have a recorder.
	➤ We didn't resolve disagreements.
➤ We expressed benefits and consequences	➤ We didn't tackle the problem or provide a rationale.
➤ We were fast to agree on task assignments.	➤ We stuck too much to our own individual "agendas."
➤ We learned from our experiences.	➤ We used majority vote, not consensus.
➤ We prepared a report at the end.	
➤ We injected some humor.	➤ We were poor listeners.
➤ We built on others' ideas.	➤ We didn't check the expertise in the group.
	➤ We made too many assumptions.
	➤ We didn't have, nor did we encourage, full participation in discussions.

or apathy and a smokescreen for disagreement. Don't assume silence is consensus—it could signal disengagement. As one team member said, "Silence isn't golden!"

We all know that healthy disagreement can turn into unproductive and dysfunctional conflict if it is not managed effectively. Team members can begin to attack each other, get defensive, and/or become polarized on issues.

How do you develop a team to a point where team members can vigorously debate issues and create a wider range of creative options to choose from when evaluating issues and making decisions? Along with the Resolving Differences Guidelines in Toolkit 10.6, we have found, over the years, that the following principles can guide world-class teams toward functional and productive conflict management.

Sources of Conflict

```
              SOURCES OF
               PROBLEMS


   PERSONALITY          CONFLICT          VALUES


              SOLUTIONS TO
               PROBLEMS
```

10.6 Resolving Differences Guidelines

Demonstrate Understanding	1. Listen nonjudgmentally. 2. Summarize. 3. Check for your understanding. 4. Explain your point of view.
Identify Areas of Agreement and Disagreement	1. Where do you agree? 2. Where do you disagree?
Explore Alternatives	1. What are all of the possible alternatives? 2. Are there any new alternatives?
Evaluate and Select	1. What are the "must haves" for each party? 2. Where is there room for compromise? 3. What are the consequences if no agreement is reached?

Reprinted with permission from MICA and Management Research Group©.

1. *Build a strong foundation of trust and respect among team members.* When team members are operating from the vantage point of what's best for the team and not just for themselves, their disagreements will have trust and respect as a backdrop.

2. *Share—and continually return to—common goals.* Throughout this book, we have indicated that *sharing common goals* is the glue that holds teams together. When team members disagree on a course of action, they can always resort to asking: What is the best alternative to achieve *our* goal?

3. *Keep feeding the dialogue with facts.* Someone once commented to us, in describing arguments he had with a colleague, "The louder we get, and the more right each of us believes we are, the clearer it is how little each of us knows." Many disagreements result from teams making assumptions and sharing individual perspectives without having the requisite information. The mind-set then becomes: "You're attacking my opinion [me]" and the result can be interpersonal conflict. When you begin to hear team members say, "I think . . . ," it's time to cut off debate and turn the focus toward what you all *know.* Keep the issues in focus, not the personalities.

4. *Brainstorm your options.* Teams frequently become polarized on issues as if the options are black and white, or either/or. Practice forcing your team to develop at least a third alternative. Openly brainstorm ideas, or, to guarantee candor, ask the team to write down their preferred alternative and submit it anonymously. (See Toolkit 10.7 for Brainstorming Ground Rules.) Invite the team member whose current role is The Contrarian or The Magician (see Chapter 7) to give his or her opinions. This may trigger a very different alternative.

5. *Decide how to decide.* Later in this chapter, we provide you with a decision-making model. One of the main reasons teams get into conflict is that they lack understanding or agreement about how and by whom decisions will be made. Consensus decision making is not always the best way for teams to resolve issues. Most reasonable people know that their ideas are not always the ones that will prevail, but they want their opinions to be heard and acknowledged.

6. *Challenge group think.* As Team Leader, your task focus and your natural inclination to avoid the "messiness" of conflict may lead you to fall into the trap of "seeing consensus" where there is actually only what we refer to as "group think." Jerry Harvey, in his book *The Abilene Paradox and Other Meditations on Management,* tells the story of his family's misguided trip to Abilene. They were all sitting on his in-laws' porch, having a pleasant time, when the suggestion was made to drive the 53 miles to Abilene. Off they went in a non-air-conditioned 1958 Buick, through a dust storm and 104˚ heat. The trip consumed four exhausting hours and

10.7   Brainstorming Ground Rules

➤ Define the "task headline" (i.e., the specific issue for which the team needs ideas).

➤ Build on others' ideas—"piggy-backing."

➤ Seek quantity (versus quality).

➤ Be nonjudgmental.

➤ View every idea as a good idea.

➤ Give everyone time to express his or her ideas.

➤ Encourage ideas from everyone.

➤ Listen and don't interrupt.

➤ Use a "facilitation."

➤ Keep the scope of ideas totally open (no limits).

➤ Record all ideas.

➤ Create a safe environment.

➤ Set a time limit.

---

accomplished nothing. While everyone was complaining about it afterward, it came to light that not one of those who'd taken the trip had had any desire to go in the first place. Everyone had gone along simply because everyone else was going along, too.[2] Unfortunately, this happens a lot in groups—and in world-class teams. As an antidote, use strategies such as "individual writing" or "subgrouping" to break down large group discussions, if you suspect that a topic should be generating more controversy.

7. *Call "Time out" when you observe nonproductive conflict.* In many cases, conflict occurs because team members are not really listening to each other. (See Toolkit 10.8 for Ten Ways to "Listen Up.") When you see team members "lobbing tennis balls over a ten-foot wall" (continuing to reiterate their own point of view, or attacking others' views) or "recycling" (repeating themselves), call "Time out" and ask the team, "What's going on here?" Usually, someone has been observing the interaction. Force some structure so that the conversation can become more of a dialogue.

Conflict among remote teams poses an even greater challenge. It is very easy to register disagreement by not responding to e-mail messages or telephone calls. As team groupware becomes more sophisticated (see Chapter 17), we will be able to use electronic polling techniques and interactive technologies to record team members' opinions or votes on

10.8   Ten Ways to "Listen Up"

1. Ask short questions.
2. Listen actively by making mental notes of what the other person is saying.
3. Paraphrase main ideas to make sure you understand them.
4. Review verbal areas of agreement to be sure there are no misunderstandings.
5. Show nonverbally that you are present.
6. Don't jump to conclusions, make assumptions, or evaluate prematurely.
7. Listen for the emotion behind the words.
8. Ask for more information; draw out others' perspectives and rationales.
9. Ask about other concerns; be empathic.
10. Keep an open mind so that you can see the world through others' eyes.

---

issues. However, we are far away from managing remote dialoguing and conflict resolution. Until then, when a team has important decisions to make, either hold face-to-face meetings or be very clear about how decisions will be made and what process will be used for communication of opinions and/or votes.

■ TEAM DECISION MAKING

Today, Team Leaders (and team members) need to be able to demonstrate effective team decision-making skills by managing and facilitating the decision-making process, analyzing and identifying ways to improve the team's decision-making process, and recognizing and utilizing the decision-making approach that is most appropriate for the situation at hand.

We have learned, from watching teams, that effective decisions stem from a combination of quality thinking and acceptance. In other words, the thinking behind a particular decision may be highly rational and extremely creative, but if the people who have to implement the decision do not accept it, the decision will suffer in its implementation. However, the reverse can also be true. Irrational thinking may lead to an inappropriate decision that is very acceptable to the people who have to implement it, in which case a poor decision will be effectively executed.

The ideal, of course, is high-quality thinking that is very acceptable to the people who have to implement it. This combination produces a

10.9   Steps in the Decision-Making Process

1. Analyze the situation.
2. Identify objectives.
3. Consider alternative strategies:
   —Generate strategies/solutions (brainstorming/mind mapping).
   —Evaluate strategies/solutions (force field analysis).
4. Reach a decision.
5. Implement the decision.

---

synergistic effect on the decision and leads to better results than would be expected from the available resources. Synergy is defined as the interaction of two or more agents or forces so that their combined effort is far greater than the sum of their individual parts. In the organizational sense, synergy can be described as a cooperative interaction among groups, especially among parts of a corporation or organization, that creates an enhanced combined effect (from the Greek word *synergos*, meaning cooperation or working together).

Two processes need to be managed when a team is engaged in decision making. The first is the *Interpersonal Process*, which involves the skills of working with others cooperatively. With effective use of these skills, people behave more creatively and rationally when interacting.

The second process is the *Rational Process*, which involves the different skills we use in thinking a problem through to a decision. One of the purposes of following the Rational Process for decision making is to slow down the tendency of individuals to jump to conclusions and quickly leap into action. The Rational Process for decision making suggests that team members look at their dilemma from various perspectives. What are we faced with and what are we trying to accomplish? What are the possible ways we could deal with this situation? What are the shortcomings of each alternative? After considering such questions, team members are more likely to take into account all relevant factors before making a decision.

Toolkit 10.9 lists the steps in the decision-making process. The first step is: **Analyze the Situation.** This means separating and sorting out the facts from the assumptions. In most situations, all the facts are not known; nonetheless, those that are known should be distinguished from assumptions and factors that are uncertain. Analyzing a situation requires:

➤ Delineating those aspects of the situation that appear to be certain (i.e., facts).

➤ Identifying uncertain factors (or assumptions), and then discussing and assessing them.

The second step in the process is: **Identify Objectives.** It is important for a team not only to identify its objectives, but also to distinguish them from *actions*. Again, we must be careful to distinguish *what* the objectives are and then decide *how* we are going to achieve them. When strategies or actions are mistakenly viewed as objectives, team members can get so caught up in them that they lose sight of the results that the activities are supposed to accomplish. To avoid this "activity trap," it is important to:

➤ Clearly identify the end result as the objective.

➤ View actions not as objectives but as possible strategies for reaching the objectives.

Think for a minute about a problem or dilemma you are trying to resolve. What is your objective? What are you trying to achieve? What results do you want to achieve?

The third step in decision making is: **Consider Alternative Strategies.** Because the first strategy proposed for reaching an objective is not necessarily the best one, you must *generate* several strategies and then *evaluate* them. (If you fail to generate and consider multiple solutions or ideas, you run the risk of accepting a suboptimal, or potentially even fatal, course of action.) Then, by using good interpersonal processes (which we will describe shortly) among the team, you can fully discuss and evaluate the multiple strategies and thus avoid missing or prematurely rejecting a viable course of action.

When the goal is to generate strategies, it helps to first list, specify, and understand alternative strategies *without* judging their merits. You have probably heard this referred to as "brainstorming." (Recall the Brainstorming Ground Rules in Toolkit 10.7.) Once you have generated, proposed, and clearly understood all the strategies or solutions that emerged from your brainstorming, the team can begin to evaluate them. Thus, an effective and rational process requires that team members:

➤ List and clearly define possible alternative strategies or solutions.

➤ Seriously consider the feasibility and relative merits of the alternative courses of action and then categorize/prioritize them according to some set of criteria.

All of the brainstorming items should be reviewed and classified in some way for further consideration. A simple classification method assesses each proposed solution/strategy as being either possible or impossible/highly improbable. This method eliminates some ideas from consideration. The group might then be asked to select the top five strategies by an individually weighted vote; that is, each individual proposes five, and the five with the highest number of votes become the select group of alternatives.

After you have considered and categorized the alternative strategies, based on their merits, you need to choose the three most outstanding strategies. This is where the real evaluation portion of the process comes into play. It is always important to examine whether the proposed strategies are likely to lead to the objective. In critical situations, it is also important to identify the possible adverse consequences of each alternative, and consider the likelihood and severity of these consequences. The team will then be more likely to reject alternatives that are superficially attractive.

After you have selected the optimum strategy/solution, you have *made a decision*—congratulations! Now you need to take the final step: Identify the strategies/activities/tasks that will enable you to put your decision into action.

➤ Who Makes the Decision?

So far, we have explained *what* the general decision-making process is. As a Team Leader, what is your role in managing the *how* of the decision-making process? A decision can be made—and the decision-making process can be managed—in many ways. The Team Leader can make the decision alone or after receiving advice from the team. The team members can make the decision by themselves, and so on.

When it comes time to "decide on how to decide," the "Team Decision-Making Continuum" in Toolkit 10.10 may be helpful. This model was adapted from the research of two organizational psychologists, Warren Schmidt and Robert Tannenbaum. Basically, it suggests that there is a continuum of *Team Leader behavior/team decision-making style* that can result in your receiving "compliance" from your team regarding acceptance of a decision, but you may not have developed your team's "commitment" to the decision. The psychologists' research has shown that when a leader makes a decision, announces it, and expects others to do what they're told to do, there is *compliance.* This is in contrast to the other side of the continuum, which allows a team *consensus* form of decision making (see Toolkit 10.10). When a leader asks a group to make a decision by consensus, there is more commitment to the decision among the individuals in that group.

10.10　Team Decision-Making Continuum

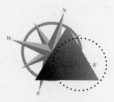

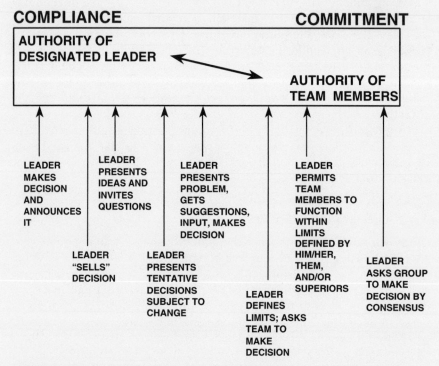

| COMPLIANCE | | | | | COMMITMENT |

AUTHORITY OF DESIGNATED LEADER

AUTHORITY OF TEAM MEMBERS

LEADER MAKES DECISION AND ANNOUNCES IT

LEADER PRESENTS IDEAS AND INVITES QUESTIONS

LEADER "SELLS" DECISION

LEADER PRESENTS PROBLEM, GETS SUGGESTIONS, INPUT, MAKES DECISION

LEADER PRESENTS TENTATIVE DECISIONS SUBJECT TO CHANGE

LEADER DEFINES LIMITS; ASKS TEAM TO MAKE DECISION

LEADER PERMITS TEAM MEMBERS TO FUNCTION WITHIN LIMITS DEFINED BY HIM/HER, THEM, AND/OR SUPERIORS

LEADER ASKS GROUP TO MAKE DECISION BY CONSENSUS

Adapted from W. H. Schmidt-R. Tannenbaum "How to Choose a Leadership Pattern," *Harvard Business Review,* 1958, No. 36, pp. 95–101.

Consensus, although it sounds optimal, is not always the best decision-making process and it should not be regarded as the solution to every situation—particularly in emergencies!

In Toolkit 10.10, the first approach has the leader making and announcing the decision. In the next approach, the leader makes the decision but thinks, "I had better *sell* the decision, not just tell it." The next options have the leader presenting ideas and inviting questions or presenting tentative decisions that are subject to change. Another possibility is that the leader will present a problem, get suggestions and input, but still make the decision. Or, the leader might permit the team members to function within limits defined by the leader, the team, and/or superiors. The most empowering decision-making style occurs when the leader asks the team members to make the decision (and he or she is willing to live with their decision!).

With this continuum, the notion is that *if* you have competent people on the team, you can and should turn the decision making over to the team. That strategy produces more commitment than if you make the decision yourself and then announce it. How difficult is it to make a decision and tell people to carry it out? What happens if they do not want to do what you tell them to do? The consequences of having made a solo decision, especially the emotional reactions of team members, can be harder to deal with than making the decision alone.

Decision Making: Questions to Ask

➤ What are the risks associated with the decision? (How visible is the decision? How costly is a mistake?)

➤ Does the team have the ability to make the decision?

➤ Is the team willing to be held accountable for the decision?

➤ What is the confidence level of the team regarding the decision?

➤ What is the complexity of the decision?

➤ What constraints are associated with the decision?

➤ How much time does the team have to make the decision?

➤ What is the size of the team?

➤ Consensual Decision Making

Most Team Leaders would agree that making decisions alone is fairly easy to do. However, when reaching a decision, it is helpful and important to have all team members agree with and support the team's decision. Your team is unlikely to be fully committed to a decision if they don't accept it; yet the coordinated and cooperative efforts of all team members often are necessary for effective implementation.

Consensus translates to: "I might not have made that decision myself, but I can live with it, support it, and defend it." Do not confuse consensus with majority-rule decision making or voting. An example of when you should get consensus among team members is: approval of the Charter/Vision. The Charter is vital to the entire team. On a less important issue, it may be more appropriate to use majority rule. For example, on the issue of "Where are we going to meet the next time—Hong Kong or Korea?", you may want to only seek opinions or take a vote.

Because unanimous agreement and consensus are the most difficult decision-making processes, we suggest these "Techniques for Team Consensus":

➤ Let everyone have the opportunity to voice his or her opinion and knowledge of the issue. (Perhaps record individual ideas on a flipchart.)

➤ Actively listen (e.g., paraphrase, summarize individuals' perspectives).

➤ Look for opportunities to link contributors' ideas.

➤ Keep the group focused on its goals and on the issues that need to be resolved.

➤ Ask people for their rationale behind an opinion/perspective.

➤ Make the group's or individuals' assumptions explicit.

➤ Don't let people change their minds or drop out just to avoid conflict.

➤ Don't let the group slip into one-person subgroups, or majority-rule votes, or horse-trading, unless they consciously decide to do that.

➤ Help individuals and the team examine consequences/implications (pros and cons) of positions.

➤ Don't let the group get polarized on positions or stuck in "either/or" decisions. Look for alternatives.

➤ Look for areas of agreement/common ground first, then move on to issues of disagreement.

➤ Ask people who are not in consensus with the majority: "What alteration of this position *could* you accept/support?"

➤ Poll people to determine their initial position. (Use a fist for "no support," high five for "full support," and three fingers for "needs modification.")

➤ After consensus has apparently been reached, ask each person individually: "Will you endorse this decision with key stakeholders when you leave this room?"

➤ Don't jump too quickly into decision making. Evaluate and analyze the issues first.

➤ Let people do their own "picture building" from their perspective before jumping into arguments, disagreement, or reality testing.

➤ If necessary (and possible), postpone the decision to allow for new ideas or rethinking of positions.

➤ Reassess with the team whether consensus is necessary or desirable for this decision.

■ KNOWLEDGE MANAGEMENT

Four questions should be answered that are key to helping a team manage its team performance:

1. How do we establish goals that align organizational, team, and individual performance?
2. What communications and reporting are needed between team meetings?
3. How do we track projects and goal-setting progress?
4. How do we manage allocated resources?

In Chapter 11, we take you through a Team Alignment Process that can help you develop team goals that really add value to an organization. It also provides a means by which you can ensure that individual team members' objectives and assignments are aligned to achieve the team's goals. But what processes should you use to ensure the team's work is facilitated and reported toward those goals, particularly between team meetings?

For world-class teams, communications and project management processes and technologies are of critical importance because so much of their work is done remotely rather than face-to-face. Consequently, there is a propensity for miscommunication, mistrust, and missed deadlines, and for work to fall sway to the "out of sight, out of mind" syndrome. (See Chapter 17 for information about team technologies.)

➤ Reporting/Communications Strategies

Meetings are typical forums in which teams meet to review goal progress, share information, and track project status. But world-class teams, because of distance and time, do not have the "luxury" of frequent meetings to perform these functions, so they must look at developing alternate strategies.

Another challenge for world-class teams is how to manage the complexity of communications when team members are "networked" in a myriad of matrix relationships.

Early in the team's formation (after Charter, Boundaries, roles, and goals are sorted out), the team must systematically examine what we refer to as its Communication Strategies and its Project Management Strategies. There are no pat formulas for these processes; rather, teams need to create or find processes and systems that match their team's needs. These, in effect, become tools with which to help manage their work and their Operating Agreements with each other.

Toolkit 10.11 shows how one world-class team, with 35 team members from Asia, the Middle East, France, the United Kingdom, Latin America, and the United States, decided to approach the issue of their communication difficulties. At their first meeting, they formed a task force charged with answering the questions listed. During their first year, they attempted to develop technological resources as well as clear guidelines for defining who provides what information, to whom, and when.

Another team—again, made up of members from all over the world—was making extensive (and productive) use of e-mail technology, but realized that *how* they used it needed some improvement. Accordingly, they developed the list of "Team E-Mail Guidelines" shown in Toolkit 10.12.

➤ Project Management

Myriad books and software programs are available to assist teams, particularly those that have numerous and/or diverse projects to manage. (See Chapter 17 for suggestions for working with team technologies and "groupware.") One team we worked with was building a customized project management program (there are hundreds on the market) to help

10.11 Team Communication Processes Task—Draft Plan

➤ Standard Reports
  — What information should be included?
  — Frequency of distribution?
  — Distribution to whom?
➤ General Communication Process
  — What critical pieces of information do specific team members need?
  — Who needs to be informed?
  — How/through whom do we communicate issues?
  — What mechanism of communication do we use (systems)?
  — How are best practices to be shared across the team?
➤ Subcommittees
  — Frequency of meetings?
  — Report format, content, and distribution?
➤ Meetings
  — Frequency?
  — Format?

10.12   Team E-Mail Guidelines

Sending Rules	Response Rules
1. Use "ABC" [abbreviated team name] as the first word in the subject line.	1. Don't use the "Return Receipt" default.
2. Classify the type of message being sent: —"Action." —"Record." —"FYI."	2. Turn off the "Reply to All" default. 3. Reply only to sender (whenever possible). 4. No response is expected from "FYI" messages.
3. Identify the topic.	
4. Identify the addressee: —"To"—to whom the action is being requested. —"cc"—everyone else, but they will not necessarily be the "action" parties.	
5. Be aware of distribution lists; be selective and don't overcopy.	

track over 190 projects (and subprojects) that were on their plate for 1997–1998. Toolkit 10.13 shows one page from their report; any team member has ongoing access to this report and can also "go inside" the report and examine the details for any of the 190 projects.

As we have said throughout this chapter, each of the sections herein could fill a separate book. Listed below are some critical steps in the project management process:

➤ Write a goal statement for the project.

➤ Define all deliverables/work products.

➤ Assign responsibility for each deliverable/work product.

➤ Identify constraints/contingencies.

➤ Define all project activities.

➤ Identify what is needed to accomplish each activity (people, equipment, materials, and so forth).

➤ Identify all milestones/approvals/sign-off points.

➤ Identify all dependencies for milestones.

➤ Create a preliminary project management activity bar chart.

10.13 Product Team Activities Draft

ID	Project	Start	Finish	1997				1998			
				QTR 1	QTR 2	QTR 3	QTR 4	QTR 1	QTR 2	QTR 3	QTR 4
51	Product Awareness Materials Development	Fri 12/13/96	Mon 12/28/96	X	X	X	X	X	X	X	X
52	Video	Fri 8/15/97	Fri 2/13/98		X	X	X	X	X	X	X
53	CD Rom	Fri 8/15/97	Fri 2/13/98				X	X			
54	Brochure	Mon 1/13/97	Mon 1/13/97								
55	Slide kit	Mon 1/13/97	Mon 1/13/97								
56	Other (to be defined based on MR)	Mon 1/13/97	Mon 1/13/97								
57	Publications Development	Mon 9/15/97	Tue 12/15/98								
58	Advocacy building	Mon 1/13/97	Mon 1/13/97								
59	Publications (submission dates)	Fri 12/13/96	Mon 12/28/98								
60	Refinement of creative, begin planning market research	Thu 5/1/97	Mon 5/12/97								
61	Testing	Tue 5/13/97	Mon 5/26/97								
62	Compile results and revise creative	Tue 5/27/97	Mon 6/2/97								
63	Submit creative for review and approval	Mon 6/30/97	Fri 7/4/97								
64	Testing	Wed 6/4/97	Tue 9/30/97								
65	Develop graphic standard manual, (logo, color, typeface, etc.)	Wed 8/20/97	Fri 10/24/97								

Toolkit

➤ Assign resources to scheduled activities.

➤ Adjust the preliminary schedule so peak requirements don't exceed resource availability.

➤ Create a list of the total resources needed to complete the project within the set time frame.

➤ Establish project monitoring and review the responsibility schedule.

■ COACHING TEAM MEMBERS

As a Team Leader, unless you decide to be both chief cook *and* bottle washer, much of the work that gets done is accomplished by your team members—whom we have referred to as the "raw materials" of a team. How do you nurture and shape these raw materials in such a way that they create world-class team products?

The most fundamental step is to work with your team to establish a clear Charter and Boundaries and to develop targeted goals for which team members assume responsibility. Nothing fosters team identity and team members' commitment more strongly than to have a performance challenge that matters and a way to recognize that team members play a vital role in meeting that challenge.

Once those factors are in place, along with the goals (Chapter 11) and rewards (Chapter 13) that support them, what softer, less tangible tools can you use to bring out the best in your team members?

We think they can best be implemented through your role as team coach.

➤ What Is Coaching?

A coach, as defined in *Merriam Webster's Collegiate Dictionary,* Tenth Edition, is "one who instructs or trains a performer or a team of performers . . . in the fundamentals of a competitive sport and directs team strategy." Even in the dictionary, the role is closely associated with the world of sports. We've all seen "The Coach" on the sidelines, directing and admonishing team members to score or otherwise produce results. But change the phrase "competitive sport" to "world-class team" and you've got a good working definition of a world-class Team Leader. Compared to their counterparts on a football field or basketball court, however, Team Leaders are usually "player coaches"—that is, in addition to coaching a team of performers, they themselves are "in the game" and have specific team tasks/assignments they are accountable for delivering.

Unfortunately, many Team Leaders are more comfortable performing their own task assignments and merely checking on their team's
progress than they are in performing the role of coach with people who
are their peers.

■ WHY TEAM LEADERS RESIST BEING COACHES

After working with many Team Leaders who were reluctant to take on
the role of coach, we can sum up the reasons for their resistance as originating from:

1. Skills ("I'm uncomfortable and I don't know how").
2. Role conflict ("Too many other demands on my time, development's not *my* job").
3. Values ("You make your own bed and breaks").

Yet, as their title implies, Team Leaders are *leaders*—so why don't
they see "developing effective followers" as their job? For answers to this
question, consider the key characteristics of the best coaches in the
world of sports. Perhaps, first and foremost, is the fact that the best
coaches operate comfortably on the sidelines. They are not on the playing field throwing the ball or making the catch; they don't put the points
on the scoreboard. They are coaches because they are passionate about
the game, and they derive the deepest satisfaction from developing competitive game plans and then cultivating players who will successfully
execute those plans.

The best sports coaches create "learning organizations." They oversee continuous practice sessions that include both hands-on rehearsals
and video-based feedback reviews of their own and their competitors'
performances. They not only hold their players accountable for their
scoreboard performance, but, as Pat Riley did when he was coach of the
New York Knicks, they may bench or suspend players who have broken
ranks with the team's values. They know that while they may win in the
short term with individual superstars, they need a fully functioning *team*
to make postseason playoffs.

There is no doubt that sports coaches' primary focus during the playing season is their players. They spend the majority of their time with
them—motivating, drilling, and strategizing. Time spent on administrative tasks with the front office and even "marketing" to the fans is limited
to press conferences or periodic radio/TV appearances. Team Leaders,
on the other hand, typically give much less time and attention to their

"players." Instead, they spend more of their time (perhaps by choice) in meetings with bosses, internal stakeholders, or key customers.

Don Shula, former head coach of the Miami Dolphins and one of the most winning coaches in the National Football League, once claimed, "I think goal setting is overrated." Not that, when he was coaching, he didn't focus on winning games, which is the ultimate goal for football teams. But he put more emphasis on his players' learning the fine points and details, and drilling and practicing the basics. Shula said that "to be effective as a coach, you have to have credibility and patience [with your players]. . . . There's no magic formula. You can't get away from the basics."

Reflect instead on what many Team Leaders in business do. They try to get on the field, hog the star role of their team players, and finally spend very little time doing what coaches such as Pat Riley, now with the NBA's Miami Heat, do with a *lot* of their time—namely, coaching. Both types of coaches make use of current technology not only to prepare detailed game plans before each game, but also to review and provide feedback to the team immediately after each game. This points to an area where sports coaches have an "in-person advantage." Team Leaders of world-class teams also make use of technology, but that's because they must often engage in "long-distance coaching"—giving feedback or instructions electronically, such as by e-mail or fax, or over the phone. With e-mail or fax, the good news is that a team member has a chance to think before he or she responds. The problem with all long-distance coaching is that there is no chance for face-to-face dialogue and feedback or for being able to read the emotions of the team members.

You may be saying to yourself: "Coaches like Shula and Riley coach games, but I'm coaching professionals who are participating in projects or ongoing professional activities, so where's the application?" Our response: "Pro sports coaches see coaching as a *business,* and they're in the business of helping professionals develop and use their potential." Are you still seeing such a big difference?

One of the distinct advantages of creating teams is that you provide midlevel managers and professionals with opportunities to learn how to be world-class team players, while also teaching them how to lead. As product champions or individual contributors, they have had to persuade and influence others with their ideas, but by being on a team and coaching to influence others, their value to the organization increases and their career opportunities are enhanced. Winning companies such as GE, Motorola, Hewlett Packard, and ABB (Asea Brown Boveri) invest considerable amounts on developing leaders throughout their organizations. An excellent example of what can happen when a team player is coached to expand his or her skills and become a team leader is found in the legend-making success of the Chicago Bulls. When Phil Jackson took over as head coach, he knew he had a superstar talent in Michael Jordan, but he also aimed to coach Jordan to assume a leadership role on the team. As Jackson describes in his book *Sacred Hoops,* Jordan took to the role and had a pivotal effect on elevating the team's level of play— enough to lead the team to a record series of championship seasons.

Many businesspeople eschew sports as an inappropriate metaphor for business. But let's look again at what constitutes a world-class team: a group of diverse individuals who are recruited to become a cohesive unit with an intense loyalty to the team. That sounds a lot like a professional football or basketball team.

One of the ironies of the business world is its lack of recognition that businesspeople are, in fact, playing a game with a defined playing field and set of goals. So far, the parallel to the sports world holds true. The analogy breaks down with the fact that we rarely see our Team Leaders acting remotely as coaches. They call team meetings, but where is the relentless attention to game plans and providing team members with the kind of coaching that is required?

What is the "art" of coaching? We think it lies in understanding the motivation of team members, delegating assignments that challenge and develop their potential, and, finally, providing them with feedback for course correction.

➤ Motivation

What motivates world-class team members? Among the many valuable theories of motivation that have been put forth over the years, we believe psychologist Abraham Maslow's hierarchy of needs continues to have practical value today as workers in the Industrial Age evolve to become workers in the Information Age, or "knowledge workers." Simply stated, Maslow's theory suggests that not everyone is motivated by the same incentives. Applied to a world-class team, the key is to find out what motivates *your* team members and then build strategic incentives accordingly.

The focus here is on motivating individuals. As a backdrop or starting point, however, you can glean some hints about how to motivate individual team members by considering traits they tend to share as a group of knowledge workers. Carol Stephenson, president and CEO of Stentor Resources Centre Inc., a Canadian telecommunications company, offers this perspective:

> I've observed four characteristics that make knowledge workers creative and appealing:
>
> ➤ They tend to be more work-focused than job-focused. Work must provide growth and accomplishment, as well as remuneration.

➤ Knowledge workers are fiercely autonomous. To manage them, you must surrender authority for day-to-day task control.

➤ They are aware of their own worth. They can leverage their skills and determine where and how they work.

➤ They are impatient with standard routines and protocols. But they will give you their best "out-of-the-box" thinking.

On the whole, most people on world-class teams already have met what Maslow refers to as their "physical and security needs," such as money, physical work environment, confidence in their competencies. What they want likely falls into the needs categories of affiliation (belonging), ego (personal status and recognition), and self-actualization (ability to realize and use their skills and grow). Being and feeling part of the team addresses affiliation; rewards and recognition address ego. Learning, growing, and being an involved and valued team member are critical elements for self-actualization.

When looking to generate enthusiasm, loyalty, and top performance from *your* team members, don't make *assumptions* about what will do the trick. For example, with incentives such as different types of compensation and recognition, find out what your people want individually—for instance, promotion, learning, travel—and then give them what they find most valuable or meaningful.

In addition, remember to keep in mind the crucial differences between *compliance* and *commitment,* and emphasize participation as one way of motivating team members. For self-actualization, a primary objective is freedom, which has been referred to as delegation and empowerment. In short, you need to give people important work to do, and then the freedom to do it.

➤ Delegation and Empowerment

"Never do what you can delegate" sounds great. However, the biggest challenge facing Team Leaders is to let go of their work.

The first reaction of most new Team Leaders is to take on more work. It's a powerful reflex. How else can they be sure that their project, the most important assignment they've ever had, will get done right? Like all reflexes, the do-it-yourself model is also a substitute for thinking.

Delegation refers to the team tasks a Team Leader gives a team member to do, and empowerment refers to the amount of freedom team members have for making decisions and taking action. We know this about world-class team members: If they are going to achieve role efficacy and be highly motivated team members, they must have meaningful work that is challenging and is perceived as truly adding value, and freedom to use their competencies as they choose (more or less).

You can use different leadership styles as you coach team members toward their full potential. CAUTION: As with motivating individual team members, there is no one *best* style—the choice depends on the motivation and competencies of a particular team member. As a framework for assessing and developing effective leadership styles, you may want to draw from a theoretical model, such as the Transformational Leadership model presented by Bernard M. Bass in *Bass & Stogdill's Handbook of Leadership: Theory, Research and Managerial Applications* (The Free Press, 1990). We have found Blanchard and Hersey's Situational Leadership Theory, which we mentioned in Chapter 9, to be a straightforward tool for helping Team Leaders choose which delegation/empowerment style is best used for which team member (see Toolkit 10.14). The four leadership styles that make up the Blanchard/Hersey model are as follows:

1. The *Telling* style is useful for teams at startup or where team members have a lot to learn about the task. The Team Leader has a high level of interaction with the team, and most communication from the Team Leader to team members consists of giving information and directions. The Team Leader chairs meetings, allocates work, and is the main source of feedback for the team.

2. The *Selling* style is useful for teams as they begin to perform their tasks and learn to manage their borders. The Team Leader has a high level of interaction with the team. Most communication from the Team Leader contains positive feedback and emotional support; the Team Leader does continue to provide task coaching on occasion. Team members may chair meetings, allocate work, and so on, but the Team Leader will take over if the team is too busy or is unsure of a given topic.

3. The *Participating* style is useful for competent teams that may face new challenges or lose their motivation. The Team Leader's level of interaction with the team is highly variable—he or she may interact or be distant, depending on the needs of team members. Most communication from the Team Leader is of a more visionary and strategic nature; the Team Leader represents the team in the organization. The Team Leader may or may not chair meetings and tends not to get involved in details of tasks.

4. The *Delegating* style is useful for very competent and experienced teams. The Team Leader has a low level of interaction with the team. Most communication from the Team Leader consists of responding to proposals and suggestions from the team; the Team Leader is occupied with broader organizational strategic issues. Team members chair meetings, allocate work, give each other feedback, and seek feedback directly from outside the team.

10.14   Situational Leadership Model

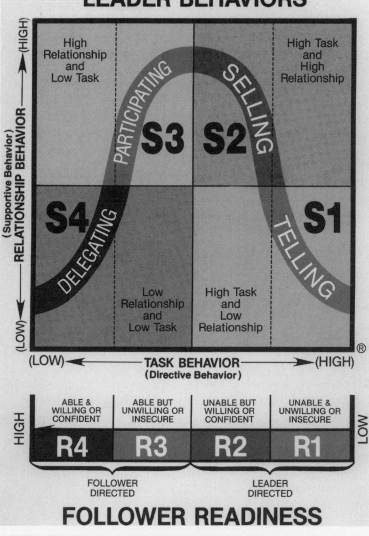

The operative thought is: In order to have motivated and committed employees who continue to grow and develop, you must match your style to what your team members need.

➤ The Art of Feedback

We often hear it said that "Feedback is a gift." Like a sweater that doesn't fit or is a color you don't like, you can always give it back or put it on a shelf.

Anyone who has watched pro football coach Bill Parcells pacing the sidelines and then yelling at one of his New York Jets for dropping a pass could question whether the coach saw the gift he was giving as "optional." Unfortunately, we've come to believe that when it comes to world-class teams, too few gifts are being offered and, therefore, team members (and Team Leaders) often are left in the dark or caught like deer in headlights when they receive unanticipated feedback.

Among the reasons team members fail to give feedback are: they are uncomfortable with how best to critique (or praise) their peers, and they fear repercussions. With those reasons in mind, here are some points for "team coaches" and "team players" who may be giving and receiving feedback:

Giving Feedback

➤ Focus on the behavior of the individual or the group, not on the personality or character.

➤ Be specific (what, when, where, etc.).

➤ *Describe* the person's behavior; do not *judge* it.

➤ Direct advice at behavior that can be changed, not at permanent characteristics of an individual.

➤ Make the comments timely; deliver them either at the moment the behavior is occurring or as soon afterward as possible.

➤ Remember that people are uncomfortable receiving feedback, even if you are handling it the best way possible.

➤ Whether the person agrees to continue (you gave positive feedback) or to change (you gave negative feedback), express your appreciation for his or her listening to your concerns.

Receiving Feedback

➤ Actively listen to the person's description of your behavior and to recommendations to either continue what you are doing or make changes that would be helpful. (This is hard!)

➤ Do not get defensive; trust that the intent of the feedback is to help, not hurt you.

➤ Paraphrase or summarize the feedback to make sure you have understood it correctly.

➤ Give the feedback serious consideration. Do not dismiss it as irrelevant or unimportant.

➤ Communicate to the person any changes in his or her behavior that may be needed to help you change.

➤ Whatever your reactions, express appreciation to the other person for caring enough about the relationship to give you the feedback, and request that he or she continue to do so periodically.

■ ALL FOR ONE AND ONE FOR ALL

As we noted in the previous chapter, some people find "can walk on water" the most important qualification for Team Leaders. However, even though the buck does stop at their desk to a large degree, Team Leaders don't have sole responsibility for leading and aligning the team for high performance. All team members bear a shared responsibility for keeping their spotlights in balanced focus. As a final tool for those who are in the helicopter, here's a set of "how tos" (and some "shoulds") that perhaps can serve as an "Alignment Checklist."

➤ Develop a clear set of team goals and team accountabilities for each team member, and a process (project management) for monitoring team progress. Encourage both independent and collaborative projects among team members.

➤ Develop strategies for keeping the team Sponsor and key stakeholders "in the loop." Remember they are your "customers," and their needs and expectations must be met.

➤ Take periodic time-outs to reflect on how the team is functioning, what the team is learning, and how to build better collaboration.

➤ Travel only with a clear goal, and examine other cost-effective meeting/communication alternatives.

➤ Avoid being technology-driven and do hold some face-to-face meetings.

➤ Use social events to celebrate team and individual milestones.

➤ Provide individual team members, who must balance individual and team roles and responsibilities, with performance feedback and career/professional development opportunities.

➤ Value team diversity, but also openly discuss cultural differences that may be adversely affecting the team's functioning.

➤ Formally seek out feedback from key stakeholders regarding your "measures of success."

➤ Develop rewards and recognition strategies for both the team and individual team members.

➤ Create an interdependent network of independent local experts who think globally and act locally.

➤ Be committed to continuous improvement in processes and out-puts—"How can we do better?"

➤ Develop the ability to deal with difficult, subtle, and conflict-provoking issues.

➤ Provide a mechanism for teams to share "best practices" and achieve transfer of knowledge among team members and between and among teams.

➤ Find creative ways to keep remote team members unified and motivated.

➤ Provide a project management system that allows everyone to stay on track and keep on schedule with their accountabilities.

➤ Provide a technological communications platform (such as Lotus Notes and Internet-access databases) to help manage the "remote" factor.

➤ Rotate meetings to different team members' locations (that is, countries/regions).

➤ Encourage team members to "nurture" each other—to communicate between meetings about things other than work. Harvey McKay, author of *Swim with the Sharks,* recommends that you develop a database for your key customers that includes birthdays, names of family members, favorite hobbies, "hot buttons," and so forth. Why not do something like that for your team members?

➤ Include in team meetings some form of "cultural education." For example, have team members, on a rotational basis, give a cultural "lecturette" or demonstration that would help people understand what they would need to know to feel comfortable and knowledge-able in their country.

➤ Don't assume that any team dysfunctions (e.g., conflict, burn-out, lack of commitment, unproductive meetings) will just take care of themselves.

STRATEGY

4

Measuring, Managing, and Rewarding World-Class Team Performance

Chapter 11

Team-Based
Goal Setting

After a team has developed and agreed on its team Charter and Boundaries, it is ready to establish its team goals—the statements that reflect the results and outcomes the team intends to achieve. The team goals reflect the vision of the team as it moves toward creating a "new reality" that will make the organization substantially better than it is today. The team goals must be aligned with the team Charter and serve as the benchmarks for which the team will be held accountable by its Sponsor and stakeholders.

In Chapter 1, we introduced our definition of a world-class team and suggested that the major difference between a working group and a world-class team is that the latter shares a commitment to achieving a common set of goals. Therefore, the team's goal-setting process is absolutely critical to the team's success, and all the team members and key stakeholders need to be part of the process if they are expected to be committed to the team's outcomes. How vital are goals? In a survey titled "1995 Team-Based Pay Survey (U.S.A.)," conducted by the Hay Group, the top three reasons for the failure of teams were: goals not clear; change of objectives; and inadequate management support.

■ MEETING SPONSOR AND STAKEHOLDER EXPECTATIONS

As indicated in Chapters 3 and 4, the *raison d'être* for world-class teams is to meet the Sponsor's and other key stakeholders' expectations. The Sponsor and key stakeholders, through expression of their expectations, reflect what the organization intends to be the "value-added" provided by the team.

Prior to establishing the team goals, the Team Leader, with appropriate participation from team members, should meet with the Sponsor and key stakeholders to develop an understanding of the "vision" and expected outcomes for the team. During such meetings, the Sponsor and key stakeholders should be asked questions such as these:

➤ A year from now [or another time frame, as appropriate], what would it take for you to enthusiastically recommend that this team continue working together?

➤ What do you want and/or expect from this team that you have not been able to obtain or achieve with any other organizational unit so far?

➤ What added value do you expect this team to contribute?

In these meetings, it also may be interesting and worthwhile to conduct a "SWOT Analysis": Each individual offers his or her perspective on the *Strengths*, *Weaknesses*, *Opportunities*, and *Threats* perceived in the marketplace (external) and within the organization (internal), toward which the team should be prepared to address its work. (See Chapter 5 for more guidance on how to identify stakeholder expectations.)

With candid responses to these types of questions and exercises, the team is in a good position to begin to structure its goals.

■ CREATING A TEAM VISION

When the team begins to shape its team goals, a review of all the Sponsor/stakeholder needs and expectations should be the first step. The second step is to create a team vision.

Lynda McDermott, in her book *Caught in the Middle,* describes this process as follows: "Setting a vision simply means understanding where your part of the organization is today, and where it needs to be headed in the future, again, in support of the overall direction of the business. It means becoming the conductor of your section of the orchestra and ensuring that it's in harmony with the rest."[1]

McDermott goes on to say: "Creating a vision [for your team] gives personal meaning to the work you perform. It describes a desirable state for [the team], as well as the unique contributions and added value that you and your team bring to the table."[2]

To create your team's vision, ask your team to participate in an exercise similar to the one below.

Imagine we have come to the end of our work. Our team Charter has been successfully fulfilled. As we reflect on the team and its work, how would we answer the following questions:

➤ What are we proud of having accomplished?

➤ What results did we achieve?

➤ What is different and better that exists now as a result of our team's efforts and was not present when we began our team's work?

➤ What value has the team contributed to the organization?

➤ What are the Sponsor and key stakeholders saying about our accomplishments?

➤ What are the team members saying about this "Dream Team" experience? What did we learn and achieve?

➤ When we first set *these* targets, others said that they were virtually impossible to achieve. [Identify the targets.]

The answers to the above questions make the ultimate work of the team tangible and set the stage for more specific planning and goal setting. In fact, a three- to five-year "strategic plan" may be developed as a result of this visioning process. (See the model in Toolkit 11.1 for an overview of the team goal development and alignment process.)

11.1 Team Goal Development and Alignment Process

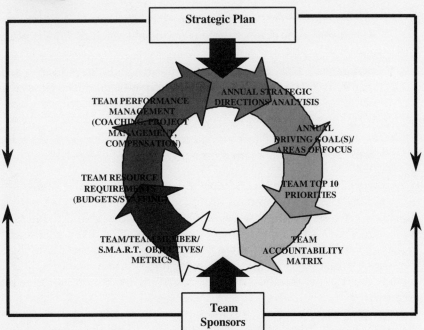

■ THE TEAM ALIGNMENT PROCESS

When a broad and inspirational team vision has been established, the team can begin to develop a more detailed goal-setting framework for its work. A Team Alignment Process can be used to bring focus, discipline, and structure to the team's goal setting. The process can help the team:

➤ Choose primary goals for the year and agree on five to ten key priorities.

➤ Focus on major team initiatives and align them with resources.

➤ Clarify how each team member will contribute to, and be accountable for, team achievements.

➤ Serve as a vehicle for communicating team and individual team member performance expectations throughout the organization.

➤ Provide a mechanism for benchmarking and monitoring team and individual performances.

Because teams exist within an organizational context, their performance should be measured and evaluated based on goals that are aligned with the other organizational units surrounding the team. Generally speaking, three levels of performance goals need to be aligned:

1. *Organizational goals.* These are the strategic measures for which the corporation is held accountable, such as ROI, profits, and market share.

2. *Team goals.* These measurements are both quantitative and qualitative. They measure the work directly produced by either business unit teams or cross-functional teams whose work supports the corporate strategy.

3. *Individual goals.* These should measure the results achieved by both the individual team members and the team.

Why worry about alignment? Because dealing with a lack of goal alignment among the components of an organization is like driving an unaligned car. When even one wheel is not coordinated with the others, a very bumpy and "off-balance" journey lies ahead. The Team Alignment Process provides team members with the opportunity to see how their work has a direct impact on the corporate organization's success, and it ensures that the organization has maximized its investment in the team members.

Goal setting is always important, but the Team Alignment Process is *critical* for world-class teams because they face particular issues related to the remote locations of team members and to their multiple reporting relationships. A world-class team that relies on computer networks and other technologies for much of its interaction needs to be operating against shared, explicit goals and expectations in order to facilitate its remote project work and decision making.

➤ Alignment: What Is It?

Anthea Scott was overwhelmed. She was lead person on the majority of marketing projects for her product, which was scheduled to launch in several countries over the next six months. She was buried in work and saw "no light at the end of the tunnel."

"What can I do?" she implored us. "Management isn't going to give us any more resources, and they don't stop with their requests for information and fire fighting. I can't get to the really important projects on my desk." Knowing we were about to start the Team Alignment Process with her team the next day, we begged off giving her any advice other than: "Be patient."

After only a one-day session, during which she actively participated and we saw her on more than one occasion talking dynamically with her Team Leader, she approached us and said, "Thank God you did this for us." We felt honored by the feedback, but, in reality, we had simply provided a very systematic and practical tool for prioritizing and aligning their work. They now had a plan. They would go to management and ask for either more resources to prioritize their projects (not everything is critical), or permission to eliminate projects. They had a rationale and a process for allocating resources and accountabilities. They also had a strategy and tool for warding off, or at least slowing down, the fire fighting in which they had been embroiled.

The very foundation of the Team Alignment Process is to provide a sense of common purpose and direction for a team. It means taking a collective "stand" with regard to the future. Moving beyond their own personal agendas and decisions, individual team members can choose how best to spend their time in order to fully support the implementation of the team's agenda.

What prompts individual team members to align with each other and the broader team agenda? First, team members must feel comfortable with "switching hats"—taking off the "functional/national" hat (symbolic of that part of the organization that a team member traditionally represents) and putting on the "team" hat. Individual technical and country perspectives and expertise are valued commodities for the team, but, when setting team goals, each team member must keep the team's Charter in perspective and not be concerned about how a particular goal will affect his or her department's or country's agenda. This focus may be difficult for some team members, and the team needs to watch for signs of "siloism" (pushing one's own agenda). Everyone on the team must invest personally in the big picture, not his or her corner of it.

Being a high-functioning member of an aligned team carries several implications for an individual team member's identity. If alignment is to be achieved, he or she must learn to operate from the point of view of the team's success rather than personal success. In addition, team members may need to give up some of the power and control they have traditionally wielded. They may feel the "cost" of collaboration in the loss of autonomy and freedom to act.

We have noticed that when functional or country managers of team members serve on world-class teams, they experience the loss of control more than the team members themselves. Consequently, team members who are in the process of trying to align their functional/country work with the team's work may get pulled in different directions. However, if the team can set sufficiently lofty goals that, if achieved, will truly add value, the goals can be a strong force in balancing this potential tug of war.

Bear in mind that achieving team alignment will exercise new team "muscles." Rugged individualism will be replaced by a spirit of collectivism as individuals work together in a joint effort. Parochial agendas will give way to an agenda that emphasizes the good of the entire team. Where before the territory was marked with "Stay Off My Turf" signs, alignment demands that those various territories be integrated (or at least the boundaries relaxed) to achieve common goals.

One of the things that happens in the Team Alignment Process is that the team makes conscious, and sometimes tough, decisions that they haven't been able to make before. They gain confidence to tackle the difficult resource issues that all teams face, and they begin to develop competence and skills in what real teamwork is all about. If the Team Alignment Process is to be successful, they will begin to clearly distinguish between operating from their own functional/national concerns and operating from the perspective of the whole team.

All team members should actively participate in the Team Alignment Process. This involvement will help to create a sense of ownership and accountability, which should lead to the team's full commitment to achieving its goals. As we learned in Chapter 10, not all of a team's decisions require consensus. However, when a world-class team makes decisions about its goals, *these* decisions must be consensual.

Depending on the team Charter and Boundaries, the team may need to involve the team Sponsor and key stakeholders in the process. Their involvement, if only in a review-and-approve capacity, helps ensure their "buy-in" and support of the team as it works towards its goals. World-class teams, which must compete for resources (primarily, money and people), frequently need to "cross their borders" to influence others for support. If, during the goal-setting process, the team engages key stakeholders and negotiates both goals and resources, the team will be in a much better position to achieve its goals.

As your team prepares for the goal-setting process, ask these questions:

➤ Do we know what our Sponsor(s) expect of us?

➤ Do we know what our stakeholders expect of us (results/outcomes)?

➤ What have we done to involve our Sponsor(s) and stakeholders in the goal-setting process?

➤ Who has the final decision-making authority over our priorities/goals?

➤ Where will we obtain resources/support to achieve our goals?

➤ Driving Goal and Critical Success Factors

The first step in the Team Alignment Process is to establish the team's "Driving Goal" or "theme" for the year. One European product team we worked with made this their Driving Goal:

TO ENSURE THAT THE PRODUCT AND THE 1998 LAUNCH COUNTRIES ARE READY, FROM ALL ASPECTS, FOR SUCCESSFUL LAUNCH.

In essence, they were saying that, for this particular year, virtually all team resources needed to be focused on achieving that broadly stated goal.

To illustrate how you can creatively use the Driving Goal, consider Lynda and Bill, partners in life as well as business, who, every year at a New Year's Eve dinner, decide on their Driving Goal for the year and give it a "Chinese New Year" name. For example, in 1990, after having spent considerable money refurbishing their office and home, they declared 1991 the "Year of the Profit." In 1995, as their business continued to grow and they needed additional professional resources, they named 1996 "Year of the Strategic Alliance." In each of these years, whenever they were forced to make choices about time or money, they bounced the choice against the current Driving Goal.

After you have established your Driving Goal, look at your Charter and Boundaries. What Critical Success Factors for *this* year will enable you to achieve your Driving Goal? Critical Success Factors represent the major issues that must be addressed by a team during the annual planning period. For example, for a product development team, it may be one of the Four Ps—Product, Price, Promotion, Place. No matter what other Critical Success Factors you select, we would include, for *all* world-class teams, a Critical Success Factor called Team Performance.

A strategic management system that has tremendous value for assessing the performance of world-class teams—and should therefore strongly influence the team's goal-setting process—stems from a concept called the "balanced scorecard," which was introduced by Robert S. Kaplan and David P. Norton in a *Harvard Business Review* article, "Using the Balanced Scorecard as a Strategic Management System."[3] The balanced scorecard was developed to counteract the weakness that most organizations have in limiting their "measures of success" to traditional financial measures. The balanced scorecard tracks the key elements of a company's strategy by using both financial and operational measures. The operational measures are viewed as being the drivers of future financial performance.

According to Kaplan and Norton, four key areas of organizational performance are driven by answers to these basic questions:

1. How do we look to our stakeholders? (Financial perspective)
2. How do customers see us? (Customer perspective)
3. What must we excel at? (Internal perspective)
4. Can we continue to improve and create value? (Innovation and learning perspective)

The balanced scorecard helps ensure that *all* the Critical Success Factors are evaluated. It provides checks and balances so that one area isn't overemphasized at the expense of another. Because a team's Critical Success Factors are derived from the team Charter and team vision, a balanced scorecard approach ensures that the measures used and the areas for goal setting will help strategically manage the team for both short- and long-term results. The more the team's goals and results are aligned to the broader organizational strategy, the more the team will contribute value.

The European product team cited earlier, whose Driving Goal was a successful launch, selected these Critical Success Factors:

➤ Product registration.
➤ Commercialization.
➤ Clinical development.
➤ Evergreening (extending the life cycle of a product).
➤ Team development.

Other potential Critical Success Factors include:

➤ Market share.

➤ Financing.

➤ Customer satisfaction.

➤ Quality.

➤ Cycle time.

➤ Productivity.

➤ Operations.

➤ Product.

➤ Top Ten "S.M.A.R.T." Goals

The next step in the Team Alignment Process is to establish no more than ten goals for the year. Is ten a "magic number"? Not at all. In fact, we might argue that having ten priority goals for a team that is partially staffed by part-time people may be overly ambitious. Selecting *only* ten can be tough, but when individuals realize how many "to do's" are added to their team accountabilities, anxiety creeps in and they worry about not having enough resources. (Toolkit 11.2 presents several statements of goals from world-class teams.)

The rationale for "no more than ten" is linked to the common complaint among team members, particularly in new teams, that their initial work program is too ambitious. In trying to accomplish the goals, they are prone to burnout or to substandard performance on one or more of the goals. To avoid these disappointments and to leave room for the "strategic

11.2   Sample Team Goals Statements

➤ Ensure product pricing is optimal for the region.

➤ Establish strong product branding/image.

➤ Develop and implement regional market research.

➤ Maximize commercial potential of regional product sales.

➤ Seek commitments from governments to register product without mandatory waiting period.

➤ Develop and promote *strong* but segment-oriented branding for this product.

11.3   Team Alignment Process Sample

DRIVING GOAL

Prepare product and countries for product launch

TEAM TOP TEN GOALS

(Examples)	Goal Guide	Support
1. Maintain Publication Program	K.R.	J.P.
2. Complete and Deliver Pricing Policy	A.S.	S.M.

opportunities" that are certain to present themselves, we strongly suggest that the team limit itself to ten goals.

After determining its goals, the team can move on to creating a team accountability matrix. In this step, each team member, including the Team Leader, either volunteers for, or is assigned, the role of Goal Guide. Each Goal Guide takes the lead in (1) ensuring that one (or more) of the Team Top Ten has a specific set of objectives and a work program, and (2) focusing the team's resources on achieving those objectives.

Toolkit 11.3 shows an abbreviated sample output from one team's Team Alignment Process through the stage of identifying the Team Top Ten and assigning Goal Guides and support personnel. This example, which identifies the key person for a particular goal and the person who will provide support, develops a picture of how the team's work will be balanced and how team responsibilities have been allocated. (See Toolkit 11.4 for an example of one team's work program.)

The first task of the Goal Guide involves developing one or two S.M.A.R.T. goals for the Team Top Ten item that is his or her assignment. As the team begins to finalize the team goals, make sure they can pass the "tests" listed below.

➤ Goals must be S.M.A.R.T.:
    SPECIFIC.
    MEASURABLE.
    ACTION-ORIENTED.
    REALISTIC.
    TIME-BOUND.

11.4 Area Teams Work Program

Team Leader: ____ Team Members: CAB CB FLM IWH JK MDM TS

Project	Actions	Timing	Responsibility	Country Involvement*
Completed				
Planning Conference – NY		6-May-96	CAB FLM IWH	Europe
Team Meeting with France		5-June-96	IWH	*France*
Differentiation Strategy Templates		29-May-96	ISH	Headquarters
Ongoing				
Area Team Meetings	On-going	Monthly	IWH	Area Team
Team Meeting with Norway	Identify date	16–22 Sept 19	IWH TS	*Norway*
Team Meeting with Germany	Identify date	17/18 July 199	IWH CB FLM	*Germany*
Switzerland	Comarketing issues and positioning follow-up	TBD	IWH	
Netherlands	Re-Launch follow-up	TBD	IWH	
Symposium – Tromso	Review proposal & prepare country bulletin	18-Jan-97	FLM	*Norway* UK Canada Italy
Symposium Nov. 96	Prepare country bulletin	1-Jul-96	FLM	*Italy*
Symposium – Melbourne 1996	Finalize symposia presentations	23-Jun-96	IWH	Headquarters
Symposium – Madrid 1996	Finalize symposia presentations	23-Aug-96	IWH	Headquarters
Sales Management Planning Conference	Identify date	Nov-96	IWH CB	Europe
Major Country Planning Conference	Identify date	Aug-96	IWH	Europe
Advanced Workshops	Identify plans and needs	Jul-96	TS	Europe
European Advisory Board	Establish proposals for Planning Conference	Aug-96	TS CB	Europe
Symposium	Liaise with NYPT for preliminary workshop	27-Aug-96	CB	Europe
Consensus Meeting	Discuss Feasibility	22-Jun-96	IWH	NY Team

* The Sponsor Country is indicated in bold italic.

➤ They are possible to be accomplished.

➤ They will fulfill the team Charter and vision, and will meet Sponsor and stakeholder expectations.

➤ They leap over present obstacles and describe a positive future that is different from today.

One team listed the following as its team goals for the year:

1. Register faster.
2. Determine and meet specific regional marketing needs.
3. Ensure strong product image.
4. Meet or exceed sales expectations/goals.

These may be targets or priorities, but they are not S.M.A.R.T. To make them S.M.A.R.T., we recommended restating goal 4 to include an actual sales dollars figure and restating it as: "Meet or exceed $1.5 million in sales for this product."

What about goal 3: "Ensure strong product image"? This goal is harder to make S.M.A.R.T. because it is not dealing with something that is totally objective.

Another product team decided to focus its first-year efforts on Industry Opinion Leaders. Some of its S.M.A.R.T. goals were:

1. Develop a *Speakers' Directory* for first-quarter publication.
2. Develop innovative symposia formats to encourage more diverse supporters for '98 Congress candidates by 3rd Quarter '97.

In both cases, the goal was improved by stating a time frame, but more specific criteria would have defined whether the goal had purpose and would be successfully achieved beyond just meeting a deadline.

Keep in mind that the work of white-collar employees (usually found on world-class teams) is often difficult to measure. They tend to resist attempts at management by objectives (MBO) because they think their knowledge-based work can't be reduced to quantifiable numbers. You conquer a major hurdle when you tell them the goals have to be results-focused, and that the results must be observable according to some measurement that a third party could evaluate or verify. Merely asking "How would you or one of your key stakeholders define your success in achieving this goal?" usually pulls out qualitative goal definitions.

Review your team goals for this year. Are they as S.M.A.R.T. as they should be? Could an outsider evaluate whether you have achieved them? Challenge your team to make all your team goals S.M.A.R.T.

➤ Team Member Objectives

When the top ten S.M.A.R.T. goals have been developed and agreed on by the entire team, team members should develop their individual objectives as members of the team. Although a team member might not be the Goal Guide for a certain goal, he or she may have an individual objective to provide some type of support. The objective becomes part of that person's Annual Individual Objective package, which includes team goals, individual team objectives, and functional (nonteam) objectives. (See Chapter 13 for a Toolkit example of goal weighting for a team member.)

One way to ensure that accountability and work programs are balanced across the team is to review the individual team members' accountabilities and allotted time for work on the team. For example, if a team member has allocated only 25 percent of her time to the team, but is a Goal Guide on three major team goals, either the assignments or the time allocation should be questioned. If these "misalignments" can be worked out in the goal-setting process, misunderstandings and frustration can be prevented when the team begins its work.

When establishing both team goals and individual team member objectives, stay focused on *accomplishments* and *results,* not the activities needed to achieve them. The results from both teams and individuals also should be directly linked to the organizational goals. For example, if market share is a corporate Driving Goal, and a product team sees market share slippage for their product in Europe, then their Driving Goal (or at least a high-priority area) should be "Improve product market share position in Europe."

➤ Team Process Goals

The team may want to move beyond the more traditional task-related goals and develop some team process goals. In one organization that pioneered setting up a regional product team, the world-class team set these process goals in addition to its task goals:

1. Create a new way of working together and be a "trailblazer" for other product teams to follow.
2. Do together, as a team, what can't be done alone in the various countries.

3. Speak with one voice for the region.

4. Focus on the strategic issues of a new product introduction, and be a model for others.

5. Be admired and respected throughout the global organization as a "high-performance team" that overcame challenges to do what has never been done before in this region.

These types of goals are difficult, though not impossible, to measure. Alternatively, the team could have developed a more specific objective: Achieve recognition for high-performance teamwork among key stakeholders through the publication of articles.

Team process or "soft" goals are the most difficult goals to measure. We often resort to saying, "I'll know it when I see it" as a measurement methodology. For each of the five team process goals listed above, create one S.M.A.R.T. goal.

➤ Stakeholder Goal Management

The final stage in the goal-setting process is to decide how and with whom the goals, work program, and so forth, will be communicated. As part of the stakeholder expectations process described in Chapter 5, agreement on communication may already have been reached. However, a word of caution. This is the point in the team's development where border management must take place. The team goals, and the accompanying work program, will dictate the work and resource allocation of the team. If there is not agreement or buy-in from key stakeholders at this point, the success of the team is potentially undermined.

We recommend that some form of communication briefing be given to key stakeholders, perhaps with the advice and counsel of the team Sponsor. The briefing should provide a forum for questions and for clarification of the team goals and other aspects of the team's work.

Team Alignment Process: Questions to Ask

➤ Do we have a broad vision to accomplish and a Driving Goal for *this* year?

➤ What currently are the Critical Success Factors for our team?

➤ Where can our team best contribute to achieving them? What are the priorities for the team? (Have we limited ourselves to the Team Top Ten?)

➤ What can each team member best contribute to achieving the team objectives? Do we have clear accountabilities assigned? Does everyone have a role?

➤ If each of us meets our objectives, will our team have made a significant contribution to the success of the company?

➤ Do we have *team* goals versus broader organizational goals, or just one individual's goals (e.g., the Team Leader's)?

➤ Are the goals S.M.A.R.T.?

➤ Are they realistic as well as ambitious? Do they allow small wins along the way?

➤ Do they call for a concrete set of team work products?

➤ Do all members agree with the goals, their relative importance, and the way in which their achievement will be measured?

➤ Will the goals meet our stakeholders' expectations?

➤ Do we have a "team learning stop" built into our agenda for the year?

➤ How will we celebrate our team's accomplishments?

■ TEAM PERFORMANCE MANAGEMENT

Many teams spend a large part of any meeting time reviewing "results to date." For many team members, this status review appears to be a waste of time because it can be accomplished simply by looking at charts. In the spirit of *team learning,* we recommend that the team convene, at least at the midyear mark, for the specific purpose of taking a "team learning stop." This would include an assessment of goals both to celebrate significant results accomplished and to identify any "killer gaps"— performance gaps that will make a critical difference in achieving the team's Driving Goal (and, ultimately, the team's vision). Launch an open discussion and ask these questions:

➤ What, if anything, most worries us about not achieving this goal?

➤ If the goal is not achieved by year end, what is likely to be the cause?

➤ What didn't we know that could have led to this shortfall?

➤ What would it take for us to turn this around? What do we need to learn/do before we start?

The art of handling this type of review lies in minimizing individuals' defensiveness and maximizing team dialogue, problem solving, and learning. You may find in the process that the original goals were unrealistic, given the level of resources, or that external forces drastically altered either the results or the desirability of particular goals. On the other hand, you may uncover some element of either an individual team member's performance or the team's process that is contributing to the performance gap. The team can then address the problem.

Even with a clear Charter and well-defined team and individual accountabilities, there will be times when performance expectations are misunderstood or are not met. Although it presents a major challenge for most teams, dealing with performance and accountability issues is essential to a team's success. If such issues are not resolved, the team will experience the following problems:

➤ Team members will begin to mistrust one another.

➤ Team members will "drop out" or show other forms of apathy.

➤ Performance will slip, either in quality or missed deadlines.

➤ The team will lose its credibility.

The following three-step process will help you to analyze team performance issues and to decide on the best strategy for resolving them. For purposes here, a performance issue arises any time a team member's behavior and/or work products are not on track with what is expected of that team member.

1. Identify the performance gap. Where there is a gap between expected and current performance, ask the following questions:

   — Were performance expectations clearly established and communicated?

   — Are the performance expectations realistic?

   — Has the team member received any previous feedback?

   — Does the team member have the skills and resources to meet the performance expectations?

2. Based on the above analysis, determine why the issue exists and what approach to take with the person, or decide that you have insufficient information with which to make a conclusion.

3. Discuss the performance issue with your team member, with the goal of gaining mutual understanding about the issue; then develop a Plan of Action (POA) for how to resolve it. Make it a point to monitor progress on the POA and to provide positive feedback or additional coaching as required.

In the excitement of the team's formation, getting the team to spend time and energy on developing its goals and work program is usually not a problem. The challenge is to also develop (and enforce) a process by which the team will review and evaluate its progress and results, and, perhaps, adjust its goals or objectives at a later time.

Team Alignment Framework

Team vision: A broad description of the value-added unique contributions that will be created by the team.

Driving Goal: For the planning period, the primary area of focus.

Critical Success Factors: Those four to five issues that *must* be addressed to achieve the Driving Goal.

Team Top Ten: The maximum number of goals that should be assigned/accomplished during the planning period. Each of these goals should be as S.M.A.R.T. as possible.

Objectives: The specific and measurable priorities that will focus the individual team members' tasks and activities and allow the team to achieve small wins in pursuit of the broader goals.

Tactics and work programs: The specific actions and outputs that team members, either alone or jointly, will carry out in order for the team achieve its goals and objectives.

■ CHARTING YOUR TEAM'S COURSE

A team committed to achieving its team goals stays focused and is constantly asking itself: "If we continue on this path, will we achieve and fulfill our team Charter and vision?" The goals are the navigational course required to help the team reach its destination. Just as unexpected changes in the weather may cause you to reevaluate and, in fact, chart a new course, having a clarity around your Driving Goal helps to keep the team focused and aligned.

When you keep the team spotlight on *team performance,* it can energize the group, even when results aren't up to expectations. Most team members want to be on a winning team. When you can get them to share both personal and collective accountability for results, you spontaneously light the fire that drives team commitment.

Chapter 12

Measures of Success for World-Class Teams

"You get what you measure," and teams are no different in this regard than any other management challenge. But creating measurements that define whether a team initiative is successful is easier said than done! Unfortunately, much of the organizational change that world-class teams create can't be measured strictly by numbers. Why (and how) we measure them is therefore difficult.

■ WHY MEASURE WORLD-CLASS TEAMS?

World-class teams set goals or objectives for themselves that relate primarily to the specific outputs or products each team will produce. This form of measurement was described in detail in Chapter 11. We differentiate measures of success from a specific world-class team's goals; these measures indicate whether the team or team structure has really *added value to the organization,* as perceived by key stakeholders.

In the process of defining *how* to measure, both the teams and their key stakeholders define in objective terms what "bottom line" they expect from the team. We believe that this process of establishing clearly defined value-added expectations is a vital component in setting up a team for success.

What Measures of Success Can Do for a Team

➤ Produce high-performance results with clear and verifiable goals, even for hard-to-measure "knowledge-worker" teams.

➤ Align a team's measures to its organization's measures.

➤ Create measures with which to link individual team members' goals to team goals.

➤ Define the value-added results or accomplishments that the team produces.

202

➤ Involve key stakeholders in defining expectations and sharing in the ownership of the team's success.

➤ Force definition of "measures that matter," even for hard-to-measure functions such as market research or product design.

When one organization decided to initiate a regional team structure in Europe, the new team structure was viewed by some, optimistically, as providing the needed link between headquarters and the individual countries in the region. However, many viewed this new structure with wariness, referring to it as an "experiment." As we began to work with the new teams, we asked some key senior managers: "How will you know if the 'experiment' is successful?" They could not give us a response and, in fact, seemed reluctant to pursue the issue further.

Another organization had made a decision that, in order to successfully launch several new products over an 18-month period, they needed the full collaboration of all departments around the globe. Unfortunately, although the need for a *fast* culture change was critical, the company's culture had a history of being extremely hierarchical. Their solution: Form cross-functional/cross-cultural teams that would focus on leveraging interdisciplinary resources. We asked the three Sponsor groups to define how they would measure the success of these teams after one year. Here are some of the actions/results they would expect from "successful" teams:

➤ Launch products ahead of schedule.

➤ Reduce time gaps to launch across companies in region.

➤ Reduce cost of launches.

➤ Introduce new and creative marketing strategies; use nontraditional ways of reaching target markets.

➤ Realize/exceed sales and P&L objectives.

➤ Improve market share.

➤ Produce continued stock growth.

➤ Surpass the objectives for awareness and usage of products; make products "household names."

➤ Improve the company image.

➤ Become a "model company" in organization development, as acknowledged by the industry (e.g., in a *Harvard Business Review* case study).

➤ Benchmark the Gold Standard for teamwork and communications.

➤ Increase the international perspective of managers.

> Improve the multilingual proficiency of team members.
> Pay record bonuses.

An important step in determining measures of success for teams is to take such "brainstorming" lists and identify certain Critical Success Factors—the areas that will drive the team's performance. For example, one of the Critical Success Factors for a reengineering project might be: reducing cycle time while also reducing costs and maintaining employee satisfaction. Some related Critical Success Factors might be: reducing customer complaints, announcing no layoffs due to reengineering, and so forth.

The metrics you finally select will work best when:

> They matter—that is, they reflect the team's added value.
> The team has control over what is measured.
> They are easily quantified, either numerically or through observation.
> Key stakeholders are involved in the measurement process.
> They are viewed as information for continuous improvement.

■ A PLACE TO START: FORCES FOR CHANGE

In Chapter 3, we emphasized the importance of identifying the Performance and Business Challenge rationale for establishing world-class teams. We stressed the importance of conducting this examination *before* proceeding with building a team-based structure. This is also the place to start when you begin the process of measuring world-class team performance.

In one region of the world, a company listed the following "forces for change" as the challenges to which it needed to respond:

> Manage, support, and exploit the profitable life of four major new products.
> Monitor, influence, and respond to the changing industry environment and customer base in the region.
> Expedite the product registration process.
> Capitalize on economies of scale, and improve profitability.
> Develop the organizational infrastructure and culture to manage change.
> Keep the team focused on strategic issues.
> Be respected and admired as a high-performance team.

If you went no further, you could use these forces for change as a starting point for defining your measures of success.

■ CRITERIA FOR MEASURES FOR SUCCESS

The old adage "You can't please all the people all the time—only some of the people some of the time" should be remembered when selecting the most appropriate measures of success. We always suggest that our clients think of their teams as a separate business unit(s) and ask themselves: *"You are seeking funding, or permission to stay in business. Whom would you seek funding/permission from first, and what would convince your potential 'investors' to support the investment?"*

This exercise helps the team(s) to focus on two important issues:

1. Who are the most important stakeholders?
2. How will *they* judge our success?

By honing in on these issues, the team(s) should be able to identify three to four key stakeholders and determine the primary expectations each has toward the team's ability to provide "value-added" results.

Soon after launching three product teams in Europe, we gathered together the Team Leaders, their Sponsors, and three other key functional stakeholders. We first took them through an exercise in which they were asked to construct a "stakeholder pyramid" for the team—that is, to identify the teams' key stakeholders in a hierarchy of their importance, beginning with the stakeholder group whose perception of the team is success is ultimately most crucial. (See Toolkit 12.1 for the pyramid.)

We then provided them with a model for selecting measures of success. Don Kirkpatrick's model for measuring training programs can be used when setting up any system to measure a change initiative (see Toolkit 12.2). Using the four levels of measurement described below, his basic premise is that the closer you can get the measure to the "bottom-line" results (Level IV), the better.

➤ Level I measures *reaction*. The most obvious metric associated with it is what we refer to as the "smile test." The primary purpose of Level I evaluation is to measure people's perception of satisfaction and acceptance.

➤ Level II measures *learning*. Kirkpatrick observes that learning happens when attitudes are changed, knowledge is increased, or skill is improved. The primary metric associated with Level II is some

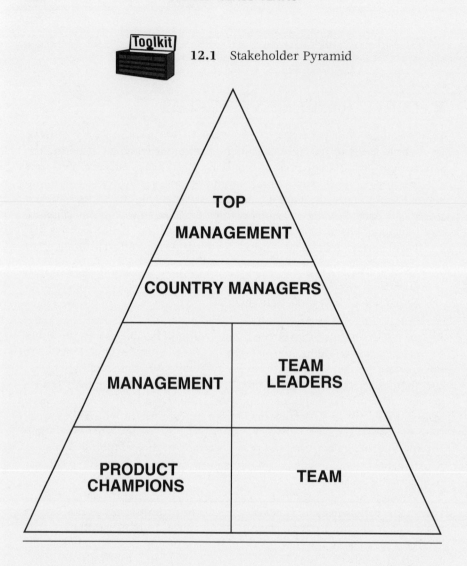

Toolkit **12.1** Stakeholder Pyramid

form of a "test" or "survey" to gauge knowledge acquisition or attitude change.

➤ Level III measures *behavior*. This is the extent to which a person's behavior changes due to the change initiative. Usually this measurement takes place after some time has passed, perhaps three months. For better or worse, the primary tools used for Level III are surveys or observation.

12.2   Team Success Metrics

Level IV	Business impact/Bottom-line results (financial, market sales, market share, profit, rank, operational measures)
Level III	On-the-job behavior change (cultural change measures; cross-border leverage measures; increased information exchange measures)
Level II	Learning (tests, interviews, surveys)
Level I	"Smiles"

> Level IV measures *results*. An attempt is made to link the change to some form of objective organizational results. The tool most often associated with Level IV evaluation is a financial analysis (typically, an ROI or a cost/benefit analysis), to gauge the impact on the business. The idea generally is to "prove the change effort was worth it."

Kirkpatrick strongly suggests, however, not limiting the effort to purely financial results. As the friendly number crunchers in your organization probably could tell you, ROI and other traditional financial measures have three major shortfalls:

1. They usually do not capture all of a company's strategic objectives.
2. ROI, for example, is a snapshot in time that tells you where you've been; it has no ability to predict where you'll go.
3. Because many financial measurements are lagging indicators, they are not good diagnostic tools.

In short, even if we are concerned only with hard-nosed business indicators as opposed to mushy, humanistic measures of "success," indicators such as ROI do not necessarily live up to their reputation as ultimate measures of "results."[1]

With one group of Team Leaders, Sponsors, and stakeholders, we supplemented Kirkpatrick's model with team success measures (see Toolkit 12.3) to get the group thinking strategically and creatively about the various ways they could measure the successes of their team initiative. We worked with them to develop a specific set of measures/criteria that

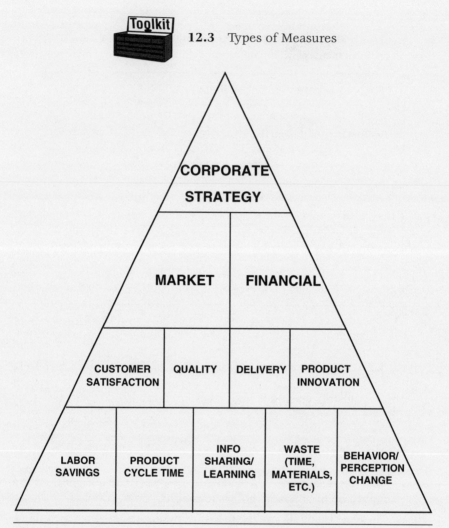

Toolkit

12.3   Types of Measures

CORPORATE
STRATEGY

MARKET   FINANCIAL

CUSTOMER SATISFACTION   QUALITY   DELIVERY   PRODUCT INNOVATION

LABOR SAVINGS   PRODUCT CYCLE TIME   INFO SHARING/ LEARNING   WASTE (TIME, MATERIALS, ETC.)   BEHAVIOR/ PERCEPTION CHANGE

Adapted from Jack Zignon, *How to Measure the Results of Teams* © 1995.

would allow them to look back after a year and objectively evaluate whether their investment of time and people had provided the intended return. (See Toolkit 12.4 for their final list of "Critical Needs/Expectations.")

Initially, the group went through a brainstorming process, asking each of the stakeholder groups: "If you were a country manager, how would *you* measure the success of these teams?" or "If you were a corporate senior manager, how would you determine whether they were

12.4 Critical Needs Expectations

Country Managers

➤ Short- and long-term results.

➤ This will enhance my P&L.

➤ This will nor hurt my P&L.

➤ I will not have to pay for this.

➤ This will improve my company rank.

➤ I will not lose control of my market.

➤ I can get new things to help my country.

➤ Reduce the workload of my people.

➤ Stop "not invented here" attitude.

➤ Free training.

➤ Maintain control of product destiny.

➤ Get added-value programs.

➤ Add more/incremental value.

➤ Improved (quicker) responsiveness.

➤ Less bureaucracy.

➤ Better communication.

➤ Find out what others are doing more easily.

➤ Better collaboration with other countries.

➤ More influence on Regional results.

➤ More input to product development.

---

successful?" From their input, we created a draft stakeholder expectations matrix (see Toolkit 12.5) to indicate what we perceived to be the primary expectations of each key stakeholder group, including areas of overlap or distinctions in terms of what each group wanted from the teams. (Keep in mind that while the final selection of key measures should reflect the combined or collective interests of all stakeholders, you should not eliminate the choice of certain measures that address the unique interests of a key stakeholder group.)

The next step was to verify, through surveys, group presentations, and face-to-face meetings, the expectations presented in the matrix. Each stakeholder group was asked to assign a high, medium, or low priority rating to the various expectations, in order to assess their level of importance and then develop consensus on the final measures to be used.

After completing that process, we suggested a "Team Success Metrics Worksheet" (see Toolkit 12.6). For each stakeholder measure, the worksheet would show both "baseline measures"—where we are today— and "benchmark measures"—where we want to be. Because many of the baseline measures were not available at that time, we initiated a formal

12.5 Stakeholder Expectations Matrix

Stakeholder Expectations	Top Management	Country Managers	Functional Management	Teams
➤ Improve product contributions to region (country) P&L and market share.	X	X	X	
➤ Company image.	X	X	X	X
➤ Better develop people and resources for accelerated growth of new/in-line products.	X	X		X
➤ Develop specific processes and methodologies to optimize preparation of management for product growth.	X	X		X
➤ Optimize resources by cross-pollinating people, knowledge, expertise, and technology.	X			
➤ Reduce expenses (head count, etc.) and workload.	X	X		
➤ Leverage and extend company resources, e.g.: —use of value-added programs. —improve information/ responsiveness. —targeted clinical studies.	X		X	X
➤ Improve involvement of senior line management in product planning and growth initiatives.	X	X		

12.6 Team Success Metrics Worksheet

Stakeholder Measures	Baseline Measure	Benchmark Measure
➤		
➤		
➤		
➤		
➤		
➤		

survey process to solicit stakeholders' opinions about baseline measures, which also provided us with a methodology for benchmarking future success.

For example, the measure of "acceptance by countries of nonlocal initiatives ('not invented here')" was not something for which we had current baseline information. The survey provided us with a scaled perception of stakeholders' attitude. In this case, they were low; that is, the stakeholders believed the organization was deeply entrenched in a silo—a "Don't share or use best practices with others" culture. Accordingly, the benchmark became to improve that scaled perception, as measured via the survey nine months to a year later.

Elements of Success for Measuring Team Success

When establishing a team or a team initiative's measures of success, follow these guidelines:

➤ Ensure that the measurements you select are aligned with and support the larger organization's mission and vision.

➤ Include team goals and objectives.

➤ Reflect key stakeholders' expectations.

➤ Include current benchmark data and Levels I–IV measures if at all possible.

➤ Finalize the measurements you select with your stakeholders.

➤ Establish the current level (baseline) for each metric. If baselines don't exist, do a survey of "perceptions."

➤ Establish an improvement goal (benchmark) for each metric. These should be set at realistic levels and pegged to a future date, such as one year.

■ MEASURES OF SUCCESS WORKSHOP

One way to initiate the quest for appropriate measures of success and to engage the team(s) with their key stakeholders in the process is to hold a Measures of Success Workshop. Before holding such a workshop, the Sponsor (and/or the team) should identify the key stakeholders. Each stakeholder group should be asked in advance questions like these:

➤ Why, from your perspective, does this team exist?

➤ What do you expect/need from this team?

➤ One year from now, what would you like to see stopped or started as a result of this team's work?

➤ What would this team have to accomplish for you to approve further investment in it?

It would be helpful for the stakeholders to see the team's Charter, Boundaries, and goals before attending the workshop. They will then be familiar with the team's initial thinking about how it should be measured. Keep in mind, too, that following such a workshop, these documents may be revised.

Toolkit 12.7 provides an agenda for such a workshop. In addition to the Sponsor and Team Leader/team members, this meeting should be attended by representatives of the key stakeholder groups.

12.7   Measures of Success Workshop Agenda

INTRODUCTION

➤ Why was this team formed? (original Performance and Business Challenge)
➤ What are the team's Charter, Boundaries, and goals?
➤ Who are the key stakeholders of this team?
➤ Our agenda: How will we measure the contribution of our team to our business?

MEASURES OF SUCCESS: GENERAL CRITERIA

➤ Two types of measurements:
   —Objective measures (e.g., financial, team goals).
   —Subjective measures (e.g., behavioral or observable).
➤ Team measurements must align with corporate/regional vision and mission.
➤ Team measurements should reflect stakeholders' expectations and needs.

TEAM STAKEHOLDERS' EXPECTATIONS/NEEDS

➤ Create a stakeholder pyramid.
➤ From each stakeholder group, and given this team's Charter and Boundaries:
   —What are your expectations of this team?
   —What needs should this team address?
➤ Large group reports (consolidate into matrix).

MEASURES OF SUCCESS: TEAM CRITERIA

➤ Review the Team Success Metrics Worksheet [Toolkit 12.6].
➤ Select three to four measures for each stakeholder group.
➤ Ask the question: "At the end of ____ [time frame], we will consider that this team initiative has been successful if. . . ."
➤ Prioritize these criteria.
➤ How will we measure success *today* and *in the future?* (See the Team Success Metrics Worksheet.)

PLAN OF ACTION

➤ *When* should we measure success?
➤ *Who* should measure success?
➤ *How* do we communicate our results?

If you don't want to (or can't) hold a Measures of Success Workshop, try this exercise:

1. Draw a stakeholder pyramid or refer to the one in this chapter.
2. For each key stakeholder group, ask: "If we were in their shoes, what do we think they would expect from our team?" (Try to get as many Level III and Level IV measures as you can.)
3. Prioritize five critical measures of success for each stakeholder group, from *your* perspective.
4. Assign a "border manager" to contact the stakeholder(s). Verify your measures of success and solicit input on both current baseline measurements and benchmark targets.
5. Develop a Plan of Action for a follow-up measurement plan.

■ BENCHMARKING THE MEASURES OF SUCCESS

As indicated earlier, one of the criteria for selecting a measure of success is the ability to obtain current baseline data. For example, if "Earlier product registration" is a key desired accomplishment for a team, then you must have or obtain data that indicate the current performance level ("Historically, the product registration timeline has been . . . .").

One organization wanted to use "People want to work on these teams" as a measure of whether the teams had been successful. Not only is that a very subjective measure, but it also violates two other criteria: (1) it is not an indication of a team's accomplishments or contribution, and (2) it does not identify a means of collecting baseline data for how people currently feel about working/not working on these teams.

Many argue that you should select only measures of success that provide for objective and quantifiable benchmarking and later evaluation. If you're working with a measure of success that appears to be more subjective, we strongly suggest that you try to gather baseline data from which you can create a form of objective measurement. One way of doing that is through surveying.

As an example, let's take the subjective measure we mentioned earlier: "Acceptance by countries of nonlocal initiatives ('not invented here')." This measure could be made more quantifiable by using a scale to assess the current level of acceptance, as follows:

What is the degree to which you believe programs developed by other parties (countries, regions, headquarters) are accepted?

Not Accepted at All		Somewhat Accepted		Very Well Accepted
1	2	3	4	5

■ PERFORMANCE, PROCESS, AND PLAYERS

When it comes to measuring the success of a team, these three questions are key:

1. *Team performance.* Are the team's work products meeting key stakeholders' expectations/needs?

2. *Team process.* Is the team becoming more competent at doing its work (making decisions, holding meetings, creating outputs, effecting change)?

3. *Team members.* Are individual team members learning and benefiting, in their personal and professional growth, by serving on the team?

In this chapter, we have focused primarily on a process to help you answer the team performance question. However, it is important to remember that the *team* and the *team members* are also key stakeholders. If you complete a stakeholder pyramid, they are critical segments.

In Chapters 7, 9, and 15, we provide you with tools for measuring your team's process effectiveness. While important, these tools do not measure results, which is what it takes to stay in business. The degree to which individuals are benefiting from team participation is not *why* teams exist. However, if you're not attending to or measuring how well your team is performing on this dimension, you may have trouble recruiting future team members!

Ultimately, your measures of success give you a starting point for evaluating the performance of your team at any step in the process. As you'll see in the next chapter, measures of success also need to be adapted and integrated into your organizational systems for assessing and rewarding both team and individual performance.

Chapter 13

Rewarding World-Class Team Performance

"You get what you pay for." This may sound harsh, but it is true. Steven Gross, an expert on team compensation, puts it quite bluntly: "By and large, people tend to behave the way they're measured and paid. If people serve together on teams, they must ultimately be paid as team members or they won't work together as a team."[1]

Teams are not a passing fad. They represent a philosophical change in how people are organized to perform work. However, the pace at which teams have been embraced into organizational life has not necessarily been matched by changes in other organizational processes/systems that can either support or sabotage a team initiative.

For example, how we reward and recognize people has not changed to reflect the changing nature of work. In the newer team-oriented structures, the more traditional pay practices—individual performance reviews and compensation—continue to exist. In one company we worked with, the Human Resources Vice President continued to insist that the team members be rewarded solely through the company's individual incentive compensation plan system, which was based on individual goal achievement. When that happens, mixed messages are being sent about the importance of working for the team. More specifically, the way in which an organization rewards—that is, provides compensation and noncompensation recognition—its teams and team members can either spell doom or support the success of team efforts.

Questions to Ask

Anyone who is contemplating forming a world-class team should think through and answer the questions below *before* forming such a team; anyone who already has embarked on the "world-class team journey" knows that these issues will emerge early, whether desired or not.

➤ What should be our reward strategy for world-class teams? Should every team be rewarded using the same basic reward structure/design, or should the reward strategies be different to reflect differences in team Charters and Goals?

➤ How can we ensure that our team reward system reinforces our corporate values and motivates high performance of the team and its members?

➤ How do we integrate the team reward system with the functional/national compensation structures to which team members may belong?

➤ How should we align base pay with additional rewards such as merit raises, incentive compensation, or noncash recognition programs?

➤ How should we adapt our current performance management systems (i.e., goal setting and performance appraisal) to fairly and accurately measure and reward team performance?

➤ What innovative and nontraditional rewards can we offer both teams and team members if we truly want them to become world-class?

➤ How do we create a team incentive plan that is simple enough for everyone to understand?

➤ What level of incentive are we able to create that will, at the end of the day, serve as a true motivator of higher levels of team performance?

➤ How can we reward for team performance and simultaneously continue to recognize and encourage individual differences in performance levels?

➤ How can we match the reward to the achievement of team results?

➤ How do we balance "formal" and more "informal" rewards?

➤ How do we train our Team Leaders and team Sponsors to provide the rewards and recognition that will motivate world-class performance?

➤ How can we involve the teams in developing our rewards programs?

➤ Should all team members receive the same level of reward?

In this chapter, we attempt to streamline the complexity of team rewards by passing on our answers to some of these questions, along with other ideas and recommendations. Our suggestion is that you seek advice from compensation consulting firms like Hay Associates or Sibson. All teams are not the same, and an organization's specific strategies, values, and culture, as well as its current compensation/reward system, should play a critical role in decisions and actions. The bottom line is that traditional reward and recognition programs will not work when you move out of functional hierarchies and begin to cross functional and country borders. You must be innovative and flexible in order to create reward systems that are both equitable and motivational for high-performing teams.

■ TEAM PERFORMANCE MANAGEMENT

Our focus here is on rewarding team performance. However, as Toolkit 13.1 suggests, these ideas should be reviewed within the context of a Team Performance Management System, which includes the following elements (see the chapters indicated for more information about the elements of this system):

➤ Goal setting (Chapter 11).

➤ Team Leader and team member performance competencies (Chapters 7, 9, 10).

➤ Team performance reviews (Chapter 13).

Toolkit 13.1 Team Performance Management System

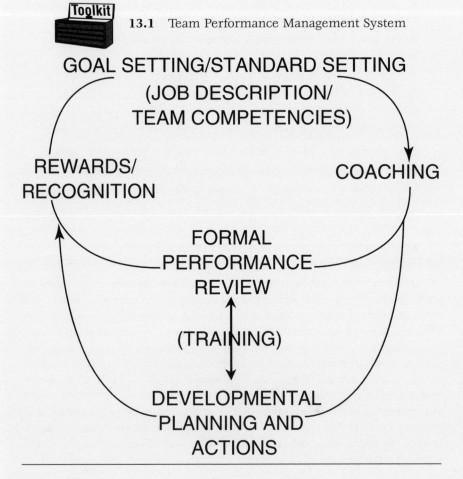

GOAL SETTING/STANDARD SETTING
(JOB DESCRIPTION/
TEAM COMPETENCIES)

REWARDS/
RECOGNITION

COACHING

FORMAL
PERFORMANCE
REVIEW

(TRAINING)

DEVELOPMENTAL
PLANNING AND
ACTIONS

➤ Team rewards and recognition (Chapter 13).

➤ Team developmental planning (Chapters 7, 9, 10).

Although we are recommending only the changes required to align your performance management and compensation systems with your new team structure, we caution you that the journey will be bumpy. Keep these three things in mind:

1. No compensation system is perfect. Do your best to create one that seems to best align with your company's values, and then be prepared for criticisms, second guessing, and the necessary adjustments after the shakedown period.

2. Although compensation issues may crop up early in your world-class team setup process, don't respond quickly with emergency aid. People's pay is an emotional issue, and you may find yourself trying to react to questions like "What's in it for me to be on this team?" with compensation-related answers, when it may be more important to sell the less tangible benefits, such as improved skill sets and a broadened company and global perspective.

3. Keep a broad focus on your options. Put as much emphasis on providing informal rewards and recognition as you do on changing formal performance reviews and compensation plans.

Just as compensation systems should be aligned to reflect world-class team-based structures, so too should the formal Team Performance Management System. In traditional functionally driven structures, performance management follows this sequence:

Step 1. The manager either sits down with you (if you're lucky) and lets you write out your goals; or, he or she passes out both the department's and the employees' goals for the year.

Step 2. One year later, the manager rates all employees on how well they have achieved the goals. (Unfortunately, too often, *this* discussion doesn't even occur. You find out "how you're doing" after you receive your paycheck and ask some of your buddies what the average merit or bonus increase was for the year!)

This performance management process is in direct conflict with a world-class team-based empowerment culture. But it doesn't need to be that way! Many performance management processes are available. We have outlined—and we recommend, in general—the types of performance management processes described in this chapter.

In Chapter 12, we introduced you to a goal-setting process that teams can use to strategize and prioritize their team goals. This process provides a foundation for managing both the team's *and* individual team members' performance. Once this groundwork is established, it can be a useful tool for the Team Leader, team Sponsor, team members' functional managers, and other managers to monitor individual team member performance, provide ongoing feedback and coaching, adjust task assignments, and so forth. Performance against team goals and individual team objectives can also serve as a benchmark for formally rewarding both team and individual performance.

➤ Annual Performance Review: Team Leader

The team Sponsor should conduct the annual performance review of the Team Leader regarding team results, particularly if the Team Leader spends 100 percent of his or her time on team activities. The Sponsor may want to ask for a second review from a key stakeholder. The review should include an appraisal of the core competencies that the Team Leader has agreed are critical for this particular team. It should also compare the team's performance against the team's goals for the year, and measure the Team Leader's performance against any individual objectives to which he or she committed. The team Sponsor also may choose to use 360-degree feedback (self-evaluation and team member evaluations) from the team members and/or other key stakeholders as input into the Team Leader's performance review.

➤ Annual Performance Review: Team Members

The Team Leader should be the first reviewer of each of his or her team members' performance on the team. Assigning Team Leaders the responsibility for the performance review of the team members (whether they are part-time or full-time members) strengthens the team concept and the Team Leader's role. The team members' functional manager (or managers, if there is a matrix relationship) should be the second reviewer of team-related performance competencies. Assuming that the team member has additional functional responsibilities, the functional manager will be the first reviewer of how they were performed. In most situations, for part-time team members, the functional manager is the person who usually compiles the review documents and has final influence on the compensation.

We recommend that a team member's *Team Performance Review* include the following:

➤ How well the team member performed against his or her team-based individual objectives.

➤ How well he or she performed the team-based competencies as assessed by the Team Leader, fellow team members, and a self-appraisal.

The overall performance rating of team members is agreed to jointly by the Team Leader and the functional manager, subject to review at the next higher management level. This shared task necessitates an ongoing dialogue between Team Leaders and functional managers regarding the roles, responsibilities, and performance of team members. This can get complicated. Imagine you are a Team Leader with five or six team members, each of whom reports to a functional manager (who is two to three organizational levels above you) and resides in a different country. Each of the countries is also likely to have a different philosophy or system of compensation. Your task of ensuring equitable compensation for your team members will be a challenge!

■ TEAM REWARDS AND RECOGNITION

When considering how to reward and recognize team performance, you have several opportunities to choose from within the three major elements comprising most compensation systems:

1. Base compensation.
2. Incentive compensation.
3. Recognition programs (compensation/noncompensation).

➤ Base Compensation

An individual's base compensation is the money received for doing the job he or she was hired to do. If a person's participation on a world-class team requires significantly different additional roles and responsibilities, consideration should be given to changing the base pay or providing a merit raise for the team assignment. To recognize an individual's or a team's efforts or activities that are above expectations, give a noncash reward.

There are two considerations when setting an individual's base pay: (1) marketplace *benchmarking* or comparability and (2) *internal equity*. With benchmarking, you want to make sure that you are paying what the market will bear—that is, what others in similar positions are paid. With internal equity, you want to make sure that individuals with comparable roles, responsibilities, and competencies within the organization are making relatively equal pay. One thing you risk when you pull people out of their functional silos or countries and put them together on a team is that they will compare their compensation packages. You shouldn't worry about changing the global inequities as you establish world-class teams, but be aware that differing pay rates can be a distraction, if not a demotivator, for a team.

Generally speaking, increasing someone's base pay as a result of a world-class team assignment is not the preferred method for rewarding the individual's team performance. Instead, some form of incentive compensation, where the reward is based on both individual goal achievement and overall team performance, is generally a better approach.

➤ Incentive Compensation

Each team member should be eligible for some form of team incentive compensation, whether originating from the company's existing formal management bonus program or another one especially created for teams. This type of incentive compensation can reward individuals for their:

- ➤ Team's performance.
- ➤ Individual contribution toward team goals.
- ➤ Individual team performance competencies.
- ➤ Performance of corporate objectives.

Individuals could also achieve incentive compensation based on their functional performance. Receipt of team-based incentive compensation should reflect the achievement of specifically outlined individual objectives that are aligned with the team's goals. (See Toolkit 13.2 for examples of individual team objectives and their relative weightings for individual team members who serve in different roles.)

Recognition Programs

One option for recognizing achievement of key results is to provide cash rewards. How much pay is considered to be truly motivating? Most experts agree that at least a month's salary for outstanding team results is considered meaningful. That can be expensive if everyone on the team receives the full reward. But if the team's results and contribution to the organization are significant—why not? Not only do the team members receive the reward, but the rest of the organization receives a powerful message: participation on world-class teams not only has the potential

13.2   Objectives for Individual
Team Members—Examples

CORPORATE BUSINESS OBJECTIVES	*Weight (%)*
To achieve sales growth of XX percent.	7
To achieve Income Before Allocations growth of XX percent.	15
To improve the ratio of operating income to sales by X.X percentage point.	4
To achieve a sales growth rate that exceeds market growth by 2.5 percent.	4
Total Business Objectives Weighting	**30(%)**

TEAM OBJECTIVES	
To achieve [product name] sales $XX (or profit of $XX, or market share of XX percent).	20
To develop a pilot program ensuring industry presentations of data; minimum of two publications; and one key industry conference.	15
To develop a Plan of Action for ensuring presentation of results of product research studies and XYZ Symposium.	10
Total Team Objectives Weighting	**45(%)**

FUNCTIONAL OBJECTIVES	
Coordinate Department Task Force to address proposed revisions to administrative procedure XYZ with recommendations due [date].	25(%)
Total Functional Objectives Weighting	**25(%)**

for long-term career enhancement, but also provides short-term financial rewards if the team performs successfully.

In general, *incentive compensation* should be tied to achieving *results,* and *recognition (noncash) awards* should be given for a team or an individual's *efforts.* For example, as incentive compensation, the team member(s) could be given a "spot cash" (one-time bonus) award if achievement of the team's Charter and goals relates to increasing company profitability.

The team compensation experts strongly suggest that, whatever the program, the "line-of-sight concept" must rule: The reward must be clearly related to the team's performance. However, the goals for which the team can be rewarded must be goals that the team can, in fact, achieve, and over which they have control. (See Chapter 11 for a more detailed discussion of the team goal-setting process.)

Accordingly, be careful in structuring an incentive compensation plan in which corporate financial measures are key. More often than not, teams do not have sole control, or even a substantial level of control, over the elements that impact "bottom-line" results. At the same time, the reward should have *some* relationship to the company's bottom line. If the team achieved its goals but the company lost money, the team should not be able to receive its maximum reward.

One form of noncash incentive compensation is to provide team members with "equity" or ownership opportunities in the form of stock or stock options. To have real value, however, the equity should somehow be linked to the work of the team. As an example, if a global product team achieves successful product launches around the world, a company could make team members eligible for higher-than-usual stock options as a means of recognizing and rewarding their efforts.

▶ All Rewards Being Equal?

An equal reward for team members (either equal money amounts or equal percentage of pay) is the simplest type of compensation scheme for teams. However, there is absolutely nothing wrong with different levels of individual rewards for team performance. Not every team member performs the same, and individual differences should be recognized so that rewards are allocated where deserved and appropriate. You need to decide, however, whether to reward the team's performance equally and then take care of individual differences through individually weighted objectives.

Jerry McAdams, an expert on reward and recognition systems, distinguishes between "group incentives"—any type of award (cash or noncash) made contingent on some measure of performance—and a bonus, which is based on largesse or another form of nonperformance criteria. Group incentives use a preannounced formula that tells people in advance what they can earn, based on each group-performance measure. They also specify *when* and *how* the plan will pay out. Importantly, *every* team member earns the award if the team achieves its goals. McAdams's research also shows that 10 to 20 percent of base pay for team participation is considered to be equitable.[2]

We do not advocate individual goal achievement as the sole source for an individual's rewards, but it may also not be appropriate to reward an individual solely because of the team's achievement. This is particularly true when a team member is not a full-time team member or functions in multiple teams/units. In that case, some combination of individual and team incentives probably works best.

If rewards are given for results and not just for effort, the cash reward needs to be meaningful and substantial. For incentive compensation to truly motivate continued high performance, the percentage increase must be significantly higher than that received by the average employee. For example, on one team, each team member received an annual increase (merit) that was twice the amount of the published average salary increase for a given year. Create a plan that offers team members an opportunity to make more money by performing their work smarter and harder, and by adding real value to the organization.

➤ Consider the Context

On mature teams, if you want to ensure that individual performance on the team is accounted for, do some form of 360-degree feedback, where each individual receives a rating from his or her Team Leader, and perhaps from a key stakeholder or two, regarding performance on critical team factors.

When individuals serve on multiple teams, as they do in companies such as Motorola and Hewlett Packard, it can be an administrative nightmare to try and keep track of time allocation, contributions, and so forth. Such an individual should receive compensation based on how the business is doing and how the various Team Leaders rate his or her performance against goals and in relation to his or her team competencies.

If some team members serve on multiple teams or are part-time team members, they might be awarded with "shares" based on their time allocation. For example, a full-time team member would receive 100 percent "shares," and a part-time team member who spends, say, 30 percent of his or her time on the work of the team would receive only 30 percent of the shares. When it comes time for the team performance bonus, the reward would be allocated accordingly.

Problems increase when there are core team members and support team members. How do you recognize those whose contribution may have been peripheral but was highly significant at the time? We know of more than one example where the core team got the reward and the support groups received nothing. If support groups have made significant contributions to the team, we recommend that you use some form of noncash reward for their efforts.

Another consideration is the "cultural expectations" of team members. For example, in the United States, we expect to be rewarded more for our individual contribution. In other cultures, such as in Asia, the norm tends to be that people receive equal compensation for team efforts. These kinds of differences can pose a unique challenge for cross-cultural teams.

■ PROMOTIONS, "PEAK EXPERIENCES," AND OTHER NONCASH MOTIVATORS

Money—whether it is base pay or some form of incentive compensation—is a controversial subject in terms of whether it is a motivator of high performance. Some organizational studies rank money as the primary incentive, but other research points out that once an employee gets it ($), it no longer motivates. Common sense would tell us that if financial rewards are perceived as being grossly inadequate, dissatisfaction is not far behind. Then, too, many complaints about money stem from the perception that financial rewards are being inequitably doled out, which seems to occur frequently in corporate organizations. Our own experience tells us that money isn't *everything;* consider and include other reward mechanisms as well, when you're looking to motivate a team.

Typically, those who are selected, or who elect, to work on a world-class team are high achievers. They are motivated by what psychologist Abraham Maslow called "self-actualization." They derive a high level of personal satisfaction from continuing to learn, to grow, and to maximize their potential. Although they tend to be highly self-motivated, the external rewards that they most value (provided that overall compensation is perceived to be equitable) come from having others recognize and publicly acknowledge the value of their achievements and contributions.

A new team member has been assigned to your team. Unfortunately, he recently was demoted, lost his title and his stock options, is making less money, and, not incidentally, suffered reduction of confidence and self-esteem in the process. As Team Leader, what would you do to motivate him to perform to high world-class levels of performance?

One world-class team clearly signaled the value that nonmonetary rewards had for them when they were asked: "How can we reward/recognize team members?" Their responses were:

➤ Have senior management make a formal announcement of the team/members to the organization.

➤ Promote global recognition for our participation.

➤ Provide to senior management, on a regular basis, feedback on how we're doing.

➤ Inform "contributor" countries of the efforts of their individual team members.

➤ Offer promotions and professional development for team members.

➤ Provide formal recognition (e.g., financial reward, special award).

➤ Offer travel opportunities, such as special events (skiing in the Alps, hiking in the bush) or seeing/visiting special places.

➤ Furnish useful equipment and/or improve working conditions (e.g., high-tech tools to work from home or virtual offices).

Interesting—the team's entire list of desirable rewards included only one mention of money!

Offering team members promotions and/or "plum assignments" following their team tour are strong means of sending a message, throughout an organization, about the importance of teams and the rewards for high performance. Susan Silberman, a product team leader for Pfizer Europe, was uniformly recognized for developing a world-class product team that involved partnering proactively with a strategic alliance. Her team's success was all the more lauded, given that the team, when launched, was considered to be an "experiment" and was perhaps viewed with suspicion by internal stakeholders. After concluding her team assignment, Silberman was rewarded for her Team Leader efforts by being assigned responsibility for all new-product teams in a major European subsidiary.

When selecting the appropriate form of reward and recognition, it is particularly critical to balance the recognition of individuals who serve on teams with the recognition of the overall team's performance. One of the inherent dangers of teams (and a factor in why some employees reject team membership and prefer to be "Lone Rangers") is the fear that individual identity and contribution will be overshadowed by the team. High individual achievers can serve on teams—but there needs to be a vehicle for recognizing their particular contributions to the team.

On that assumption, we asked organizations and teams that are seeking world-class performance to share with us some of their ideas for, and experiences with, providing creative and meaningful rewards for teams and their team members. A sampling of their responses is provided in Toolkit 13.3. Some of them may seem trivial or obvious, but before you dismiss them, imagine how meaningful they could be from the perspective of team members who are working twice as hard as they've ever worked, trying to serve multiple masters, traveling through three time zones to attend team meetings, and doing whatever else it takes to meet their team's goals.

If you've just embarked on a world-class team journey, and your organization is still operating with traditional reward/recognition systems that you believe are not sufficient to motivate the level of performance you expect and require, ask your team to brainstorm some realistic but meaningful ways *they* would like to be

13.3   Noncash Rewards: Ideas to Consider

➤ Have senior management make a formal announcement to the organization about the appointment of the team and/or team members, stressing the valuable contribution the organization expects and needs from the team and the particular individuals serving on the team.

➤ Provide visibility opportunities to the team/team members whenever possible, such as presenting papers and project results to senior management, or nominating team members to serve on highly visible corporate task forces or committees with the President or other senior executives.

➤ Keep the "contributor" functions/countries—those who supplied the team members—regularly informed about key accomplishments/efforts of the individual team members so they can individually recognize accomplishments.

➤ Provide developmental opportunities to team members, such as training programs and special assignments.

➤ Give out formal recognition for exceptional individual achievement, like "Living the Teamwork Values" awards for team members who have been caught "walking the talk" of the company's and/or team's explicitly stated values.

➤ Arrange travel and special social/cultural events that are separate from or coordinated with team meetings, and are matched to the parameters of achievement versus value.

➤ Provide state-of-the-art equipment and flexible working conditions, such as a virtual office, to facilitate flexibility and productivity.

➤ Take video shots of your team's working experiences and create a video production for use and distribution at key organizational meetings. (Another alternative is a photo collage or a slide show, either of which could be computerized and distributed on disk or made accessible online.)

➤ Take team photos and either write to or ask the company's Public Affairs department to profile the team in a corporate publication or an industry/trade journal.

➤ When a team has made a significant corporate contribution, include their photo and a description of their contribution in the annual report or some other highly public piece.

➤ Invite senior management and key stakeholders to attend team meetings and functions in order to "showcase" the team and its members at work. (Note to senior management and key stakeholders: Make the time to attend.)

➤ Write a personal note of thanks or congratulations and send it to the home of the team member(s). This should come from the Team Leader, team Sponsor, and/or other significant stakeholders.

➤ Send flowers or a gift basket to the family/significant others of team members who have been working long hours or traveling excessively.

Toolkit 13.3 *(Continued)*

➤ Hold celebration events at the completion of important milestones.

➤ Buy a gift that relates to a person's hobby, and give the person time off to enjoy its use. For major accomplishments, give this person a paid vacation to enjoy the hobby.

➤ Include team members' names on team "outputs" whenever possible. One of the biggest demotivators is when individuals do not receive personal recognition for a contribution to the team, or, worse yet, when someone else gets or steals the credit for their contribution.

➤ Take a photo of the team, or a team member, with a corporate executive or distinguished external VIP, and have it framed for all the team members and/or the VIP. Include the photo in a public recognition event, publication, or other type of "visibility vehicle."

➤ Publicly announce promotions, bonuses, and raises, and directly link them to the team/team member performance. Many recognition efforts lose their punch for both the individual and the organization because they do not clearly communicate that the reward is for an important achievement.

➤ Invite the team/team members to attend industry or professional conferences or to visit other companies to share the learnings and results of their work.

➤ Allow time to take a break. In one management survey, "time off" was listed as the third most important motivator (after money and recognition). Often, time off during a project is a luxury that the team cannot afford. However, small breaks can be planned for; and large breaks after completion of major milestones are particularly appreciated by individual team members (and their families). In some special cases, sabbaticals are deserved and necessary to avoid burnout.

➤ Create a "World-Class Team" or "Most Valuable Team Player" Award, and recognize the team or individual who is modeling the type of teamwork that the organization wants other employees to emulate.

➤ Pay tuition for an MBA or other degree or professional certification program, and adjust work schedules or provide reasonable time off for attending the program.

➤ Allow tuition reimbursement for non-job-related learning, like real estate or golf. The purpose is to encourage continuous learning and entice building loyalty to the organization.

➤ Nominate teams and team members for industry and professional association awards.

➤ Send a card or gift for a team member's birthday and corporate anniversary. Better yet, give the day off or pay for a celebration lunch or dinner with the whole team or for the team member and his or her family.

➤ Send the team to team-building activities, such as Outward Bound or Habitats for Humanity, which builds houses in the community.

rewarded *if* they achieve their results. Compile and fine-tune the responses and then make an appointment with your team Sponsor to develop a "change plan."

■ WHAT MAKES YOUR TEAM TICK?

The ideas above, or variations of them, could be used to help motivate teams to perform at a world-class level. But to get the best results, don't forget to find out what makes your team(s) tick. Different individuals are motivated by different incentives—the opportunity to earn more money, to travel to exciting places, or to learn new skills or knowledge. The task of a Team Leader or team Sponsor is to understand and creatively try to meet those individual expectations as the team is working toward its achievements. Ask your team members (individually) what they personally want to gain from the team experience, and try to structure their personal career growth goals into the team's work and experience.

Finding the most appropriate rewards and recognition for your world-class team is a tricky task. Much of what you do is influenced by both the eye of the beholder—the team member you want to motivate—and the constraints of the organization's culture and systems. As we have cautioned, you can get into real trouble if there are drastic inequities between what you expect from team members and how you compensate them overall. However, our travels around the world, from Malaysia to Chile to Boston, suggest that world-class team members, in general, derive their highest levels of satisfaction from the knowledge or belief that their personal and team efforts are truly making a value-added contribution to their organization's achievement—and that significant others outside the team are aware of it, too.

No matter how obvious it may sound, letting teams and team members truly be empowered to do their team and individual tasks and make important decisions is a powerful motivator. Team members need to know that they have the confidence and support of "the powers that be." When a world-class team in Canada was going through its initial setup and had developed its Charter and Boundaries, one team member commented, "Do you really think they [senior management] will let us do this?" He was cautiously optimistic about how this new way of working would offer him and his team the chance to make things happen.

As you create world-class teams, be aware that if you're going to change people's thinking and behavior toward more collaboration, you've got to send the message through your performance management system. People *do* what gets measured and rewarded. As proof, all you have to do is look at the success of Weight Watchers over the years!

Diagnosing for World-Class Team Performance

After listening to a presentation given by Nolan Brawley on "How to Launch a High-Performance Team," Alan Bootes, country manager for Pfizer Canada, approached the presenter and said: "Nolan, you know we've had successful product teams in Canada for several years. But, after listening to your presentation, I'm not sure that they're really as successful as they could be. Could you come up and do some training?"

Alan's assessment that his teams needed more training was not unusual. Most managers, when faced with any kind of team performance gap, first assume that the team needs additional knowledge or skills, and a "training program" is assumed to be the best solution to the problem. Unfortunately, in only about 20 percent of the cases is the real cause of the team's substandard performance a lack of skill/knowledge within the team.

Knowing this, Nolan assured Alan that we could provide training to the teams—if necessary. But he recommended that we fly up to Canada and first do a "diagnosis" to uncover the *real* source of Alan's dissatisfaction. Alan agreed and asked his Pharmaceuticals Division Manager, John Stewart, to select a cross-section of senior managers, product team leaders, and medical, marketing, and sales professionals who were currently serving as team members (or key stakeholders) of the company's six product teams. Those selected were to participate in a one-day High-Performance Team Diagnostic session.

Nolan and Lynda began the session by describing the characteristics of "working groups" and "high-performance teams" (see Chapter 1 for these descriptions). They also shared with the group their model for "world-class teams" (see Chapter 2 for the model) and suggested using it as a framework for looking at how Canada's cross-functional product teams had been operating and performing.

By 10:00 A.M. (one and a half hours into the session), there was a consensus among the 25 people present, that, in fact, for all their apparent success, the product teams were not *real teams* at all. They agreed that

231

they had been functioning as "working groups." The Product Managers from Marketing, and not the "team" (made up of representatives from various functions such as Medical, Sales, and Regulatory), had been bearing the full responsibility and accountability for the product teams' results, but without having the "authority" to secure the resources required for the teams' success.

Using a High-Performance Team Diagnostic Agenda (see Toolkit 14.1), the session participants delved deeper (nondefensively, we might add) into their examination of how the teams had been operating. They discovered—or finally brought out into the open—that the issues outlined below were seriously affecting not only their product teams' current performance, but also the country unit's future ability to successfully launch over ten products in the next several years. Among the strengths and weaknesses of these teams were the following:

Strengths

➤ Senior management is committed to and supportive of our current teams.

➤ Key people and departments are included on the teams.

➤ Communications have been continuously improving.

➤ Team members are dedicated, capable, and resourceful.

Weaknesses

➤ The mandate and authority of the current product teams are not well defined.

➤ The exact roles of the Team Leader and team members are not clear. There are varied perceptions around the company of what these roles should be, and of what time allocations are required by team members.

➤ The boundaries and jurisdictions of teams, versus the boundaries of functional groups and upper management, are ambiguous.

➤ The objectives of the teams are not formally shared by all members.

By the end of the one-day meeting, they realized, perhaps reluctantly, that the organization could not continue with its current team structure and that a major overhaul was needed in how the teams operated and were structured. The group developed a Plan of Action (POA) that called for several subgroups to take the issues that had been identified and, over the next three months, to develop their recommendations for creating a

14.1 World-Class Team Performance
Diagnostic Meeting Agenda

PREWORK

➤ Define participation.

➤ Ask Sponsor: Who has the decision-making power to determine whether and how to organize teams?

➤ Define clear expectations/objectives for the meeting and agenda.

➤ Define the Performance and Business Challenge that teams are assumed to address.

➤ Identify a preliminary vision of what the organization might look like a year from now (that is, what problems, effectiveness issues, and so on would be resolved).

➤ Record the meeting logistics.

OBJECTIVES

➤ Agree on what a world-class team should be.

➤ Obtain information and perspectives from various stakeholders about how the current organization works (SWOT: Strengths, Weaknesses, Opportunities, Threats).

➤ Identify the Performance and Business Challenge that teams will address.

➤ Identify where we are now with our teams.

➤ Determine where we want to be with our teams at the end of this year.

➤ Develop a Plan of Action (POA) and a time line.

AGENDA

➤ Overview of the world-class team development system.

➤ Diagnostic process overview.

➤ Visioning exercise: Defining the "ideal world-class team."

➤ Current reality: How are we doing (SWOT)?

➤ Where is the gap?

➤ What organizational changes would facilitate closing the gap?

➤ Plan of Action.

new High-Performance Team Model for the company. Subcommittees were organized to address the five issues that were considered critical:

1. Team Charter and Boundaries.
2. Team structure.
3. Team processes.
4. Team performance management.
5. Team training.

At the end of the three-month period, the total group reconvened to review the final recommendations. Among the most significant changes advocated were:

➤ Have all teams, through their Team Leaders, reporting to a member of the Management Committee.

➤ Clearly define the team's Charter/purpose/mission.

➤ Clearly define the Team Leaders', functional supervisors', and team members' roles and responsibilities (Boundaries).

➤ Clearly define the reporting relationships of team members to Team Leaders and functional managers, and the time-allocation commitments for part-time team members.

➤ Involve Team Leaders in the formal evaluation of team members.

➤ Have Team Leaders/team members assume responsibility for the annual product strategic plan and product P&L.

➤ Include each team member in the Management Bonus Plan.

➤ Provide formal and structured training for Team Leaders and team members, to help them learn how to facilitate team processes.

Six months after the initial diagnostic session, Alan Bootes issued a High-Performance Team Launch Document, announcing the new team-based organization structure. And eleven months after Bootes's initial request for team training, we provided the newly formed teams with training to help launch them toward "world-class performance" from the outset.

■ INDICATORS OF WORLD-CLASS TEAM PERFORMANCE PROBLEMS

As was the case when Alan Bootes first approached Nolan, sometimes you may have only a vague uneasiness about how your teams are performing.

Perhaps you suspect that the teams could be more productive, but the issues seem more amorphous than glaring. To begin to determine the sources of the "dis-ease," consider the major "symptoms" listed below. They indicate specific areas in which teams may not be performing at world-class levels.

Symptoms of Unproductive Teams

➤ Teams are unclear as to their purpose, mission (Charter), goals, and roles/responsibilities.

➤ Team Leaders don't have personal influence with senior managers and functional managers. Their input is not being considered, and they are not being included in strategic tactical discussions and decisions.

Symptoms of Unproductive Teams

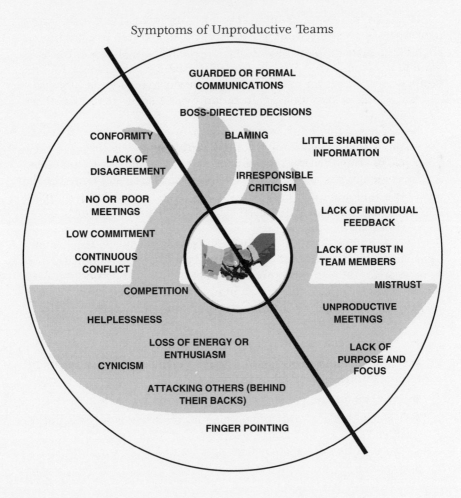

GUARDED OR FORMAL COMMUNICATIONS

BOSS-DIRECTED DECISIONS

CONFORMITY

BLAMING

LITTLE SHARING OF INFORMATION

LACK OF DISAGREEMENT

IRRESPONSIBLE CRITICISM

NO OR POOR MEETINGS

LACK OF INDIVIDUAL FEEDBACK

LOW COMMITMENT

CONTINUOUS CONFLICT

LACK OF TRUST IN TEAM MEMBERS

COMPETITION

MISTRUST

HELPLESSNESS

UNPRODUCTIVE MEETINGS

LOSS OF ENERGY OR ENTHUSIASM

LACK OF PURPOSE AND FOCUS

CYNICISM

ATTACKING OTHERS (BEHIND THEIR BACKS)

FINGER POINTING

➤ Team Leaders have no authority or impact with the team members.

➤ Team members are confused about their individual roles/responsibilities.

➤ Team members are demotivated and unsure of how their performance really matters to the organization.

➤ Team members are not showing up for meetings.

➤ The team is not receiving any training and development.

➤ Time allocations for team members to conduct or participate in team activities/tasks are not clear and/or are not being honored by their functional managers. Team members are confused: Does their loyalty lie with their team or their functions?

➤ No internal/external operating agreements have been established.

If you are uncertain about how to structure your review of a team's performance, you may want to use a Diagnostic Model. Begin with our High-Performance Team Model and create from that a team assessment to assist in diagnosing a team's performance. (See Toolkit 14.2 for sample questions from each of the high-performance team elements, and for a look at how one organization evaluated its teams on these elements.)

Regardless of the industry they work in, or where they are located in the world, teams evolve from different starting points and receive varying levels of structure, training, support, and so forth. Using some form of diagnostic process allows you to evaluate them against a model of the most critical elements of high-performing teams, and thereby pinpoint critical areas that need to be "corrected" if the teams are to evolve into high-performance teams.

Here's another example of the results of a diagnostic assessment. Soon after the formation of a new team-based, cross-functional/cross-cultural organizational structure in the Research and Engineering Division of Mobil Oil, we conducted an interview-based "assessment" among only the Team Leaders. Some of their comments were:

➤ "Our projects are on track, but there's tremendous pressure."

➤ "Management of our 'virtual' team [i.e., members residing in different countries] is a challenge."

➤ "We are learning as we're going—there are no models."

➤ "Unclear team and functional role boundaries are leading to conflict."

➤ "Very little cross-team learnings/best practices sharing and problem solving."

14.2 High-Performance Team Effectiveness Assessment: Sample Survey Questions and Scores

Instructions: This brief survey is designed to provide feedback that will help us know how the new cross-functional teams are doing. We need your frank and honest appraisal. To take the survey, read each statement below. Then select, from the following scale, the number that corresponds to your level of agreement or disagreement with the statement, and enter it in the appropriate space.

1.0–1.9   Strongly Disagree
2.0–2.9   Disagree
3.0–3.9   Agree
4.0–4.9   Strongly Agree

TEAM CHARTER/VISION

<u>2.8</u> The goals of my team are completely clear and relevant to its overall charter.

<u>2.1</u> We are clear about the boundaries (level of authority/empowerment) within which we must accomplish our goals.

STAKEHOLDERS/BORDER MANAGEMENT

<u>2.9</u> We continuously seek input and feedback from our customers, suppliers, and other stakeholders.

<u>2.5</u> We are receiving sufficient support from our Champion/Sponsor.

<u>2.0</u> We have been given sufficient time, by our functional managers, to work on *this* team's work.

TEAM ROLES

<u>2.2</u> Role definitions are clear, so misunderstandings seldom arise about who is responsible for what.

<u>2.7</u> I have received sufficient information or training to enable me to perform my cross-functional team role.

TEAM VALUES/PROCESS

<u>1.9</u> We appear to have sufficient resources to achieve expected team results.

<u>2.6</u> We are working toward becoming a high-performance team, focusing both on our tasks and our teamwork.

TEAM OPERATING AGREEMENTS

<u>1.8</u> The team has agreed-on approaches for problem solving and decision making.

<u>2.2</u> As a team, we are receiving sufficient recognition for our team's accomplishments.

They also had key questions:

> "Is there organizational commitment to the process—across the functional silos that continue to exist?"
> "What are the roles of the teams? of the team members? Are we recommenders? Planners? Doers?"
> "How will we communicate within the team and outside of the team to key stakeholder groups?"
> "How will we obtain and manage our resources (budgets, etc.)?"

Again, it was clear that although management had committed to providing training for the new teams, the issues they faced were more structurally and culturally oriented. As a result, we were able to influence them to step back and first go through a more formal team setup process involving the teams and their key stakeholders (refer to Chapter 3 for a detailed description of this process).

When was the last time your team asked each other and/or your key stakeholders: "How are we doing?" Ask your team members that question at your next team meeting. Or, ask a third party (i.e., a training and development manager or consultant) to send out a survey or to conduct some interviews. Include all team members and possibly select stakeholder groups.

■ SOURCES OF TEAM PERFORMANCE INFORMATION

A variety of strategies and techniques can be used to gather information about how your teams are performing. Listed below are some of these options, with brief descriptions of their advantages and disadvantages.

> *Direct observation.*   Watch the team as it works. For example, watch who communicates with whom, how decisions get made, and who makes them. This option has the advantage of being informal and minimally disruptive to the team. However, the assessment is in "the eye of the beholder," and much could be missed by only watching the team when they are together. It also limits your diagnosis to *only* those times when the team is together, which are apt to be infrequent. In addition, there is no objective way of presenting the information, except to report the "behavior" that is observed. You're really assessing team process and interpersonal dynamics, which are only a small part of what impacts high performance.

➤ *Interviews.* Individual interviews provide more substantial information regarding people's perceptions, attitudes, and beliefs about how the team is functioning. However, interviews take more time, and some individuals may be fearful of the consequences of being open and candid.

➤ *Questionnaires.* Paper-and-pencil, disk-administered, or e-mail surveys can accommodate a large number of respondents or team members who work remotely. The surveys can be structured to provide objective and quantitative (scaled) as well as qualitative (individual comments) information. Standardized questionnaires are available, but some of their questions may not be applicable to your team's situation. However, technology increasingly is allowing survey questions to be customized in order to highlight issues that are of particular concern. (The "Team Effectiveness Assessment" shown in Toolkit 14.2 is one type of questionnaire used to help assess a team's or a team-based organization's effectiveness and performance after team members have been working together for some period of time.)

➤ *Dynamic group diagnostic process.* This process, which is used with a cross-section of team members and key stakeholders, is administered by skilled facilitators. This is one of our preferred options; it can be used either as an initial diagnostic technique or to process information previously provided from other sources. It has the advantages of tapping the entire (or a representative) group who have a vested interest in the team's success, getting underneath the symptoms, and beginning to resolve the real issues (a "peel the onion" concept). It begins to build, with people who can make a difference, ownership and accountability for solving the issues. The obvious disadvantages are that it requires a skilled team-focused facilitator and takes the time of key organizational people not only during the diagnostic data-gathering sessions, but also during their later involvement in task groups, when they must identify recommendations for issue resolution.

There is no *one* best way to collect information about team performance; in fact, you may want to use a combination of techniques, depending on your situation.

■ ANALYZING TEAM PERFORMANCE INFORMATION

After team performance information is gathered, some form of analysis is needed before "diagnosis" and recommendation of solutions. This analysis can be done by any number of people; however, our own bias is to have the team itself actively participate. There is no surer way to trigger defensiveness, and thus impede a team's ability to learn and change, than to have the Team Leader, or even an external facilitator, "tell" the team where they have problems and, worse, what they need to do to "fix themselves." Often, a team may need help in the diagnosis, but at some point in time they need to hear or see the information and share in the team performance problem-solving.

In early summer of 1996, we helped to launch three new pharmaceutical product teams in Europe. We scheduled a Team Development Follow-up Session for early summer 1997. Prior to designing that session, we asked each of the team members/Team Leaders to complete the Team Effectiveness Assessment referred to earlier. They returned the surveys to us and we prepared a composite report for all three teams. In looking over the results, we determined that "gaining agreement on time commitments from country/functional bosses," "managing borders with stakeholders" and "paying attention to team process" seemed to be the major issues for all three teams. Consequently, we developed a two-day program to address those issues specifically. In the agenda, we scheduled time for each team to receive its own composite report and to review and discuss issues that were of particular concern. Each of the team's discussions resulted in a Plan of Action.

For example, one team that received significantly below-average scores on stakeholder/border management spent time during the follow-up session identifying who their key stakeholders were for the upcoming year, and who was in the best position to serve as "Border Manager." Each person then developed a set of key issues/questions to put before his or her assigned stakeholder. The agenda for the next meeting was to include time to present these to the team for feedback and discussion.

Sometimes, the assessment process can make the case that the teams that have been formed need more structured development. For example, we were called in by Sanofi Pharmaceuticals, Inc., the U.S. pharmaceutical unit of the global healthcare company Sanofi, just after five cross-functional teams had been formed to help launch six new products in an 18-month period. Prior to the formation of the teams, the president of the U.S. unit had announced that the company's success in America was critically dependent on the success of these cross-functional teams.

David Fisher, vice president of marketing, had primary accountability for the teams and was aware that they needed structure and development. But he also knew that this would require an investment of both money and senior executive support, which he was not sure he would get. He commissioned a brief survey of current team members and some senior executive support staff to determine the perceptions of the teams' requirements for support and structure. An analysis of the survey results indicated that the Sanofi teams, as currently operating, believed they had the following strengths and weaknesses:

Strengths

➤ We have agreement about our projects with key stakeholders.

➤ We are clear about our teams' Charters.

➤ We are in continuous dialogue with our customers.

➤ We have selected the most appropriate people for the team roles.

Weaknesses

➤ We do not have agreed-on approaches for problem solving and decision making, or for negotiating resources and priorities.

➤ Team members are not receiving recognition for team contributions.

➤ We do not appear to have sufficient resources to achieve expected team results.

➤ Team members have not been given sufficient time, by their functional managers, to work on the team's work assignments.

It became clear from this assessment that the teams required some additional "structure" to help them deal with what we refer to as "stakeholder/Sponsor" issues, as well as some "development" in problem solving, goal setting, and negotiating. This information was presented to the Management Committee, who then authorized a Cross-Functional Team Development Process to assist both new and established teams. David Fisher believes that if this assessment had not been done, he would not have been able to convince his senior executive peers of the need for a larger investment in the development of these teams.

Take an assessment of your preferences and skills.

Evaluate your preferences and skills in relation to your position.

Analyze your role on the team, including similarities and differences versus other team members.

Manage your work in balance with the team.

Work on process as well as task.

Oblige and cooperate with other team members.

Review and recognize your team's performance.

Know and practice what you need to do to build a high-performance team.

(Source: Paul Maloney, Ph. D.)

■ LEARNING AND ACTION PLANNING FOR WORLD-CLASS PERFORMANCE

After reviewing the results of some pre-team-building interviews, Kevin O'Rourke, the chief information officer of Sanofi Pharmaceuticals, Inc., said: "You know, we're going to take this team off site in a few days and we're going to look at the issues that have been identified and make a considerable investment of time and emotion. How do I know it's going to be worth it?"

Very good question. Collectively, we have been involved in well over 500 broadly defined "team effectiveness" interventions during the past 25 years. Quite frankly, we're glad we didn't structure our compensation from these clients based on the teams' performance improvement record following our work with them. Is that because, given those teams that didn't soar as high as we all would have liked, we think that we, as consultants, or the interventions we selected, or the teams we chose to work with, were incompetent and therefore doomed from the beginning of the relationship? Of course not.

But why don't teams improve once they know what it would take to become "world-class"? The simple answer is that no real consensus is reached among all team members and their management that they, in fact, want to *work at* becoming "world-class." We often find ourselves saying to the teams we assist: "There is no accident that the word *work* is in the word *teamwork,* because that's what it takes." What kind of work do world-class teams do *after* they assess their performance and find it below their own or others' expectations?

To enhance our own learning and to help teams answer this question, we stepped back and thought about teams that had openly declared that they didn't want to be "working groups"; they had a strong desire to move onto the fast track toward "high performance," but didn't get there. We also thought about the successes—teams that did become and continue to be "world-class." What differentiates them from the "pseudo-teams" that Jon Katzenbach and Douglas Smith refer to in *The Wisdom of Teams: Creating the High-Performance Organization?* A pseudo-team is defined as "a group for which there could be a significant incremental or performance need or opportunity, but it has not focused on collective performance and is not really trying to achieve it."[1] Pseudo-teams make the initial investment to examine their performance, may even ask for some help, and possibly even develop an "action plan" at the end of a teambuilding session, but nonetheless don't achieve world-class performance.

From our vantage point, here's what world-class teams work on to become gold-standard:

➤ They have a consensual commitment, as a team, to be "world-class"; they publicly commit to consistently operating at high and achievable standards, which they explicitly define for themselves and their stakeholders.

➤ Team members hold themselves accountable to operating at those standards and to receiving feedback and coaching if either individual or team performance falls below standard.

➤ They put in place, and pay relentless attention to, the "basics" (which we showed you in our model in Chapter 2 and have discussed in detail throughout this book).

➤ They periodically conduct a formal review of their performance, including 360-degree assessments from fellow team members and from their key stakeholders.

➤ They develop specific Plans of Action to improve performance, and they set specific accountabilities and time frames for review and accomplishment.

➤ They know that "world-class performance" is a process, not an end state; they are open to continuous learning and improvement.

Is your team committed to working at high-performance standards? Or are you just a "pseudo-team" going through the motions? These are hard questions to answer, but if you're willing to look in the mirror and then commit to change where necessary, you've got a chance for the gold medal. Did you conduct the assessment we described in an earlier exercise? What is your current Plan of Action?

■ KEEP LEARNING

High-performance teams—those that reach the Constructive or Esprit stages of development we talked about in Chapters 7 and 9—don't just evolve. It takes hard work and continuous commitment. It is not nirvana or some other sublime place at which you arrive to find that all's well that ends well. Teams do not exist in a vacuum. They themselves change, as does the organization that surrounds them.

Accordingly, as we've emphasized in other chapters, you need to ask—about both the team and the organization: "How are we doing?" You need to keep "checking in." Are we as committed as we claim to world-class teams? Using the terms coined by Harvard professor Chris Argyris, which we noted in Chapter 6: How well does our "theory in use" live up to our "espoused theory"? Are we actually walking the walk?

Perhaps the most fundamental element that distinguishes a high-performance world-class team is the team's ability to learn. In a *Harvard Business Review* article, "Building a Learning Organization," author David A. Garvin describes a learning organization as one that is "skilled at creating, acquiring and transferring knowledge, and at modifying its behavior to reflect new knowledge and insights."[2] When diagnosing your world-class team, that's a good standard for how closely the team and the larger organization meet this mark.

STRATEGY

5

Managing the Functional and Cultural Borders of World-Class Teams

Chapter 15

The Power of
Global Collaboration

If a company is going to attain a world-class team organization, it must create a culture of collaboration that renders functional borders and country borders inconsequential, or at least removes them as obstacles. World-class team organizations recognize the power of global collaboration in building the strength of individuals, specific work units, and the organization as a whole.

If you limit your perception of collaboration to a Webster's definition, your team's collaborative behavior will be "to work jointly with others or together especially in an intellectual endeavor." However, the global collaboration we envision between team members on world-class teams goes beyond just individuals' "working together"; it describes a synergy created by people who have mutual and synchronized goals, capabilities, and rewards.

■ THE WISDOM OF COLLABORATION

Why collaboration? Collaboration is a critical dimension of an organization's culture where there are business requirements for continuous learning and for multidimensional problem solving that integrates different points of view into a "global" solution. When companies form teams charged with finding global solutions, those teams must seek out and integrate ideas and knowledge from around the globe.

Many organizations today experience a clash between the need for differentiation and the need for integration. On the one hand, we require specialists to help us deal with the immense complexities of our marketplace. And on the other hand, the complex nature of problems requires the integration and application of knowledge from a variety of experts. Collaboration is required to resolve the creative tensions between the two.

But in the words of Percy Barnevik, president and CEO of ABB (Asea Brown Boveri), "Global managers are made, not born. This is not a natural

The Hierarchy of Collaboration

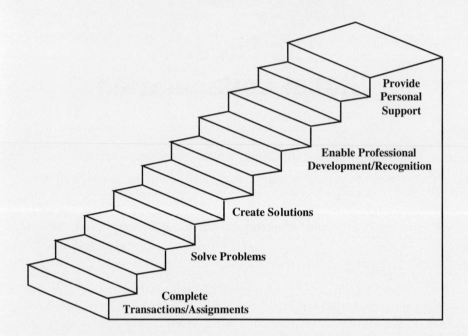

Provide
Personal
Support

Enable Professional
Development/Recognition

Create Solutions

Solve Problems

Complete
Transactions/Assignments

process. . . . This is why we put so much emphasis on teams in the business areas [BAS]. If you have 50 business areas and five managers on each BA team, that's 250 people from different parts of the world—people who meet regularly in different places, bring their national perspectives to bear on tough problems, and begin to understand how things are done elsewhere."[1]

When people come together to collaborate, they are doing it with a purpose in mind. They mutually desire to create, produce, or decide on something. Their desire for collaborative effort with one or more other parties, as opposed to individual effort, arises out of different needs. For instance, they may not have sufficient expertise or experience to go it alone, or they may not have the required resources of time or money.

What does true collaboration "buy" a world-class team?

➤ Improved conflict resolution.

➤ Easier consensus decisions.

➤ Enhanced creativity because of "openness."

➤ More efficient task completion.

➤ Fun, and comfortable working relationships.

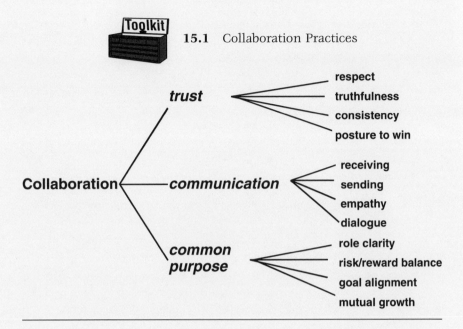

15.1 Collaboration Practices

Who wouldn't want to pay the price? But a high price it is—it requires *work*. (Our collaboration model, in Toolkit 15.1, depicts the key elements of collaboration.)

The desire for collaboration moves teams beyond what is commonly known as teamwork and toward what we call gold-standard teamwork, which presumes and relies on collaboration. When people are truly collaborative, they are working to create something of added value for the organization and themselves. They are willing to put their own agendas on the back burner in the interest of achieving something greater than the sum of parts. As Michael Shrage, in his book *No More Teams,* suggests: "Formal collaborations can involve structures and processes (like meetings and new-product reviews); informal collaborations can involve instances and episodes (like scribbling on a napkin over lunch at the cafeteria). The thing these collaborations have in common is people who realize that they can't do it all by themselves. They need insights, comments, questions, and ideas from others."[2]

Collaboration: The "Basics"

➤ *Collaborators must be competent.* Collaboration, by definition, is designed to make up for some type of knowledge gap. However, collaboration cannot compensate for fundamental deficiencies of knowledge or expertise.

➤ *Collaboration requires the existence of a superordinate goal or Charter.* The focus of collaboration is on adding value, not just collaboration for the sake of having a collaborative relationship.

➤ *Collaboration relies on a baseline of mutual respect, trust, and tolerance for individual differences.* Successful collaborations do not require that the individuals involved have a particularly strong friendship. We all have our unique idiosyncrasies that can be annoying to others. However, when the focus is on the task at hand and the goal line, we are generally able to ignore annoyances.

➤ *Collaboration requires a common playing field.* A shared understanding of the environment in which we work, an agreed-on set of rules, and a common "language" are key aspects of collaboration. These define the environments (formal and informal) in which we work and the tools we use to do the work. This is why we advocate spending time defining the team's Charter, Boundaries, goals, Values, and Operating Agreement.

➤ *All collaboration is not consensus.* As we noted in Chapters 7 and 9, consensus is one form of decision making. We can collaborate and pass decision-making authority around if trust and competence are present.

➤ *Collaboration is not timeless.* Because collaboration is driven by the need for goal achievement, the collaboration can and should end when the goal is achieved, unless the collaborators identify another common reason for working together. Those in a collaborative relationship may develop such strong personal bonds that they seek other opportunities to work together. However, in the absence of this common work, the collaboration ends, but perhaps not the friendships.

North American Philips (NAP) has used world-class teams to change the attitudes of subsidiary managers who have had a long history of independence. A senior manager in NAP's consumer electronics business reflected: "We have . . . transformed the defensive, territorial attitude of NAP managers into a more collaborative mindset."[3] How? By giving them a sense of purpose that they were contributing to the global corporate strategy. That is the power of global collaboration.

Our experience working with world-class teams tells us that most people truly want to collaborate—at least it sounds good as an "espoused value." But *wanting* doesn't always lead to *getting.* For instance, in interviews we conducted prior to the first team meeting of a new global product team, the primary objective that people had for the meeting was the opportunity to get to know and learn from each other. The individual team members recognized that, together, they could make something special happen for this product on a worldwide basis. But when these individuals from around the world arrived for the meeting and began to discuss their own particular interests/agendas and respective areas of authority, which in some cases overlapped, it became obvious that alignment of their interests, goals, and capabilities was going to take significant work well beyond this first meeting.

Unfortunately, collaboration is not a value that is shared by everyone. Recently, a Wall Street broker said that he thought he reflected the *real* current values of at least American, if not multinational, businesses when he said: "The only deal worthwhile is the one you steal." Not exactly the voice of collaboration.

If this viewpoint reflects the dark side of organizational life, then collaboration may be the "espoused ideal" but certainly will not reflect organizational or team reality. Particularly in Western-influenced cultures, people seem ambivalent about turning anything over to anyone else. In fact, the relatively high value placed on individualistic behavior in some ways can have the effect of supporting or reinforcing *noncollaborative* behavior.

15.2   Team Collaboration Practices Survey

	Seldom	Occasionally	Frequently	Regularly
Team members perceive me as:				
—Being candid and forthright with helpful information.	0	1	2	3
—Having a high regard for my team members' expertise and problem-solving capabilities.	0	1	2	3
—Honoring and meeting my commitments to the team.	0	1	2	3
—Giving honest feedback about others' performance or behavior.	0	1	2	3
—Accepting responsibility for problems that occur, even when they are not directly my fault.	0	1	2	3
—Operating with high levels of integrity.	0	1	2	3
—Having genuine interest in the team's achieving its goals.	0	1	2	3

Using the model in Toolkit 15.2, evaluate how *you* are collaborating with your team members: seldom (0), occasionally (1), frequently (2), or regularly (3). Then, using the same scale, ask one (or more) team member(s) to evaluate how well he or she perceives you to be collaborating. Discuss any "gaps" that may exist, including possible reasons why, and develop a Plan of Action for closing the gaps.

■ SHARKS AND DOLPHINS: CAN THEY COEXIST?

Dolphins are often used as a metaphor for teams. Dolphins tend to travel in "schools," demonstrate "group skills," and appear to be a "kinder, gentler" species. Conversely, sharks travel alone and are anything but tame and trustworthy. If dolphins personify collaboration, and sharks represent competitors, can they live together in teams and organizations? They can and they do.

Although we are spending considerable time discussing the merits and strategies of collaboration, we would be naïve and unrealistic to ignore the competitive realities that exist and can, in fact, be healthy for a team. Udai Pareek, in his comprehensive description of collaboration and competition, defines competition as "one or more persons working against other persons for the attainment of mutually exclusive goals."[4] Although often viewed as being negative and unproductive behavior, competition can provide value to both individuals and organizations. If competitive rivalry is used to achieve higher standards of performance, it can benefit the organization and increase the competency, creativity, and accountability of the rival groups.

Not all world-class teams need to be *highly* interdependent and collaborative. As we have indicated in earlier chapters, work gets done even if you're a working group in the "polite" stage of team development. However, we strongly believe that teams need to be clear about (1) the degree of interdependence they want, and (2) how well they are performing/working against that interdependence, and what they need to do to bridge any gap.

One world-class team without much history of working together used a simple "test" to evaluate "What's Our Need for Teamwork?" Their "Where We Need To Be" score ranged from 60 to 100, and their "Where We Are" score ranged from 40 to 100. When asked what would "close the gap," their responses were:

➤ Clarify our common goals.
➤ Clearly define and agree on our roles.

> ➤ Improve our communications process.
> ➤ Get buy-in from our respective senior managers.

The team's views on "Where We Need to Be" led to particularly interesting results. The range of scores indicated that not everyone felt the same about the degree of collaboration needed—not at that point, anyway. The team then worked together on creating their Charter, part of which read:

We are responsible and accountable for maximizing the commercial success of this product. . . .

Discussion about whether they wanted to collectively hold themselves "accountable" created the power of collaboration. After their Charter was developed, everyone agreed that the need for teamwork was at the 80 to 100 percent level!

Much value can result from collaborative behavior, but when collaboration is used to conform to others' demands, to avoid conflict, or to escape task demands, Pareek calls this "dysfunctional collaboration." Others refer to it as "group think." We call this type of behavior "false collaboration." How many times have you sat in a meeting during which the team ostensibly makes a decision—collaboratively and in consensus. Then, two weeks later, one or more team members make sharklike decisions or take actions that are in direct conflict with the team's decision. That's not collaboration. It's an indicator that their own self-interests were not mutually aligned with the interests of the team.

In world-class teams, where the focus is on high performance, sharklike behavior is not appreciated. A team of dolphins will ostracize sharks who appear to be out to attack their own agenda. Rosabeth Moss Kanter states, in her article, "Collaborative Advantage: The Art of Alliances": " . . . being a good partner has become a key corporate asset . . . a company's *collaborative advantage.*" In studying external partnerships, Kanter and her co-researchers arrived at three fundamental conclusions that we believe apply to collaborative efforts *inside* organizations as well:

1. There must be benefits for all parties as a result of the collaboration.
2. The benefits must involve creating "new value together rather than mere exchange."
3. The collaboration cannot be controlled or forced nonchalantly and relies heavily on "interpersonal connections."[5]

Kanter goes on to suggest that "the best organizational relationships, like the best marriages, are true partnerships" built on mutually beneficial behaviors and attitudes. In a collaborative relationship, it is recognized that all team members bring valuable assets, knowledge, and skills to the team. What they can achieve together is more than what they could achieve on their own. Interacting in an open manner, they are willing to exchange information, examine issues, and work through any conflicts that arise. Trust is a vital element and is reinforced by treating each other with respect and integrity.

Such behaviors and attitudes are not achieved by simply gathering a team together and telling them: "Start trusting and sharing now." Sune Karlsson, a vice president of ABB, points out: "Sharing does not happen automatically. It takes trust, it takes familiarity. People need to spend time together, to get to know and understand each other. People must also see a payoff for themselves. I never expect our operations to coordinate unless all sides get real benefits. We have to demonstrate that sharing pays—that contributing one idea gets you 24 in return."[6]

Ten Truths about Collaboration

1. Collaboration requires a mutual alignment of interests.
2. Collaboration requires a mutual investment of resources (such as time, money, information).
3. Collaboration results in increased leverage and synergy for both/all parties.
4. If the goal can't be shared (i.e., only one person can win), competition, not collaboration, is the result.
5. With collaboration, a group achieves results beyond the total of all individual resources.
6. Most people are motivated to relate to others and be helpful to them.
7. Collaboration is not a zero-sum game.
8. Collaboration requires a perception of equal, or relatively equal, power.
9. Collaboration requires the trust that another's power will not be used in a selfish or malevolent way.
10. Collaborators honor their commitments to each other.

Ten Myths about Collaboration

1. Collaboration just happens over time.
2. Collaboration is simply a matter of trust.
3. Collaboration is always better than competition.

4. Collaborators will not compete to achieve results.

5. "Unconditional cooperation" leads to the development of collaboration.

6. All team members prefer to operate in collaboration with one another.

7. Collaboration comes "naturally."

8. Collaboration does not require an investment.

9. Collaboration does not require explicit agreements.

10. Collaboration means never having to say you're sorry.

■ ANATOMY OF A COLLABORATOR

Collaboration results when there is agreement around a mutually beneficial goal; a belief that each party has power; and a base level of trust that the power each has will not be used against the other. But what motivates a person to be a "collaborator"?

Social psychologists say that individuals who have high *extension motivation*—a basic need to relate to and be helpful to others—have a greater tendency to collaborate. This concern for others goes beyond individuals and extends to caring about the greater good of the organization to which one belongs, and perhaps even the community or society in which one lives.

World-class teams, which are cross-functional/cross-cultural and often operate in a matrix form of organization, require the highest level of collaboration. With these teams, there is a tendency toward:

➤ Increased stress (meeting the demands of multiple masters).

➤ Greater potential for heightened conflict and power struggles.

➤ More difficulty monitoring and controlling resources and outputs.

Collaboration does not mean just meeting together and sharing individual goals and work products information. That's what a working group does. Highly collaborative teams plan together, scope out projects together, and decide on individual tasks together. They then communicate with and watch out for each other, keep the goals in focus, and celebrate their mutual accomplishments. Collaboration doesn't mean you have to *do* everything together—which would be nearly impossible (and costly) for "virtual" teams. But interestingly, teams that are highly collaborative *want* to *be* together.

As noted above, collaboration revolves around *power* and *trust*. Let's take a closer look at these two significant elements.

➤ How Do You Get Power Today?

Max Weber, a world-famous sociologist, described three kinds of power:

1. *Charismatic:* People follow the leader because of his or her exemplary character (e.g., a religious leader).
2. *Traditional:* People follow and are obedient to someone who occupies a traditional or inherited position of authority (e.g., a patriarch or a queen).
3. *Bureaucratic:* People follow persons who have been elected or selected by others to hold an office or a position of power (e.g., a national president or a prime minister).

Since Weber's original theoretical research, other researchers have simplified the sources of individual power within organizations, categorizing them as either:

➤ *Positional power*—derived from one's formal authority, the relevance of one's position to the organization's objectives (Sales versus Human Resources), centrality (role in key networks), autonomy, and visibility.

➤ *Personal power*—derived from one's expertise and competence, track record, character/style, and commitment.

These sources of power are not merely "Western" phenomena. They cut across cultures, just as what motivates people (e.g., achievement, money, power) tends to transcend cultural values.

The biggest change in the use and style of power in organizations today is the decline in the amount of influence that one has because of "formal authority." "Do it because I'm the boss or Team Leader" doesn't get action these days. Organizational hierarchy is eroding in favor of cross-functional teams and borderless organizations, and the authority of a senior-level title has given way to deference to people who have knowledge and connections to others who have resources. Most cross-functional/cross-cultural teams depend on collaboration among people over whom the Team Leader has no strong authority.

It's not just because it's now stylish to "make nice" that more value is placed on collaboration. As with most organizational change, the marketplace is driving it. Companies cannot be fast or global unless people in the field are empowered to make judgment calls. To do that, they need the resources and the authority to act. Today's most successful power players know that they must share their power. As William Bratton, former police commissioner of New York City, put it: "Power is all about empowerment."

In today's "networked organizations," power derives heavily from influence, and influence is subject to continuous shifts. It's hard to know or predict who will have power (resources and information) because the context keeps changing.

➤ Where Does Trust Come From?

Thomas Jefferson once said: "An honest man can feel no pleasure in the exercise of power over his fellow citizens." The same could be said of a good collaborator on a world-class team. Knowing how to use—and not abuse—power can bind team members together through trust.

Trust is a required ingredient for collaboration. Individuals must learn to, and be able to, rely on and respect each other and accept each other's judgment and competence. Without trust, the team depends on higher levels of authority—people who make unilateral decisions and pull power plays on each other. Also, keep in mind that trust is not formed or broken on the basis of personality. A trustful collaboration only breaks down when one of the parties does not perform up to agreements—in other words, betrays a "trust."

During a team development session that we conducted with a world-class team made up of Americans and Europeans, several trust-related issues emerged as the result of a comment made by the Team Leader. We were going over the collaboration model shown in Toolkit 15.1 when she blurted out: "I'm having trouble with this. When I was in business school, I was taught 'Don't ever trust people you work with,' and now you're trying to tell me that I'm supposed to just assume that people won't do me in?"

Her comment prompted another team member to add, "It seems like the ground rules are changing around here. We're hearing that *this* is what management wants, but I haven't seen any evidence that they [senior management] are willing to model and stand behind what they're saying, or provide us with any training on how to do something we've never had to do." We quickly pointed out that part of the reason we were there was to provide them with at least an initial awareness of what collaboration is all about and how to put it into practice. We then went a step further.

Prior to the meeting, we had asked each person to (1) complete a Team Collaboration Practices Survey (see Toolkit 15.2 for excerpts) and (2) select one team member they worked with from "across the pond" (i.e., an American with a European) to complete a similar "observer" survey. We asked each pair to exchange their surveys, to rate how each perceived the other in terms of their collaboration over the past year, and to compare the observer's view with how they saw themselves practicing collaboration.

Some were pleased with their scores. Others were surprised or disappointed. Before asking the team members to sit together, discuss their findings, and resolve any issues that had been raised, we asked a subgroup of the team (people who had worked on a few projects together) to come to the front of the room and openly examine how well they thought they'd collaborated on these projects and what, if anything, they could do to improve their collaboration.

From the outset, it was clear that the Europeans were not happy with how the Americans had "collaborated" on the project. They felt that they had been asked for their ideas but had received no feedback on work they had done for the project, nor any recognition for their contributions to the project. As the discussion proceeded, it became clear that the American team members had not been aware that their behavior had caused these consequences. They then began to dialogue among themselves, seeking ways to work together more effectively in the future.

Interestingly, the Team Leader (the woman who, earlier, had questioned the model) had been actively taking notes during the process. She then initiated a thorough summary, for the team, of what she had observed in the dialogue, and she encouraged all the team members to engage in this type of communication with each other. Had this experience changed her views of "trust"? Probably not—but it began to move her from the realm of the theoretical to the behavioral. To talk about collaboration in the abstract has limited value. Instead, you must create opportunities for collaboration—give people mutually beneficial goals/rewards, help them to define "collaboration" according to their own ground rules, and then periodically have them provide each other with feedback on how each views the relationship, and correct the gaps that are uncovered.

Anatomy of a "Team Collaborator"

➤ Places high value on communications.
➤ Listens actively and works at understanding others' interests.
➤ Cares about developing solutions that are mutually beneficial.
➤ Keeps self and others focused on the common goal.
➤ Has high achievement and low control needs.
➤ Assumes responsibility for resolving issues.
➤ Suspends judgment before facts and perspectives are reviewed.

Anatomy of a "Team Destroyer"

➤ Does not share information.
➤ Avoids conflict.
➤ Dominates group discussions.

➤ Actively resists or sabotages team efforts.

➤ Refuses to compromise.

➤ Puts his or her own agenda over the team's agenda.

➤ Lacks self-discipline.

➤ Blames others.

➤ Is concerned with individual "star" power.

■ MOTIVATING COLLABORATION

Earlier, we suggested that not everyone is a "born collaborator." Some people are socialized early in their development to learn and practice collaboration. Others are taught and/or surmise through experience that competitive behavior can get them more of what they want and/or protect them from harm. As we've indicated, however, world-class team success is dependent on a healthy dose of collaborative behavior from both within the team and among the team's stakeholders. How can you motivate and develop collaboration in your team and stakeholder network?

The following strategies can build collaborative behavior, even among groups and individuals who traditionally have operated with a more competitive style.

1. *Create a structure that "forces" collaboration.* It may seem a bit ironic, but some organizations have strategically created cross-functional/cross-cultural teams for the express purpose of proactively fostering collaboration. When people only report up through their geographic and/or functional organization's chimneys, imploring them to work together usually isn't sufficient.

As an example, Pfizer had, for years, three separate silos that were responsible for development and commercialization: (1) Central Research, (2) U.S. Pharmaceuticals Group (USPG), and (3) International Pharmaceuticals Group (IPG). By 1997, one silo (Central Research) remained, but USPG and IPG were merged to form Pfizer Pharmaceuticals Group (PPG). In addition, Global Development (Product) Teams (GDT) were formed which not only formally named team members from Central Research and PPG Headquarters, but also included formal representation from Area Product Teams assigned to Europe, Latin America, Canada, the United States, Asia, and Africa/Middle East.

2. *Encourage and reward senior managers for modeling collaborative behavior.* When senior managers model collaborative behavior and do not implicitly condone competitive behavior, this sends a strong message down the line. Doing the opposite, of course, will have the opposite effect.

One organization had reworked its organizational Values to include a strong emphasis on teamwork, yet the president continued to condone the noncollaborative behavior of a key senior executive. This double message (an organizational message versus an executive behavior) "permitted" team members who reported to this executive and to a global team to continue to operate in favor of the executive's own—and his organization's—self-interest. Other team members kept asking: "Why doesn't he have to play by the same 'new' rules we have to play by?" Good question. Until all of senior management gets on the same page of music, those noncollaborative behaviors will continue.

3. *Hold joint goal-setting sessions to create a consensus on goals among all parties.* As we noted in Chapter 11, tangible goals are the first "glue test" for teams. If there is no alignment of purpose nor any perceived need to work together to achieve those goals, collaboration won't happen. Developing a matrix that shows the respective and mutual accountabilities for specific goals is a powerful way to gain consensus on both the goals and team members' responsibilities.

4. *Create goals that require mutual dependency.* The goal is the driving force that each person evaluates before engaging in collaborative behavior. Collaborative goals:

➤ Should be desirable to each party.

➤ Should not be zero-sum; that is, one team gains only if the other loses.

➤ Should be structured so that the goal cannot be achieved by a single individual or group working alone.

Most research on collaborative behavior suggests that the results when two or more individuals or groups work together are better than those that would be achieved by working alone.

5. *Create team/stakeholder Values and Operating Agreements that require conformity to collaborative standards of behavior.* When individuals mutually define their "ground rules" for working with each other, they have an implied contract that governs their behavior. Conformity can be effected both within the team and among the team and its stakeholders.

6. *Create a "payoff" for collaborative behavior.* We often hear people say: "They want us to work in teams [and be collaborative], but the performance review system doesn't evaluate teamwork, and the compensation system still only evaluates me on my individual accomplishments." If the organization's culture is skewed toward rewarding competitive behavior, then these two organizational systems need to be changed to support a collaborative culture. Psychological payoffs also can result from collaboration—for example, increased recognition for performing a useful role together can reinforce collaborative behavior.

(Chapter 13 suggests various strategies for rewarding world-class team performance.)

7. *Alter the power system.* Over the tenure of his stewardship, Jack Welch, chairman of General Electric, has developed a healthy perspective on the value of teamwork. In fact, he terminated several key executives who apparently were not willing to play "team ball." This sent a serious message, throughout the organization, about the importance placed on teamwork.

8. *Expose team members to simulations that demonstrate the value of collaborative versus competitive behaviors.* For example, many exercises regularly used by line managers and training professionals, such as "Prisoner's Dilemma" or "Win as Much As You Can," are aimed at demonstrating that the best results come from cooperation and collaboration. Survival exercises, such as "Outback" or "Lost at Sea," demonstrate that group problem solving generally produces better results than individual problem solving.

■ COLLABORATION: NOT AN OVERNIGHT SENSATION

Organizational reality dictates the need for and the existence of both competitive and collaborative behavior. World-class teams, particularly those that must work with stakeholders and with borders that span cultures as well as functions, must work very hard at leveraging the power of collaboration.

Knowing how to nurture relationships is one of the critical challenges facing world-class teams that envision true collaboration as their goal. As Rosabeth Moss Kanter indicates: "The effective management of relationships to build collaborative advantage requires managers to be sensitive to political, cultural, organizational and human issues. . . . As the saying goes, success comes not just from what you know but from who you know."[7] We would add that success relies also on how you manage that relationship for mutual benefit and to create added value.

Developing collaboration also takes time and requires personal commitment. For true collaboration to exist, all members of a world-class team need to be committed to telling the truth. According to Peter Senge in his book, *The Fifth Discipline:* "Commitment to the truth does not mean seeking the 'Truth,' the absolute final word or ultimate cause. Rather, it means a relentless willingness to root out the ways we limit or deceive ourselves from seeing what is, and to continually challenge our theories of why things are the way they are. It means continually broadening our awareness, just as the great athlete with extraordinary peripheral vision keeps trying to 'see more of the playing field.'"[8]

Chapter 16

Beyond Matrix Management: Crossing the Borders of World-Class Teams

Cross-functional teams and, even more, cross-functional/cross-cultural teams that operate in a matrix organizational structure represent the most complex, difficult, and potentially frustrating forms of structure in which to work. As if managing the diversity of the team itself were not enough, these teams must also serve "multiple masters" and build bridges to a wide variety of key stakeholders outside of the team.

We refer to the process of managing the interfaces between a team and other stakeholder groups within the larger organization in which the team operates as "border management." It begins with these elements:

➤ Clarifying the roles and responsibilities of the team and particular stakeholder groups.

➤ Agreeing and committing to the team's Charter.

➤ Developing Operating Agreements for how the team and the specific stakeholder groups will work together (for example, how they will exchange information and other resources, make decisions, and benchmark the team's progress).

➤ Identifying the expectations/needs of the stakeholder group vis-à-vis the team.

Ongoing border management involves operating within the framework of the Operating Agreements and working toward meeting their expectations.

We can think of no team we have ever worked with that was self-contained—that is, had no relationship to any other organizational unit. Most teams are interdependent on other teams or functional groups within the organization. Unfortunately, once a team has been formed, team members have a strong tendency to put their focus solely on the internal goals and tasks of their team. They tend to forget that their work needs to be performed within a larger organizational context and integrated with other individuals or work groups, and that they are to share information about their work that may affect the decisions or actions of others.

When border relationships are not managed effectively, cross-functional and cross-cultural teams have the potential for creating myriad political skirmishes. Considering that most middle managers and professionals, when surveyed about what they like least about organizational life, answer, "The politics," doesn't it follow that doing what it takes to prevent and/or minimize such skirmishes is a worthy cause for any team? In this chapter, we examine the various types of border management issues that world-class teams face, and proven strategies for successfully navigating their channels.

■ DEFINING AND APPROACHING THE BORDERS

Border management implies a proactive and not just a reactive role on the part of the team. As we saw in Chapters 3 and 5, early in its formation, a team should identify its key stakeholder groups—those individuals or groups, either internal or external to the organization, that have a significant impact on the team's ultimate success. We refer to the relationship interface between the team and any one stakeholder as the "border."

There are formal and informal ways to manage your team's borders. One of the formal ways is described in Chapter 5, where we recommend that, early in the team's formation, the key stakeholders hold a Stakeholder Team Launch Meeting, together with the team, to clarify their respective Charters and Boundaries and share operating expectations with each other. The Operating Agreements that emerge from this process serve as border management contracts for how the stakeholders and the team will work and interact.

Other methods for developing strong linkages between the team and its key stakeholders are:

➤ Informal and social interaction. It is easier to work with people whom you know on a personal basis. In fact, when conducting preliminary interviews with virtual team members from around the world, the one objective for the meeting that was consistently mentioned was: "I want to put a face to the name."

➤ Formal meetings of the team and Team Leader with senior management. For example, at a meeting of European senior managers, European Team Leaders were invited to provide updates of their products, as well as their team's issues and requests for support, to the senior management group.

➤ Electronic communications, such as shared databases, e-mail, voice mail, and Web sites, through which people can have access to other team members and stakeholders and circumvent some of the limitations related to different time zones or languages.

➤ Team Sponsor meetings at which the Sponsors, along with their respective Team Leaders, meet periodically to discuss mutual issues and learnings.

➤ Use of liaison persons who are aware of the work of the team and of other units and who can call for meetings or communications of necessary parties when issues arise.

➤ Overlapping team membership so that an individual team member can serve as a communications link to both teams of which he or she is a member.

As organizational structures become more complex, the number of stakeholder borders that a team has to manage may increase, and the team may need to spend more time on border management than perhaps it feels necessary.

Border management is designed to facilitate *trust building*. In Chapter 15, we described trust as a required ingredient in collaboration. Trust can be destroyed if team members/teams/stakeholders:

➤ Are left out of the loop on communications that are considered relevant.

➤ Are not included in decisions that affect work and goals.

➤ Feel, based on other people's behavior, that others are out to "win" at their expense.

➤ Learn that previously agreed-to border management contracts have been broken.

➤ Discover that others are taking credit for their ideas.

If, over time, a "collaborative" relationship develops between the team and its stakeholders, the "formal" border management process can become less formal and tedious. In new relationships, however, we recommend initiating a more structured border management process so that all parties go into the relationship with their needs and expectations clearly communicated and with necessary agreements solidly formed.

As traditional organizational boundaries decrease, differences (and conflicts) over authority, control, resources, and perspectives may, in fact, increase.

■ BORDER ISSUES

Dr. William C. Shutz, a psychologist and trainer, has described these stages of group or team development:

➤ *Inclusion.* Who's in and who's out?

➤ *Control.* Who's got the power over what?

➤ *Affection.* Who supports and trusts each other?[1]

Once a world-class team's formation has been announced, these issues begin to surface, not only within the team itself, but also in relation to the stakeholder groups. Stakeholders want to be "in the know" about exactly what the team is up to and what role/relationship they themselves have with the team. They want to be "in control," some more so than others, in terms of having either direct or indirect influence on the team's membership, goals, and processes. They want to make sure that the team is meeting *their* expectations, perhaps even to the extent of having their needs hold priority over those of another stakeholder. Only when these issues are adequately resolved will they become true advocates and supporters of the team, which means that the team must spend whatever time it takes to deal with these issues!

Let's look at an example. In early 1997, a Global Product Development Team (GPDT) was formed. This team, under the direction of marketing, replaced a product development team that was led by the Research Department. At the same time, regional teams, focused on local product launch issues, were formed around the world and their Team Leaders were added to the GPDT. As expected, not only did control issues emerge between marketing and research because of the shift in the GPDT leadership role, but the new team organization raised other inclusion and control issues among senior management's key stakeholder groups. Who should really be on the core team and who is just a stakeholder? Who controls the funding—the GPDT, or the countries that are the ultimate customers? What control would regional teams have over customization of "global strategies"?

To move through the inclusion, control, and affection stages, the team must address and build consensus around these issues:

➤ *Charter and goals.* Is there agreement between the team and its stakeholder on the team's Charter and goals? Are there overlapping goals between the team and its stakeholder?

➤ *Roles/Boundaries/Responsibilities.* Are there clear definitions of the role(s) and responsibilities of the team or team members vis-à-vis

the stakeholder? How will the roles, responsibilities, and work activities of the team be differentiated and integrated?

➤ *Resources.* How will the team receive, give, or share resources
with the stakeholder?

➤ *Results.* How will the stakeholder measure the results and success of the team?

➤ *Communications.* How will the team communicate with the
stakeholder on both its process and its results?

➤ *Decision making and empowerment.* Are there clear agreements
about the processes and boundaries for the team to exercise its
authority?

As you can imagine, if these issues are not openly discussed and mutually resolved, the result may be what we refer to as "border skirmishes." Here are some examples we have witnessed over the years:

➤ *Differences of opinion on team priorities.* Who will determine
team projects, the team or its stakeholders? Which stakeholder's
needs take precedence? One team thought it was empowered to develop its own priorities but discovered that two key stakeholders had
different sets of priorities—different from those of the team and of
each other.

➤ *Initial misunderstandings or disagreements about the team's and
its stakeholders' roles and responsibilities, resulting in work duplication
or lack of funding for team activities.* One team initially thought its
Charter was to oversee and coordinate certain tasks that would be
done by other functional units; instead, it discovered that it would be
responsible for actually completing those tasks, which required a different level of funding than was initially budgeted.

➤ *Functional bosses' "talk" of team support not matched by "the walk."*
Team members who had 50 percent of their time officially allocated
to team activities found that their country/functional bosses continued to expect 100 percent of their time to be spent on "back-home"
responsibilities.

➤ *Role and empowerment disagreements.* Role interference often
occurs when functional bosses, believing that team members are
still their "property," want to continue to supervise their role and
their work done on behalf of the team. In one blatant case, a functional boss in Germany removed a team member from a European
product team without notifying the European Product Team Leader.

➤ *Power and control disagreements.* Who will visit/present to senior
management? Who will manage the budget? The latter indicates a

prime area where power and control issues often emerge. Who will fund the team? Will the team have to answer to stakeholders and "grovel" for funds?

If the key stakeholder is *external* to the company, as happens where there is a corporate strategic alliance, the border management issues can be even more complex and costly if they are not understood and resolved as early as possible in the relationship. One Team Leader, whose company's product was being marketed by another company, resented the "subservient role" she thought she was forced to assume at jointly held product meetings. Her resentment continues to this day because she refuses to initiate a "stakeholder expectations" exchange that might resolve some of her frustrations.

Another Team Leader, whose firm was in a strategic alliance with a Japanese company to market a licensed product in Europe (with much attention from her corporate headquarters group in New York), characterized her role of "border manager" as seeming at times "like I'm fighting for a piece of the Golan Heights and the West Bank . . . OK, not that violent, but you get the picture."

Border managers are like stage directors: they must learn to recognize the people who are (or should be) in the "cast" of their team's "play," what roles (and expectations) those people are to assume, and how to facilitate their full participation toward making the "production" a smash hit that will get rave reviews!

Although some people believe that total chaos or anarchy seems like a built-in problem for world-class teams, this outcome rarely happens. However, there are two specific areas in which team-based matrix structures have problems that seem endemic and can be predicted.

The first area is *power struggles*. Whenever two parties believe they have control or authority over one domain—whether people, decisions, or resources—the potential exists for win–lose power struggles with constant jockeying and shifting. One thing is certain: The balance of power never stays in one place. And the overlap is "natural." You can't avoid or prevent power struggles. You can only minimize them by:

➤ Attempting to clarify roles, responsibilities, goals, and resource allocations.

➤ Having all parties establish a problem-solving "what's-good-for-the-organization" win–win orientation.

➤ Sending strong and consistent messages from the top that teamwork is expected and is an organizational *value*.

The second area is the *complexity of decision making*. Another potential problem for world-class teams is that the decision-making process can get bogged down by the weight of the team structure. With more than one reporting relationship, how empowered are team members to make decisions in one context (the team) without checking with the boss from the other context (functional/country manager)? What if all the bosses of the team members won't support the team's decision? Does the decision get escalated up to the boss whom they all share in common?

Given how far down in some organizations the team-based structure has cascaded, this suggests that if a regional team in Argentina (which reports to a Regional Marketing Manager, who reports to both the Regional General Manager and the Latin America Area President) wants to decide on how to package or promote a product locally, but is in strong disagreement with how it is being done by the team that is in charge of the product globally (which reports to the Vice President of Product Development, who reports to the President), then the decision must go up four levels before it is resolved!! The most effective strategies to address decision-making difficulties are:

➤ Call those in conflict together and attempt to resolve issues *before* they escalate.

➤ From the top of the organization, send strong messages about empowerment and reward those who take accountability and deliver results.

If you drew a stakeholder organogram in Chapter 5, refer to it now. What is your current relationship with each of your key stakeholders? How do you know? Have you asked? Are there any issues "festering" on your borders? What kind of communications are you maintaining with your stakeholders?

■ BORDER MANAGEMENT STRATEGIES

In the traditional functionally siloed organization, the primary stakeholder for a team is the functional manager. In cross-functional/cross-cultural team-based structures, there are multiple masters (stakeholders) for the team to serve, and therefore multiple borders.

We highly recommend that teams select, for each stakeholder, a "border manager"—someone who is responsible for managing the stakeholder relationship in order to maximize the team's contribution to the stakeholder and the larger organization. The team should then engage in a dialogue about how best to manage the border and develop a collaborative working relationship with this stakeholder.

In developing a specific strategy for border management of a key stakeholder group, you can use the World-Class Team Stakeholder Border Management chart shown in Toolkit 16.1. Complete each column— that is, for each key stakeholder group, answer questions such as these:

➤ What does this stakeholder need and expect from the team? What are the stakeholder's key goals/motivations? What help/benefit should the stakeholder receive from the team?

➤ Conversely, what does the team need and expect from this stakeholder? What help/benefit does the team want to receive from this stakeholder?

➤ What are some of the potential obstacles to an effective relationship with this stakeholder? What political, competitive, and resource issues and parameters need to be considered?

➤ On what basis can we get the stakeholder to buy into our team's Charter and goals? What's in it for them ("WIIFT") to work effectively with the team?

➤ What kind of progress or results are we achieving with this stakeholder?

Border Management Skills

The key skills required to be an effective border manager are those that enhance one's ability to *influence*. These skills include:

➤ Strategic skills.

➤ Facilitative skills.

➤ Information-seeking skills (knowledge is power).

➤ Networking (relationship-building) skills.

➤ Consensual skills.

➤ Flexibility.

Remember, being a border manager "ain't easy." With world-class teams, you face a full range of border management issues related to both the cross-functional and cross-cultural composition of the team. With regard to the latter, our detailed discussion in Chapter 8, about dealing with potential "culture clashes" among team members, applies to developing effective border management strategies as well. You may want to seek out resources focused on this particular area, such as *Managing Cultural Differences*, by Philip R. Harris and Robert T. Moran (4th edition, Gulf Publishing, 1996), to facilitate your managerial journeys across national borders. The good news is that it's worth the effort. If you can master the

16.1 World-Class Team Stakeholder Border Management

Key Stakeholder	Border Manager	Key Needs/Results from Team	Border Issues and Parameters	WIIFT	Border Management Strategy	Date	Progress Results

art of building collaborative relationships (like those we described in Chapter 15) around the globe, while achieving world-class results, you will have developed a competency that is in much demand as we move out of our siloed provincial worlds onto the larger global stage.

The role of the Team Leader in the process of border management cannot be overemphasized. The Team Leader is the person who ultimately bears the responsibility for ensuring that the stakeholders' needs and expectations are fulfilled, and that their relationships with the team are productive. As you can see from the types of issues that arise, the Team Leader is often "out on a limb" in trying to resolve what are sometimes highly charged and/or political issues. In this case, the phrase "It's lonely in the middle" applies. At times, the level of influence of the Team Leader is just not sufficient for issue resolution. Having a good coach to provide strategic guidance, or someone who can use greater power or influence to work through the issue, is then greatly appreciated.

The ultimate border management strategy is to continually refer back to your team's stakeholder expectations and Operating Agreements. Listed below are some additional general strategies that teams have found useful:

➤ Practice good communication—for example, provide copied correspondence on each project, and extend invitations to attend team-sponsored project events.

➤ Listen, *really* listen, to each other's needs and ideas. Ask for project input and ideas during the planning phases, not after the fact, when you will only get reactions.

➤ Early in the team's formation, clarify roles and responsibilities of team members, as well as time (and other resource) allocation issues, with functional managers. If issues arise, the Team Leader should not put a team member in the position of confronting or negotiating with his or her boss—the person who probably still has the greatest influence over his or her career. The Team Leader, perhaps with help from the team Sponsor, should manage this "border skirmish."

➤ Get early buy-in and commitment from key stakeholders to the team's Charter, Boundaries, goals, and other agreements. (See Chapters 3 and 5 for strategies to enroll them early in the team's setup/startup phases.)

➤ Have the Team Leader hold individual meetings periodically with each team member's functional/country manager to review the team member's contributions and discuss any win–lose issues that need resolution.

➤ Develop trust and respect for each other's roles, expectations, and perspectives.

> ➤ Develop shared goals toward which you can align your mutual interests.
> ➤ Share or pool resources or specific team projects.

As we mentioned in Chapter 1, research conducted with cross-functional teams suggests that the most effective teams (even more than teams that have good internal team processes) are those that manage their "organizational context" interfaces effectively. During its first year, it is not unusual for a team to place its focus internally, that is, on getting organized, getting some work done, working out the kinks in its process. However, from the time of the team launch onward, we strongly advise teams about the "proper care and feeding" of their stakeholders. In nearly all of the one-year-anniversary team development sessions we have facilitated, we have observed teams evaluating themselves lowest on stakeholder border management categories (compared to other areas of team effectiveness).

A good example of how a team can step up to its border management responsibilities comes from a product team we worked with in Asia. Anticipating with this team an outcome similar to the one we described earlier, we suggested that the Team Leader invite one or two key stakeholders to come to the team development meeting and talk with the team about their expectations and about how they perceived the team to be performing.

The result was outstanding. Not only did the team receive some valuable feedback (not all of it positive), but it also heightened their awareness that they needed to focus their "spotlight" up and out during the next year. An added benefit was that it enabled the stakeholders to gain a perspective on the team in its "work setting" (which, for many virtual teams, when they're not working together via cc:mail or other technology platforms, is often a hotel meeting room) and to strengthen their relationship with the team.

Have the border manager contact the stakeholders to ask: "How are we doing?" If you developed some stakeholder expectations and Operating Agreements when the team was formed, use them now with the stakeholders as a "team performance report card." If not, just ask for their general response.

➤ Border Management Strategies for Sponsors

In the hierarchy of stakeholders, your team's Sponsor is probably the most weighty—that is, he or she has the highest organizational authority, more organizational clout, and the most to lose if your team fails. Although other key stakeholders may squeak loudly, this is the proverbial wheel that needs to be continuously oiled. Here are some basic guidelines for nurturing your Sponsor:

➤ *Give Sponsors what they want.* This assumes that you've done your homework and asked your Sponsor (as you should ask all your stakeholders): "How will you measure our team's success?" One Sponsor was very clear in answering that question: "If this team can help us achieve our product market share and sales goals, you can meet wherever and whenever you want."

➤ *Don't deliver surprises.* Without previewing the recommendation with the Sponsor, one Team Leader we know delivered a presentation at a senior executive planning meeting that recommended outsourcing a major function of his Sponsor's department. Needless to say, Sponsor support was not forthcoming, and any trust that had developed between them previously was severely damaged.

➤ *Remember—Sponsors have stakeholders and border conflicts, too.* Most Sponsors also have bosses, as well as colleagues who reside in other silos with their own sets of border management issues. Before tossing a border management monkey onto your Sponsor's back, ask yourself: "Have I done everything strategically that I could to resolve this issue?" Sponsors are there to support you, but they're not spending their time waiting for you to bring them a "shoot-out" opportunity.

➤ *Find ways to "sell" the team's value-added achievements.* Just because someone is your Sponsor, don't assume you don't have to show him or her what you're doing and let him or her take some credit for your achievements. For example, invite your Sponsor to team meetings to both speak to the team and observe the team at work. Ask your Sponsor how best to communicate the team's progress to his or her key stakeholders.

➤ Border Management Strategies for Functional/Country Managers

A senior executive who was assigned the role of team Sponsor ended a presentation to his team, which had representation from at least seven functions and five regions of the world, by saying, "If you think this is matrix management, then think again. You don't have a solid-line reporting relationship back to your functional boss in your country and a dotted line to your new Team Leader, or vice versa. You have a solid line to both of them—so hang on for the ride."

The most common definition of matrix management that distinguishes it from more traditional organizations is that it eliminates the one-person/one-boss reporting relationship in favor of multiple bosses. In addition, as the executive quoted above pointed out, traditional matrix management relationships implied that you had more responsibility and accountability to your solid-line boss than you had to your dotted-line boss. With world-class teams, which may be both cross-functional and cross-cultural, if you work part-time on the team, you must treat both reporting relationships as equally important. Some strategies for managing the relationships with functional/country managers include:

➤ Lobby actively with your Team Leader and functional/country manager to win support from both of them for your team-specific objectives, projects, and time allocation.

➤ Negotiate to win support on key issues that are critical to accomplishing both the team's and your functional manager's goals.

➤ Emphasize specific ways that your participation on the team can benefit your functional manager.

➤ Understand both the team's and your functional manager's position in order to determine where tradeoffs can be negotiated; understand where your objectives overlap.

➤ Maintain frequent communication with your functional manager about team activities; to avoid surprises, keep him or her in the feedback loop regarding the team's progress, key decisions, and so forth.

➤ If all else fails, consider going, or threaten to go, or actually go, over your manager's/Team Leader's head to a top-level boss. (Before traveling this road, however, consider your timing. How much testing and negotiating should be done before calling for senior support? Does the top leadership want to be involved? Is it realistic to expect support and encouragement for your approach? Does escalation represent failure?)

➤ Encourage your Team Leader to review your performance with your functional manager.

Remember, your participation on a team that lies outside of your functional/country manager's domain is a potential threat to his or her status, authority, and control over you. "My 'high levels' [functional and country management] think they're 'giving up' something when I do my Area team work," described Katherine, a product manager who was serving on a European team 50 percent of her time, while continuing her job in England. "They don't understand that we're right at the heart of decision making about this product. When I go to team meetings, I bring back to England fresh, new, and up-to-date insights. The bottom line is: England wins and the product wins."

As Katherine's comments suggest, part of managing this border is to ensure that "back-home" bosses are aware that they could gain status and power through the information brought back by the team members they contribute—and through those team members' success.

➤ Border Management Strategies for Support Groups

In Chapter 3, we suggested that not everyone who performs work for the team is a *team member*. Some resource people and technical experts are participating with the team in support roles. Because they also perform work for others in the organization, just as part-time team members do, priority or time conflicts often emerge between these support groups and the team. For example, when we surveyed a group of functional specialists who support multiple teams, what came through in their comments was overwhelming frustration:

> ➤ "Where's my 'home'? Am I 'in' or 'out' of the team?"

> ➤ "If I don't have a 'home,' how will I get recognized for the work that I do for the teams I serve?"

> ➤ "I'm feeling pulled in umpteen directions. How do I manage multiple tasks, priorities, and masters?"

> ➤ "How do I keep my functional boss happy while trying to serve my two [or more] team bosses?"

These comments indicate the kinds of issues that can stem from a team's support groups and for which the core team needs to develop border strategies. To manage this border successfully, you may want to:

> ➤ Develop a contract between the team and the support group, not unlike project contracts or engagement letters used between outside vendors and their clients. This contract would specify the types of services the team requires, the time expected, due dates, and so forth. This may seem to be too formal for internal working relationships, but it can be useful in avoiding misunderstandings.

> ➤ Develop a methodology for accounting for—and perhaps even cross-charging for—the services of the support group.

> ➤ Include the support group in the goal-setting process we described in Chapter 11, to avoid or plan for overlapping team requirements from multiple teams.

> ➤ Create an information process for keeping support groups up-to-date on team activities without requiring them to attend team meetings solely for that purpose.

➤ Provide periodic and appropriate recognition for support groups' contributions, which too often go unnoticed because they are not official team members.

Teams need to be conscious of the valuable and sometimes critical role of support groups in the team's success. Because they probably support other teams and have their own functional responsibilities, it is important not to overburden them, nor to overlook their work demands and priorities beyond those of your team. Keeping support groups in the loop about the team's activities, and acknowledging their contributions, helps to meet their "inclusion needs" by making them feel they are part of the team.

Now that you've read about how some teams have strategically managed their borders, why not pick one or two of your stakeholders and complete the Stakeholder Border Management chart in Toolkit 16.1.

■ BORDER MANAGEMENT ACROSS THE ORGANIZATION

Six months into the formation of eight major product development teams in one company, we discovered that although these teams worked for the same boss, they had never met as a total group to share their concerns and learnings. We suggested that the Team Leaders from each product team meet initially to share their learnings across their teams and to identify any issues on which they were experiencing conflict. During the meeting, it became evident that much could be gained and leveraged for the benefit of the total organization if they could meet periodically. It had been assumed that because they were responsible for uniquely different products, there would be no benefit in cross-team linkages.

Similarly, in another company, we reached out to various department heads to serve as Sponsors (and together formed a Sponsor Committee) of project teams that were exploring several key human resources issues in the organization. The rationale in letting the Vice President of Information Services or the Vice President of Finance, for example, "own" each of those teams was to facilitate their understanding of the value of teams (which were critical to the company's success), as well as to encourage cross-team and cross-functional interactions and learnings. The idea is not to create committees on top of teams and produce more bureaucracy that could and sometimes does disempower teams; instead, the objective is to increase organizational learning.

Paul Lawrence and Jay Lorsch, two well-known organizational experts, introduced in the late 1960s the concept of the tension that is created given both the need for differentiation and the need for integration between and among different organizational units. This tension may get exacerbated with world-class teams. Once an organizational unit such as a team is formed, the members seek out ways—and, in fact, we encourage them—to distinguish themselves uniquely from other units with the organization. Potentially at odds with this dynamic is the need for collaboration (or integration) of the world-class team with other organizational units (teams, support groups, senior management).

No world-class team is an island. World-class teams exist within the context of a larger organization and industry. They must not merely provide "product" to others; they must also obtain resources from others. These are their stakeholders. Teams that can successfully manage the tension of differentiation and integration *and* serve multiple masters will outlive the rest.

Chapter

Technologies for Teams

Imagine two research scientists sitting in a local pub arguing the merits of a new drug. During their heated debate, one of them picks up a napkin and pen and begins to sketch out the formula like some "mad scientist." His colleague grabs the pen out of his hand and with a few arrows and additional formula notations, adds to the work on the napkin. Almost simultaneously, they cry out: "That's it!" What you've just envisioned is a case of "low-tech collaboration."

Now think of another scenario of two scientists at work. One is in the United States and one is in France. They also need the help of a pharmacologist product specialist in Asia and a regulatory expert on European registration issues, who is based in Italy. How might you best leverage the intellectual capital of these four experts and create the same opportunity for synergism with this group, using something beyond the technology of a felt-tip pen and a napkin? This is the challenge facing world-class teams.

World-class teams require efficient use of resources, and state-of-the-art technology is essential. This group of teams' technological tools, either electronic or nonelectronic, is commonly referred to as "groupware."

■ LEVERAGING INTELLECTUAL CAPITAL WITH TECHNOLOGY

Any number of technologies are available that serve the purpose of reducing costs and speeding up the creation of outputs. But teams require technologies that do something more. They must enable teams to be *synergistically and productively creative.* Unfortunately, many of our tools for the new "knowledge worker" are conveniently designed to support the work of individuals, not teams. When the authors took an inventory of our own "team toolkit" for collaborating on this book, here's what we found:

➤ Telephone with voice mail.
➤ Personal computers.

> ➤ E-mail.

> ➤ Internet/World Wide Web.

> ➤ Palm Pilot™ for personal calendaring.

> ➤ Cellular phone.

> ➤ Fax machine.

> ➤ Photocopier.

Missing from our particular "team project" were tools designed explicitly for "true team collaboration." Thus, the process of writing this book was truly linear and "functional." One of us would do research or interviews, write up our findings, and then depend on the "main author" for a particular chapter to fully understand and integrate the information. Then the chapter would be photocopied, faxed, or downloaded via e-mail for review and editing. The technology we had at our disposal did not allow for jointly and simultaneously creating the document.

The technology *does* exist. For example, engineers have used technology to design simultaneously, in real time, such complex products as aircraft engines—a major step up from the old way of designing individual components in isolation and later making them fit together. Certain industries and groups of professionals tend to have access to the latest, greatest technology, but, for most organizations—including some of the biggest multinational corporations—such technology is prohibitive because it is too expensive, not user-friendly for the average end user, or not efficient or practical for everyday use. In particular, tools designed to facilitate collaboration, particularly across geographic and language borders, are on the horizon but are still relatively hard to find. In addition, tools used specifically for collaborative projects are qualitatively different from those used to help individuals be more productive and creative.

■ WHY DO TEAMS NEED TEAM TECHNOLOGY?

Before you can determine the kind of technologies that would be valuable to teams, you need to look at what teams *do*. The work of teams can be broken down into these components:

> ➤ Evaluating issues and information.

> ➤ Establishing goals.

> ➤ Making decisions.

> ➤ Implementing and completing projects and tasks.

➤ Developing team relationships.

➤ Managing stakeholder borders.

➤ Monitoring results.

The work of world-class teams, of course, is even more complex because team members may be in different geographic locations and time zones, and may speak different languages. Another important factor is that teams—and world-class teams in particular—often require different technologies at different times as their work progresses.

To consider that factor, take another look at Toolkit 9.3, Stages of Team Development, in Chapter 9. At certain stages in a team's journey toward high performance, team members need to be physically together ("same time/same place")—for example, during the team's early formative stages, when they're moving from the Polite to the Why We're Here stage. However, as they move toward the Constructive and Esprit stages, the work can get done when team members work in different time zones and different places. However, if the team is facing "regeneration" issues, such as when a new Team Leader or team members come aboard, team members need to come together again at the same time and same place.

■ WHAT IS *GROUPWARE?*

The origin of the term *groupware* is unclear. However, it has come to refer to a set of tools that teams can use to facilitate the kinds of work we summarized above, as they move through their stages of team development with different requirements to be together. (See Toolkit 17.1 for a depiction of various technologies that can be used, depending on the team's time/place requirements.)

Although these tools are generally thought to refer to some form of technological "software," experts in team processes would likely include the old standard flipchart as a form of groupware—particularly those of us who can relate horror stories of working with teams at a Red Sea resort during an unprecedented rainstorm that left us with no electricity or telecommunications for five days. A lot of good a high-tech computer conferencing system would have been!

By one definition: "Groupware is any information system designed to enable groups to work together electronically." For example, it is intended to help groups make faster and better decisions; plan and track projects; facilitate communications; and produce reports.[1]

In addition to enhancing productivity and communications, groupware is a critical tool for organizations that want to become "learning organizations." Internet and intranet databases can be used to share best

17.1 Technology to Support Teams

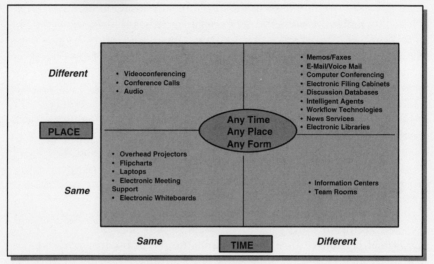

Adapted from R. Johansen, "An Introduction to Computer Augmented Teamwork," in *Computer Augmented Teamwork,* edited by Robert P. Bostrom, Susan T. Kinney, and Richard T. Watson (New York: Van Nostrand Reinhold, 1992).

practices instantaneously and access knowledge and expertise faster than a New York minute!

The most basic elements of groupware are the telephone, the computer, and the conference room. Teams that want to move beyond the basics can use these tools as "building blocks" for more advanced ways of interacting and working. For example, from the telephone you can move to conference calls and videoconferencing. For the conference room, invest in an "Electronic Whiteboard"—a movable flipchart that can copy flipchartlike notes for everyone in the room. Or move the computer into the conference room and use software applications like decision support packages to help structure a team's problem solving. Or use electronic polling devices to help capture the group's opinions (while minimizing the influence of an outspoken team member).

Those who are looking for computer software systems to support their teams should inquire about programs and systems referred to as:

➤ Group Decision-Support Systems.

➤ Computer-Assisted Communication.

➤   Interactive Technologies for Multiperson Tasks.

➤   Computer Conferencing.

For a more detailed description of groupware products and their capabilities, we highly recommend *Technology for Teams: Enhancing Productivity in Networked Organizations* by Susanna Opper and Henry Fersko-Weiss (New York: Van Nostrand Reinhold, 1992). One groupware product is an Electronic Meeting Facilitator, developed by Bernard DeKoven, founder of the Institute for Better Meetings in Palo Alto, California. This product combines hardware, computers, printers, and screen projection with off-the-shelf software (e.g., word processing, drawers, graphs) with the skills of what DeKoven calls a "technographer," a technical cofacilitator who uses real-time computer capabilities to enhance group productivity.

➤ Cross-Cultural Groupware

If your team is having difficulty working through problems, making decisions, or communicating effectively when team members are in same time/same place meetings, you can imagine the difficulties of doing this type of teamwork when teams are spread around the globe in different time zones and calendar dates. "Because virtual team members can't drop into each other's office or meet in the coffee room, there is a need for more formal communication updates," says Susan Sowers, a Hewlett Packard manager who manages a distributed work team of 21 people spread over three U.S. sites.[2]

In fact, several teams we have worked with have come to realize the importance of highly structured communication processes with regard to the use of technology—including explicit agreements as to how, when, what, and to whom information is to be communicated. One aspect of the need for formal procedures is that, although technology offers obvious advantages in dispersing information widely and easily, a potential downside is *information overload*. For example, if team members are typically barraged with e-mails, time-sensitive or other critical team communications that are sent via the e-mail waves can get overlooked or ignored. Among other considerations, teams may want to determine the proper means of delivery, regular timetables, and distribution lists applicable to the different types of information they will be managing, as well as measures to verify that communications are received. Establishing a protocol to distinguish, transmit, and regulate the flow of information can help keep a far-flung, world-class team operating effectively.

Unfortunately, many of the sophisticated groupware configurations and applications available are still focused on same time/same place teamwork. Given that world-class teams operate much as "virtual teams"—that is, team members work in different locations and perhaps different time zones—the challenge is to find technological tools to facilitate their working *together* in different times/different places.

Any set of groupware for world-class teams must meet various demands:

➤ It must accommodate a group of team members (and their divergent functions/locations) whose information technology (I.T.) sophistication and capabilities may vary enormously.

➤ It must be sensitive to internal and external security issues.

➤ It should provide the maximum amount of functionality, such as the ability to transfer files, to access common pools of information, and, ideally, to share and work collaboratively on computers located long distances apart.

The importance of the first demand above can be seen in Toolkit 17.2, which was put together by the new Team Leaders for a group of European product teams. It shows that even as recently as late 1996, in a large multinational company, there was a wide variety of I.T. capabilities! The effectiveness of groupware for teams is not, of course, simply based on the level of the users' I.T. sophistication. For example, the power of structural database technology depends on how up-to-date the information is. If knowledge is power, and team members hoard the knowledge, what's the use?

In most countries, the telephone and fax machine are common communication tools (unless a rainstorm happens to knock out all communications for five days). Most multinational companies have some form of intracompany e-mail and voice mail that can be used by teams for information exchange. The Internet is fast becoming one of the best groupware tools for world-class virtual teams, especially given the continuing enhancements of its applications by those who supply software for it, such as Microsoft, Lotus, and Netscape. However, those applications rely on personal computers (PCs), which may not be available. Portable PCs are becoming increasingly more common globally; we have found that usually at least one team member has a computer that can be brought to a meeting so that minutes and Plans of Action can be documented on the spot. However, on a recent visit to Asia, we talked about communicating back to the New York team and the response was "Not yet—not this year." Even in multinational companies, you may encounter technological limitations.

One certainty about the future is that groupware will become increasingly sophisticated and more widespread and available. Some useful

17.2   Product Team: Electronics Capabilities

	Team Leader A	Team Leader B	Team Leader C
Lap Top	All except XX [team member]	All except XX who got one on loan from XX but lost	No problems
Nokia	XX & XX do not have GSM	XX & XX have no GSM.* Check if XX has chip in phone.	No problems
cc:Mail Mobile	XX, XX and XX have no cc:mail	Only XX has cc:mail, and maybe XX	No problems
Lotus Notes Access	XX cannot access server	Do not know	Do not know
OPUS	➤ Germany and Turkey have problems with server ➤ No news yet, but think it is being handled locally		

Note:
All team Leaders would like access to:
- Monthly New Product Report.
- Country Monthly Operations Report/Quarterly Operations Report.

All of the teams need some form of PC and software training, especially Lotus Notes training for all team members. Only XYZ team members have some knowledge of Lotus Notes.

*GSM: Global System for Mobil Communication, a widely used digital mobile phone developed in Europe.

models for the groupware needs of world-class teams are emerging in various technologies now being used for "distance learning" and to create "virtual classrooms" linking participants around the globe. These include devices for simultaneous translation (i.e., for a multilingual group), anonymous polling for decision making, and immediate charting or tabulation of group responses.

All available technologies have not yet spilled over into the corporate environment for widespread use, nor are all of them able to accommodate the different time/different place scenarios and requirements of world-class teams. But they point to the kinds of groupware we can expect to become more accessible and more adaptable to the particular work being done by cross-functional/cross-cultural teams.

■ TOOLS FOR WORLD-CLASS COLLABORATION

While many of us are making use of current technologies for information exchange (such as e-mail) and for tracking task completion (like project management software), a primary element distinguishing the emerging "team technologies" is that they are attempting to design to foster *collaboration.*

As we discussed in Chapter 15, *collaboration* is an intentional process through which teams can capture the benefits of synergies and interdependence, and thereby create and produce *together* something of added value. Our definition of world-class teams presupposes this type of complex collaboration, because it requires collaboration among people from different cultures and areas of expertise. By definition, then, the technologies that would be valuable for world-class teams must be adapted to these demands.

Since the 1960s, people have been looking for ways in which technology could augment collaboration. If technology could enhance individuals' work, such as writing letters (and books!), then how could collaborative technologies facilitate the synergistic and productive work of teams?

In the book *No More Teams,* author Michael Schrage presents a window to the future by describing some of the creative collaborative technology research being done by such organizations as Xerox Palo Alto Research Center, Electronic Data Systems, Coopers & Lybrand, and Lotus Development Corporation. Each of these organizations is helping corporations to move from personal computing to interpersonal computing. Schrage notes, for example, that IBM, which makes extensive use of project task forces, uses a Decision Support Center at the University of Arizona to reduce project completion time. Using team-oriented software tools, project teams come together to brainstorm, resolve issues, prioritize tasks, make decisions, and so forth. This form of same time/same place technologies can dramatically reduce project time and increase the quality of a project.[3]

Even if your team has neither the budget nor the time to travel to a similar Decision Support Center, there is no reason why you cannot use some form of computer-enhanced meetings to enhance the quality of collaboration when the team comes together. It may be as simple as having a "computer stenographer" take down the "minutes" of the meeting on an LCD-projected computer screen for all to see and work from. This is an enhancement of the old facilitator methodology of putting points of discussion on a flipchart and posting the pages for all to see, but it allows more detail and much faster production. Facilitators who use this form of technology report that this enhancement alone increases the focus of the meeting and the richness of the content.

British Petroleum is making extensive use of new groupware technologies. Virtual Teamwork Pilot Projects connect teams around the world, and teams are making use of Lotus Notes™, the Internet, desktop videoconferencing, and shared whiteboards to facilitate and enhance communications among team members.

Price Waterhouse (PW) has well over 5,000 Lotus Notes™ users in 81 countries. The company is in the client service business, and Notes is used for internal project management and billing, e-mail, and gateways to clients. PW and the client team member can work together on engagement management and client relationships that may pull in both clients and consultants from all over the world.[4]

Those of us who have worked in meetings with Asians, Europeans, and Americans know that the barriers to collaboration go beyond those of language. Technologies, particularly if they make use of graphics and text, can be quite facilitative. In a technologically focused meeting environment, an outspoken Aussie who only speaks the language of manufacturing is "forced" to listen to, or at least read, what a reticent Asian doctor has to say about pill packaging.

However, even a computer-augmented meeting requires same time/same place social or interpersonal interaction. World-class teams need different time/different place technologies that can facilitate the same types of synergies. Much of what is referred to as groupware is mainly intended for information exchange and does not truly support synergistic creation.

With Lotus Notes™, which has become the world's most successful groupware product, we are beginning to see that groupware has the power to move beyond information management to relationship management. In the end, that is what collaboration is all about. Products such as Novell's GroupWise™, Collabra's Share™, and Group Technology's Aspects™ are all designed to facilitate human interaction. Even these software programs may be eclipsed by the growing use of the Internet. With electronic bulletin boards, discussion groups, and the increasing multimedia capabilities of the World Wide Web, the Internet has provided a technological medium that best resembles face-to-face interaction.

The biggest advantage of groupware is that as the world is getting smaller (figuratively speaking; world-class teams bring together a wide variety of people from different cultures), and as people increasingly become aware of and want to tap into the benefits of worldwide access and perspectives, then the "any time, any place" technologies can facilitate that communication. Keep in mind, however, that collaboration will not be a natural outcome of groupware, despite the many advantages it offers. In fact, the technology could actually be used as a smokescreen by rogue cowboys who "just can't find the time" to use it.

■ HIGH TECH AND HIGH TOUCH

Conflict resolution over the Internet instead of screaming at each other face-to-face? What fun is that? Will technology eliminate human contact and interaction? Some people are acting as if it could. We recently heard of two same time/same place team members who were literally sitting in offices next to each other and shooting off e-mails to each other every day (different time/different place technology). The fury in the messages could be "heard" by everyone who was "cc'd" on their exchanges.

Unfortunately, the hopeful promise of collaborative technologies assumes that the people using the technology truly *want* to collaborate. In Chapter 15, we learned that this is a myth. Even if you have all the best team technologies at your disposal, you still have to work at creating a collaborative atmosphere within the team and helping team members develop the requisite attitudes and skills for collaborative efforts.

However, imbedded in the promise of technology is a certain element of "fun" that could serve to boost the spirit of collaboration on your team. "The Fun Factor" was addressed in a paper written by Bernard DeKoven for presentation at Groupware '95, in which he observed:

> Fun (intrinsic reward) is an important, and perhaps even essential component of most collaborative efforts. By taking fun "seriously," Groupware designers and facilitators of Groupware environments can build systems that are more supportive of collaborative learning, decision-making and creativity. The "Fun Factor" is especially relevant in Learning Organizations and within those team efforts where collaboration is extrinsically recognized and supported and must be sustained over time and distance.[5]

For many people, being on a team implies or equates with going to meetings—traditionally viewed, of course, as same time/same place events. DeKoven points out that meetings have the potential for intrinsic rewards such as "being agreed with, being heard, being laughed with, being respected, being right, being supported, being understood, being welcome, being well-informed, camaraderie, debating something you know a lot about, feeling accepted, feeling intelligent, feeling powerful, getting air time, getting a free lunch, getting praised, getting something done, having something of value to add, learning something new, planning, schmoozing."[6] In other words, meetings *could* be fun. And wouldn't it be great if, through technology, we could create that type of fun environment?

■ THE BALANCED TOUCH

The extent to which your world-class team makes use of technology will be driven largely by the resources available to the team and, in part, by the willingness (or resistance) of team members to embrace technological tools. Dekoven describes a unique way that IBM has brought "The Fun Factor" into its *Team Focus* demonstration room. This high-tech meeting room—which has computers at each chair, a computer-enhanced podium with its own computer and monitor, and a wall-size rear-projected computer that can display input from any single or combined number of networked computers—also has a Koosh® ball next to each monitor! (EquiPro International has been using this "high-touch" tool for several years in our work with world-class teams, and we can vouch for its appeal. We have a growing reputation at FAO Schwartz, the renowned toy store in New York City, where we keep a standing reorder on Koosh® balls for Steve Monaghan, our office manager, who makes a visit there at least two to three times a month. One day he walked out with 90 Koosh® balls to take to work with a group of Russian managers, who loved them!)

The point is, technology may change the means of human interaction, but that doesn't take away from the fact that humans are the ones doing the interacting. You can still scream if you feel the need—you just may be venting to the computerized image of your team member in Japan while you're in Turkey, or staying "under cover" via an anonymous electronic audience-response system, or posting an all-points-bulletin on your team's electronic bulletin board.

No team can rely solely on technology as a means of interacting and getting work done. As we noted earlier, teams do need to come together physically, especially during certain stages of their work. But both at and in between those times, technology has the potential to make "discussions" between team members not only constructive, time-efficient, and cost-effective, but also lively, candid, spontaneous, less "stuffy" or formal, and, yes, also fun.

At the same time, we would do well to remember that as the level of technology becomes more complex, the need for sensitive treatment of human beings increases. John Naisbitt, author of *Megatrends,* refers to this balance as "high tech–high touch." We must wean people away from the notion that teamwork cannot be accomplished outside of same time/same place venues, but we must also keep in mind that people need and thrive on human contact. Technology expands our options for ways of working and communicating, which are especially important, given our global business environment. But unless technology adequately replicates human contact someday, we will continue to need face-to-face meetings—

and probably a screaming session or two. E-mail is *not* a substitute for effective conflict management.

For large and long-term projects, it is wise to bring all team members to what some refer to as a "bonding test" for in-person meetings. Minimally, periodic videoconferencing allows for introductions and for development of some level of trust and relationship before hitting the electronic highway together. However, for team members who have language and cultural differences in particular, this contact will not replace the value of personal interaction.

Even people who work with (and market) groupware products note the importance of team-building sessions. Chris Newell, executive director of the Lotus Institute, the research and education division of Lotus Development Corporation (the maker of Lotus Notes™), works in a virtual team and, periodically, the team members gather for ski weekends and other social events.

Romana Pylyp, who is a Director/Group Leader for the Pfizer Pharmaceuticals Group, insists that members of her far-flung team, including Ken Smith from Hong Kong, Patrick Saumont, and John Elder from Mexico attend her annual barbecue in Greenwich, Connecticut. And what better place to size people up than over sizzling steaks and a glass of wine?

Epilogue

Lessons Learned about Team Learning

As we have made our journeys around the world, not only have we logged thousands of frequent flyer miles, we have amassed a series of learnings which we've tried to describe throughout this book in the hope that you can both avoid the natural land mines and preemptively create strategies to achieve world-class success faster than others.

Throughout our journeys, we have had one underlying value: the value of *learning*. With new teams, we ask: "What have you learned from Dream Teams you've been on in the past? How can we help you to create a Dream Team with this new team?" With experienced teams, we ask: "What did you learn this last year? What lessons will guide you to become a better team next year?"

We strongly believe that world-class teams can be the vehicle that drives organizations toward truly becoming "learning organizations." As we've seen, they bring together a diversity of knowledge, experience, and perspective that can only benefit the organization if focused toward a common goal.

However, we say that with one major caveat. This can only occur if both the world-class team and the network of stakeholders around that team are willing to *learn*, or, as Peter Senge explains, create a learning organization. As we noted in Chapter 1, Senge describes "adaptive" learning and double-loop learning as the processes of learning what does and doesn't work in the organization, then making changes accordingly. The same goes for developing world-class teams.

What we have learned about team learning over the past few years is that if the organization is going to realize the benefits of teams, these elements must be present:

> ➤ *Vision.* We must be able to "see" (1) how a world-class team can *uniquely* meet a performance challenge and (2) the power that comes from leveraging diversity.

➤ *Dialogue.* We must be willing to take the time to explore issues from a perspective of real inquiry. Diversity is only a benefit when we truly try to understand another's experience and create new realities out of differences.

➤ *Strategic action.* We must not use teams as a smokescreen for allowing nonclosure on divergent thinking. We must value and manage our differences toward integration of ideas, conclusions, and action.

We firmly believe that failing to learn, practice, and master the fundamentals of the game is how you can wind up losing the game. We've provided basic blocking and tackling principles that should be followed not just by world-class teams themselves, but also by those who surround and support them.

A final learning. World-class teams are expensive. They cost the organization time and money. They cost individuals hard work and psychological commitment. Don't treat them cavalierly. If you're not willing to invest in them, nurture them, and stick with them in the face of hostile attacks, don't start. Time after time, we have witnessed the expectant faces of newly appointed team members who were eager to learn a new way of working in the world. Six months later, they were frustrated and depressed at not being able to get their work done because "management" withdrew its support.

That's why good ideas fail. Not because they were fads destined for the hula-hoop heap. But because we weren't willing to persevere with courage into uncharted waters where the wind changes and turbulence were unpredictable.

Smooth sailing on teams? Not always. But a challenging adventure—definitely.

We consider ourselves extremely lucky because we are members of a world-class high-performing team ourselves and are linked by virtue of our work to other world-class teams around the globe. We've learned firsthand that teamwork takes *work!*

Appendix A

Team Role Analysis™

■ FURTHER ROLE INTERPRETATION

➤ I. Evaluating Issues

1. The Strategist

The role of Strategist is one that may be extremely powerful in a team. It is also perhaps not one that is especially welcomed. Groups, like individuals, often like to make decisions on the spur of the moment that will bring immediate gratification or will seem to solve an immediate problem. They can become impatient with the person who is always asking, "What are the long-term implications of what we are doing?"

Nevertheless, the Strategist is often the person within the group who sees underlying issues more quickly than anyone else. He or she can point out aspects of an issue that people have not considered. The Strategist who develops credibility will usually have done so by anticipating what could have turned out to be a disaster. The group then looks back and acknowledges the fact that the Strategist has saved everyone's hide.

In the case of a team that has a clear-cut natural and appointed leader, the Strategist can serve as the right arm, working out the ways in which overall objectives can be reached by tackling the sub-priorities in a logical and systematic way.

The Strategist looks upon himself or herself as a problem solver; however, once the problem is solved, the Strategist typically wants to go on to another problem. He or she does not have much interest in the implementation phase and may assume that things are going to work out just because they have been put on paper in the proper fashion. Clearly, there is a need for other roles (the Enforcer, the Troubleshooter, the Producer, etc.) to actualize the strategy.

Strategists often times will put themselves at the service of an individual group. They see themselves as professional problem solvers and may not have any ax to grind one way or another. It is as though they say, "Tell me what your overall objectives are and I'll see what I can do to help you get there."

2. The Visionary

The Visionary is a person who has confidence and faith in his or her judgment, together with an orientation toward the future. This person will question the way things are done. The Visionary will not accept something merely on the word of authority. This role differs from the Contrarian, however, in that the latter is often more negative—refusing to accept anything, yet not putting much in its place. By contrast, the Visionary has as a goal creating a new template for his or her part of the organization.

3. The Data Doctor

The driving force for the Data Doctor is the collection of information. This is a person who would do well on a trivia quiz specifically oriented to an area of his or her expertise. The Data Doctor likes to show off his or her knowledge, and tends to gain satisfaction from serving as a resource. Data Doctors often make good consultants and, in fact, are used in this way in their organizations.

If you score low on the Data Doctor, you probably see yourself as a generalist. There are certain risks, however, to this orientation—especially if you depend on your interpersonal skills or salesmanship to impact your team (for example, High Promoter or High Politician).

4. The Traditionalist

While the Traditionalist may sometimes be a source of some frustration within the group, he or she also may be very well respected (depending upon how well the role is played). If the Traditionalist is a mere obstructionist, then clearly he or she is going to be quite unpopular and of limited value. If the role is played truly effectively, however, the Traditionalist may save the group from making costly mistakes and losing track of its priorities. Furthermore, the Traditionalist is at his or her best when the group is in a panic and about ready to make some dumb decision. The role of Traditionalist, then, can be extremely valuable.

➤ II. Making Decisions

1. The Facilitator

If a group is healthy (even one with built-in hierarchies), there should be some disagreement among the members. The Facilitator's role is to ensure that such disagreement is expressed in a positive way. The Facilitator is usually skilled at avoiding dead ends, guiding a group along paths that will prove productive.

Even if the group contains a leader with the specific position power to cut off debate and make an arbitrary decision, he or she might find that it is better to encourage the members to express their perspectives. The leader might not always be the best person to function in this facilitative role. Indeed, the leader might find that, just because he or she has this power, taking the lead is in itself intimidating. In many groups, if the leader says, "I think this . . . .", debate and discussion are effectively ended.

For groups in which the question of authority is less clear-cut, the Facilitator is indeed worth his or her weight in gold. When no one assumes this role, the group can engage in endless and pointless discussions, going up numerous blind alleys with the members all doing their own thing and not listening to each other.

With the increasing use of groups in organizations, the role of Facilitator is gaining wider and wider recognition. Many human resources departments train their personnel in just this technique. In fact, learning facilitative skills is usually helpful for any member of a group, and is almost absolutely essential for a person who aspires to professional management roles.

2. The General

The role of the General has been filled within groups since the dawn of human experience. The sight of a group milling about with no organization—and consequently no achievement—has bothered would-be Generals from the very beginning. A vacuum of power can be an anathema to the General.

Almost by definition, the General is comfortable in the exercise of authority. This person will make it clear that he or she is in charge. Humans, particularly when frustrated or scared, are quite willing to accept the authority of anyone who seems to have the focus and ability to get something done. Since the General will often appear confident and definitive, he or she is often given the authority by default.

The General, of course, may find that countervailing power centers will be set up within a group (which he or she will do everything possible to discourage). The essential thing for the General is to feel that he or she is calling the shots. While the role of the General is sometimes controversial, there is little doubt about its utility in a variety of team settings. Groups often need someone who is comfortable in exercising authority.

3. *The Promoter*

The Promoter is clearly the salesperson within the group. It is his or her function to get the group to think beyond more mundane affairs and to get it excited about possibilities it may not have considered. Clearly, the Promoter can also have a self-interest. Professional salespeople have a view of themselves as "promoters of change." Indeed, the capitalistic system is conceived by many to be a prime generator of change—making people dissatisfied with the status quo. Promoters play a major part in this whole process. They do not, however, necessarily have to be innovators. Rather, they tend to agitate for some different way of doing things. The enemy of the Promoter is usually the Traditionalist, with his or her focus on the fact that things are really not as bad as the Promoter would suggest.

There are a couple of elements that usually accompany this role:

➤ A capacity to communicate in an effective way; and

➤ The ability to generate enthusiasm and excitement for a particular course of action.

In all of us, however, there is often a certain skepticism towards salespeople. In some of us, the idea of being looked on as a "salesman" is tantamount to calling us a conniver. We reject the role out of hand as being one that is so self-serving as to be unworthy of us or of any honorable person. Clearly, this is an over-reaction and tends to reduce our own abilities for getting our point across in a group.

4. *The Contrarian*

The Contrarian carves out the role of maverick. If the group agrees something is black, the Contrarian will certainly try to prove that it is white. Needless to say, this role is not always highly valued (particularly by constituted authority within the group). Thus, it can be a risky role for an individual to undertake. (In some settings, they hang dissenters happily.)

Nevertheless, the role of Contrarian can be extremely helpful to a group. The Contrarian remembers well all the times that people in authority have confidently proclaimed X was going to happen or Y was an eternal truth and these have turned out to be absolutely untrue, or at least subject to serious doubt. As a maverick, the Contrarian can bring up things that would be out of character or unsafe for other members of the group. This person can get a group to think things through—to question its assumptions.

Clearly, the more attractively the Contrarian can present his or her views, the more likely he or she is to have increased influence. People will pay attention rather than dismissing the Contrarian's ideas out of hand.

If the basic psychological process necessary for developing as a Contrarian is time spent going through an adolescent rebellion, it is nonetheless true that this in and of itself does not condemn a viewpoint put forth by the Contrarian. After all, it has been the rebels who, through the years, have led to major changes in the ways societies function.

It is probably worthwhile for any professional to develop a bit of the Contrarian. It will prevent you from being taken too much for granted. (After all, you may not want to be counted on in every circumstance by the authorities that be or by the group.) Individuals who were members of the counterculture during the 1960s have a built-in advantage in developing as Contrarians. (It is wise to remember, however, that the rebellion of the 1960s was a mass movement with considerable peer support. Playing the role of Contrarian in your professional association may not contain the same degree of support.)

5. *The Democrat*

The movement towards democratic management appears to be gathering steam. In team settings in particular, these perspectives and skills are being valued increasingly in all organizational settings. Indeed, the democratic approach is sometimes seen as an article of faith; by contrast, any kind of authoritative approach is now often heralded as worthy of being cast into the outer darkness.

There are many strengths in the democratic management approach (besides being fashionable). Democrats almost inherently generate good feelings in group members (especially in those who have been used to being ordered about). The effective Democrat will try to make sure that he or she builds upon such good feeling.

The Democrat differs from the Facilitator in that, although the Democrat will try to gain a certain amount of consensus (like the Facilitator), he or she is primarily identified with the management role. This manager will use consensus as a vehicle for helping him or her reach organizational objectives. The Democrat is working to achieve an agenda—to set objectives. By contrast, the Facilitator is more likely to see himself or herself as a vehicle to help actualize these objectives.

There are also some inherent weaknesses in democratic management, just as there are in any management philosophy. In particular, the Democrat has to be careful not to fall into the trap of laissez-faire management (in which one gets the reputation of appearing to believe that anything will do).

If you score low on the role of Democrat, you may be somewhat less identified with the managerial and leadership role, and/or perhaps less inclined to engage in consensual processes (for example, with high

General). In either case, you may find it useful to learn more about the Democrat's bag of tricks.

➤ III. Getting Things Done

1. *The Organizer*

The Organizer is the person who rushes into the vacuum often expressed in the vague hope "one of these days we've got to get organized." The Organizer tends to have a strong ability to systematize and structure approaches towards getting the job done. This person hates loose ends and disorganization. He or she has a real capacity to make routine the things that should be routine, and is scandalized by crisis management. The Organizer may or may not have an ability to function in managerial roles, however.

The Organizer is a very useful person to have within a group. This teammate can take a list of widely differing processes and meld them into a whole. He or she also has an ability to follow up—to make sure that the things that have been started get finished properly.

2. *The Craftsperson*

The role of Craftsperson is closely associated with the idea of quality in task and production. The Craftsperson is the individual to whom one gives an assignment when a gold-plated job is really necessary. The Craftsperson takes great pains to make sure things are done just right, and cannot be rushed. He or she feels that if something is worth doing, it is worth doing well.

While the Craftsperson may have some orientation to the idea of efficiency, this is really secondary to the enterprise. The Craftsperson is usually very knowledgeable in his or her field, is quite proud of this knowledge, and produces things that are almost works of art.

The Craftsperson can function in a variety of specialties. The important element in this role is that this person practices his or her trade or profession to the very highest standards. In contributing to the group, this team member will emphasize the significance of doing a superior job on any assignment

3. *The Magician*

The crucial dimension of the Magician is an orientation towards taking imaginative approaches to problems or opportunities. The Magician emphasizes the importance of doing things on one's own but, almost like

Santa Claus at Christmas, providing for the group the solution to a problem, the achievement of a goal, the design of the system that no one knew this team member was working on.

The Magician can also be an individual who just takes on an assignment and goes off alone, keeping himself or herself motivated without a lot of need for group interaction (especially with low Team Player). The Magician, however, can be very identified with trying to do a good job for the team.

4. The Producer

The hallmark of the Producer is an orientation towards task—that is, to grinding out the work. The Producer takes great pride in counting up all of the things he or she has accomplished during the course of the day (perhaps in the form of a checklist). The Producer is also a no-nonsense person who is not much given to socializing. This team member does not like to be interrupted while off doing his or her work. Producers gain great satisfaction from setting higher and higher standards for themselves. This may be in response to outside influence, but often is internally determined. Producers are often associated with the "rate buster" phenomenon. They will often just not be bound by the average of groups. They don't necessarily have a strong interest in conforming to group pressures. Being friendly is not a necessary part of their psychology (they don't have to be unfriendly, however).

The Producer has a certain similarity to the Bottom-Liner in that both types have a strong task focus and can sometimes lack a sense of humor. The Producer, however, is someone who will feel comfortable doing the actual work.

The Producer will usually want to know, very specifically, how things are supposed to turn out. He or she will try to get people down to cases.

The Producer will often set higher objectives after performing a particular task. This person will keep pushing himself or herself. The Producer gets a certain satisfaction from coming out on top. This team member is often very competitive in terms of task.

5. The Delegator

The Delegator likes to get a variety of things going within the group. He or she will try to get people to be really focused on achieving some practical objectives. The Delegator, however, does not have to really get into the nitty-gritty of the work himself or herself. In fact, the Delegator may prefer to spend time on other things rather than doing the work itself. The Delegator will often have a short-term focus and perhaps be a bit utilitarian—getting other people to do things for him or her. The Delegator might be compared to the artist's agent, who gets a 15 percent fee and will hold other people's coats, if required.

Needless to say, there is much of the salesperson to the Delegator. This person will convince the other members of the team that it is in their own interests to go ahead and turn out the widgets.

➤ IV. Following Through

1. The Enforcer

The true Enforcer might relate well to the old mobster, Frank Nitti, of *The Untouchables* fame. It was Frank who took care of Al Capone's collection problems, He was aggressive, unsympathetic, and very direct. He also kept close tabs on Al's accounts to make sure they were collected on time.

Clearly, one would not play the Enforcer role in organizations in the same way that Frank Nitti did. Nevertheless, much of the process is the same. The reason is also very much the same—to make sure that discipline is maintained in the organization. It will not work to have a shrinking violet in charge of watching over the books.

In a team setting, one can find people who are either appointed or who appoint themselves to make sure the things that are supposed to get done actually do get done. These are the Enforcers, and they don't take "no" for an answer.

2. The Bottom-Liner

The Bottom-Liner is the person in the group who constantly reminds everyone that they are not in business for their health, and that money talks. This person supplies a focus for group concerns. The Bottom-Liner keeps the group from going too far off in Never Never Land. He or she lets everyone know that payrolls have to be met, bills have to be paid. The Bottom-Liner is likely to agree enthusiastically with the notion that "economics is everything."

The Bottom-Liner is going to play a role in looking at any of the potential outcomes or courses of action facing the group. This team member is not usually described as brimming over with the milk of human kindness. He or she has no time for that sentimental stuff—for the Bottom-Liner, performance is the *sine qua non* of organizational health.

3. The Troubleshooter

The Troubleshooter is the role that allows a person to fix things when they have been fouled up. When the team is faced with some unexpected crisis or opportunity, it will often call on the Troubleshooter to extricate it. The Troubleshooter may be looked on as the person who pulls the chestnuts out of the fire. This team member loves to be hip deep in alligators while correcting situations that are not working right. (This manager is usually, but not always, a line type.)

Impatient with grand designs and high strategy, the Troubleshooter likes concrete, specific turnaround assignments. The Troubleshooter is often restless in maintenance roles. He or she really starts to live and take nourishment when in the center of the action. Usually, the more active the Troubleshooter is, the better he or she likes it.

The Troubleshooter is also usually the supreme pragmatist. This orientation towards the practical and concrete, however, is not always associated with making sure that the problem stays fixed for the long-term (especially with low Strategist or low Organizer). The Troubleshooter is an extremely flexible person who will make do with whatever works at the time. This may mean spit and baling wire. The solution, however, will not come unglued for a period of time. Usually it is helpful to send in someone else with greater administrative interests than the Troubleshooter to make the situation secure for the longer pull.

Nevertheless, the assets of the Troubleshooter can be very vital indeed. In fact, some individuals may make a career out of their talents and interests in troubleshooting.

4. The Teacher

Many, if not all, of these team roles are almost in the realm of what the Jungians call "archetypes." An archetype is a primordial image or concept; an unconscious psychologic reality. It is ingrained deep in the psychology of the race and guides us in very significant ways. These archetypes can be found in much of organizational life.

None is perhaps a better example than that of the role of the Teacher. The Teacher is charged with the responsibility for disseminating the collected experience of the team. It is he or she who instructs new team members on the various things they need to know. The Teacher is asked to become expert to some degree about a variety of issues that are important to the team. This person usually has a strong orientation towards the communication process—informing people about things that they don't know, but which hopefully would be in their interests to find out.

Among adults, the Teacher is valued because he or she has information that is useful. In organizations, the training and development department is coming more to the fore as the need for its services becomes more and more apparent.

Usually the Teacher has to enjoy casual interrelationships with others, because people are the vehicle for the Teacher's self-realization. Information and skills are the role's reason for being.

➤ V. Building the Group

1. *The Cheerleader*

The Cheerleader is a bundle of energy. He or she really enjoys getting other people charged up to accomplish objectives. The Cheerleader, after all, is trying to get the team to win, although this person will also try to keep people's spirits up when the team is losing 50 to nothing. The Cheerleader seems to imply that, by some miracle, the game will be won 52 to 50. There is a purpose, then, to the Cheerleader's good spirits—that is, performance. He or she is not a Therapist who tries to make people feel better on general principles.

In the team, of course, the Cheerleader will work to renew flagging spirits. This group member will usually be highly identified with team goals. It is when things are not going well that the Cheerleader is most necessary.

There is another major purpose served by the Cheerleader—that of celebrating triumphs, touchdowns and goals, beating the stuffing out of the other team. The Cheerleader is supposed to lead the group in savoring its wins and piling on the dishonor felt by the team's opponents. After all, one of life's delicious pleasures is celebrating our victories over our enemies and (at least temporarily) casting them into the outer darkness. The Cheerleader serves to consecrate these events and make us feel great about them.

2. *The Team Player*

The Team Player represents the glue that holds the group together. This role emphasizes the importance of loyalty, cooperation, and just plain being a willing teammate. The Team Player will smooth out problems within the group. He or she will volunteer for the nonglamorous assignments. This team member just wants to do his or her part in bringing about positive outcomes. He or she represents the opposite end of the continuum from the temperamental, egocentric group member. When a decision is finally made, this person will dig in and do what is required.

Within the group itself, the person playing this role tends to emphasize the importance of cooperation and mutual helpfulness. If the Team Player gives allegiance to a team, it is given in full measure.

The benefits of this role for the team are clear, but there are obvious benefits for the individual playing the role as well. A desire for feelings of acceptance and being a part of a significant group of humans is built deep into our psyches. It might even be looked on as a basic drive. Feeling interconnected with others is probably a necessity for psychological health. Some may use the family as the basic unit of connection;

however, this is often not enough. The process of living and growing within an accepted group is highly nourishing as well as often exciting.

3. The Therapist

One of the crucial archetypes among humans is the role of the healer. Even in primitive human groups, there was a special niche for the person who seemed to have the power to soothe and help others recover from the onslaughts of the environment around them. The medicine man or woman was and is a very significant role in both early and modern societies. The priest also had a major part to play in rolling up the raveled sleeve of care within human groups. Descendants from these roles include physicians and nurses in medicine, and many who are engaged in the psychological rather than the strictly physical dimension of humankind's concerns. These professional roles include psychologist, social worker, and counselor.

The Therapist's role within the group is perhaps not so terribly dissimilar to that of these professionals. This team member will try to ease the pain of insult, disappointment, and humiliation that are the natural by-products of humans in groups (particularly those involved in achieving groups). Not every interaction within the group is going to lead to positive emotion. Not every attempt by the team is going to lead to a great success. Not every communication is going to be fully understood. There will be misinterpretations, and people do become angry, short-sighted, and selfish.

The Therapist's role at this time is clear. He or she must reach out in an empathetic and hopefully insightful way to facilitate the process of accommodating the negative emotions without long-term damage to the group. The Therapist will be understanding and helpful. The Therapist will provide encouragement, and will work to help the individual resolve the problem internally. The Therapist may give ideas and suggestions on how the person can deal with an ongoing problem in his or her group relations. The Therapist will attempt to limit the damage to the individual and the group itself.

4. The Politician

The role of the Politician has been with us as long as people have attempted to negotiate back and forth with each other in order to gain advantage. In an organization with a hierarchy, there is the issue of incurring favor with the hierarchy and playing one power center against another (in the same way that children will play one parent against the other if they can). With alternative organizational structures and newly defined relationships, the role of Politician is truly coming into the forefront.

Many of us, however, have very mixed feelings about the people who play this political role (whether the professional politician or the person who dons the role unofficially in organizational life). On the one hand, we feel that the Politician is not the most direct and honest person to have around. We may feel contempt for the way a Politician will compromise principles in the interests of gaining agreement among competing interests. On the other hand, the Politician can often do a considerable amount of good for our unit or for us personally.

It is always interesting to hear people complain about wanting to leave a company because there is too much politics. Usually this is a sign of naivete on the part of the individuals making the claim—they do not recognize the essential and, in the main, honorable role of the political process within organizations. Or, these people have bet on the wrong horse politically and are themselves in trouble as a result. The manager who fails to recognize the importance of having political skills is often living in a fool's paradise. Skills in understanding and maneuvering the political process, such as organizational behavior and group dynamics, are becoming indispensable.

The role of the Politician within the team is often essential. He or she may have credibility across competing constituencies. (Good early training for this comes to adolescents who refuse to get tied in with one clique and form relationships across many groups.) Because of the fact that the Politician has communication and leverage across groups, deals can be put together that are in everyone's interests. The Politician, then, can serve as a bridge for increased communication. Unless the Politician is looked on as completely self-serving, he or she may serve as an honest broker.

The political role also can be used to advance the interests of a particular constituency, to increase communication and understanding of where the group is going, to help gain acceptance for group causes, to help meld the group into a more cohesive whole.

Skills that define the role of Politician include good persuasive abilities, a capacity to relate easily to others, sharp insight into underlying individual and group dynamics and, above all, an ability to avoid being personally tied to controversy. The Politician develops tact to a fine art and avoids making statements and commitments that will alienate large numbers of the constituency. The Politician, therefore, will dance around issues and try to find common ground rather than sharpening the hard edges of controversy. While we all may admire individuals who tell us things we don't want to hear in a straightforward manner, we also cheerfully hang those people if given half a chance. The Politician understands that there is a difference between what people say they like and how they actually behave.

5. *The Comedian*

The Comedian is a role that is extremely useful but sometimes minimized in groups when the time comes to hand out power and responsibility. The Comedian serves the group by getting it over rough spots with just the right joke to diffuse tension. The Comedian also can break up mental log jams, and in this way allow the group to reframe an issue. If people are laughing, they are likely to be less intransigent about pushing for a particular outcome. We may be more in the mood for creative approaches when we share laughter with others.

The role of Comedian, when combined with the Politician and the General (or perhaps the Democrat), can be extremely powerful. Laughter can be used in the service of an agenda. It can be used to confound the enemies of one's purpose. It can be used to solidify the group on a particular course of action. (During World War II for example, humor was used by the Allies against the Germans and Japanese in a successful effort to reduce their potential to intimidate. It was harder to take Hitler seriously after listening to Spike Jones' rendition of "Der Fuhrer's Face.")

In like manner, the role of Comedian can be used to complement other roles in a positive way within the team. For example, the Teacher who is an effective Comedian will be a more effective Teacher.

The skills that define the role of Comedian include a keen sense of the ridiculous, an ability to remember jokes and to gauge the right time to present them, a certain lack of inhibition, and a basic capacity for friendly interaction with others. One would not include in this role those individuals who use particularly biting and hostile humor that is, in fact, directed at in-group members (except by accident). An essential key to success is the lack of hostility and anger, except as this might be directed at out-groups.

Appendix B

Crossing the Borders
World-Class Teamwork as a Competitive Business Strategy

■ PURPOSE OF THE PROGRAM

A critical factor in the ability of companies to realize their Mission and Vision will be how effectively people work together in teams, whether they are traditional intact teams that work together daily or cross-functional teams that focus on specific projects or processes. When senior executives are asked about their key organization development needs, they frequently mention that their managers and professionals need to "learn how to manage matrix structures that are organized around customers, as opposed to hierarchical functional organizations."

It is also becoming evident that, if managers are part of a multinational organization, they not only must move across the "functional silos" within their own companies, they must also learn to move across their national boundaries—e.g., become "Euromanagers" to more effectively respond to global market realities.

All of these forces strongly suggest that we need to provide support to people who must function effectively in these new team structures. We, at EquiPro International, are now providing team skills training for cross-functional teams in a program which we have titled: **"CROSSING THE BORDERS."**

➤ Program Objectives

The initial target population for the **CROSSING THE BORDERS** program are executives, managers, or professionals from various units within a company (sales, manufacturing, marketing, etc.) who have been formed into teams to work on short-term projects or assignments. The members of these teams come together initially to discuss issues, solve problems, make decisions or recommendations and then periodically meet to review progress. The work of such cross-functional teams usually occurs as an addition to the team members' normal job duties and responsibilities. Team members may or may not have had previous working relationships or interactions with each other before being assigned to a cross-functional team.

We would expect that the **CROSSING THE BORDERS** program would be given either before a new team begins its assignment/project or as close as possible to its inception.

As a result of attending the two-day (or 2¹/₂ day) program the participants will:

➤ Understand the importance of cross-functional teamwork in relationship to the achievement of the company's mission/vision.

➤ Be able to recognize and define the stages and process of team development.

➤ Understand and utilize the roles of:

—Team Leaders

—Team Facilitators

—Team Members

➤ Receive individual and team survey feedback data on strengths and weaknesses.

➤ Develop a set of team values.

➤ Develop a team mission and vision, including team goals.

➤ Understand the importance of both team task and process issues.

➤ Understand the critical factors that contribute to a team's success or failure.

➤ Identify and prioritize the critical skills required for team effectiveness.

➤ Develop action plans for individual and team skills development.

We will use a variety of training methodologies, including the *Team Role Analysis*™ assessment survey, small group discussions, a case study, team activities, and other experiential learning activities customized to the program learning objectives. Participants will be able to use the program materials as their cross-functional teams continue to work on their projects. The program is intended as an "orientation" to cross-functional teams, but will also provide for team skill-building. As the need for additional team skills training arises, these can be addressed in 2–4 hour add-on modules.

■ PROGRAM MATERIALS

➤ Seminar Pre-Work

➤ TEAM CONTRACT WITH SENIOR MANAGERS AND STEERING COMMITTEE

From the research conducted on cross-functional teams in a variety of organizations we know that there are several factors, beyond teaching teamwork skills to team members, that contribute to these teams becoming successful. Among them are:

➤ *Establishing the Team's Vision* by setting forth the overall purpose of the team and the performance results you expect the team to accomplish.

➤ *Selecting Team Members* who have both a working knowledge of the business issues, as well as teamwork skills, e.g., interpersonal communications, running effective meetings, conflict management, and so forth.

➤ *Empowering the Team* by defining their authority levels (including budgets) for decision-making/task accomplishment.

➤ *Providing Management Support and Commitment* for the team's efforts, including giving them a) the resources they require; b) the time they need from you to review progress or discuss issues; c) recognition for the team's efforts and individual contributions; and d) if necessary, help in prioritizing their own functional and cross-functional goals.

In establishing the mandate for the cross-functional team, the Steering Committee should examine each of these critical success factors and the sponsoring executive should address these issues and refer to this Team Contract as part of his/her Opening Remarks for the program.

➤ *TEAM ROLE ANALYSIS*™ QUESTIONNAIRE COMPLETION

➤ TEAMWORK CASE ASSIGNMENT

➤ CURRENT TEAM INFORMATION: Mission/Vision/Values/Goals/Task Assignments

➤ *HARVARD BUSINESS REVIEW* ARTICLE: "Building a Learning Organization"

■ PROGRAM AGENDA

DAY ONE

Introduction

➤ Senior executive opening remarks
➤ Program introduction
➤ "Dream Team" exercise
➤ Team introduction exercise

BREAK

Creating Successful Cross-Functional Teams

➤ Cross-functional team simulation
➤ Team case study
➤ The what and whys of teams
➤ What is a cross-functional team?

Creative Team Brainstorming

LUNCH

Warm-Up Exercise/Team Nicknames

Team Activity: Builder of Dreams

➤ Team performance skills
➤ Team process skills
➤ Border management skills

Team Role Analysis™

➤ What are the roles?
➤ Individual and team survey profiles

DAY TWO

Workshop Opening

Team Diversity: Mind Mapping

Team Development Activity: Evaluating Issues and Making Decisions

➤ Outback survival exercise
➤ Team decision making

BREAK

Stages of a Team's Development

Team Trust Activity

LUNCH

Think and Listen

➤ Team listening exercise

Team Town Meeting

➤ What is our team's mission/vision
➤ What are our goals?
➤ What are our roles? Rules?
➤ What are our values/guidelines?

Team Effectiveness Assessment

Team Appreciation Circle

Workshop Closing and Evaluation

NOTES

■ CHAPTER 1

[1] "Designing pay systems for teams" by Edward Lawler and Susan Cohen. *American Compensation Association Journal*, Vol. 1, 1992, pp. 6–18.

[2] "What's New" (column). *Training & Development Journal*, January 1996, p. 15.

[3] "Microsoft Teamwork" by Jeff McHenry. *Executive Excellence*, July 1996, pp. 6–7.

[4] *Ibid.*

[5] "Team Building a Global Team at Apple Computer" by Cole Hamlin. *Employment Relations Today*, Spring 1994, pp. 55–62.

[6] "Holistic Thinking" by Robert Lutz. *Executive Excellence*, May 1997, p. 10.

[7] "Global Teams: The Ultimate Collaboration" by Charlene Marmer Solomon. *Personnel Journal*, September 1995, pp. 49–58.

[8] "Global Teams" by Charlene Marmer Solomon. *Personnel Journal*, September 1995, p. 54.

[9] "The Trouble with Teams" by Brian Dumaine. *Fortune*, September 5, 1994, pp. 86–92.

[10] *The Fifth Discipline Fieldbook* by Peter M. Senge, Charlotte Roberts, Richard B. Ross, Bryan J. Smith, and Art Kleiner. New York: Doubleday Currency, 1994.

[11] Hamlin, "Team Building a Global Team at Apple Computer," pp. 55–62.

[12] "Chimneys to Cross-Functional Teams: Developing and Validating a Diagnostic Model" by Daniel R. Denison, Stuart Hart, and Joel Kahn. *Academy of Management Journal*, 1996, Vol. 39, No. 4, pp. 1005–1023.

[13] *Ibid.*

■ CHAPTER 6

[1] *The Book of Virtues,* edited by William J. Bennett. New York: Simon & Schuster, 1993.

■ CHAPTER 7

[1] "Developing and Increasing Role Efficacy" by Udai Pareek. *The 1986 Annual: Developing Human Resources,* San Diego: University Associates, p. 171.

[2] Adapted from "Role Clarification: A Team-Building Activity" by John E. Jones. *Structured Experience,* San Diego: University Associates, p. 171.

■ CHAPTER 8

[1] "The Concept of Culture and the Psychosomatic Approach" by Margaret Mead. *Contributions Toward Medical Technology,* ed. Arthur Weider. New York: Ronald Press, 1953, 1:377–378.

[2] *When Cultures Collide: Managing Successfully Across Cultures* by Richard D. Lewis. London: Nicholas Brealey Publishing, 1996.

[3] *Ibid.*

[4] "Cultural Synergy: Managing the Impact of Cultural Diversity" by Nancy Adler. *The 1986 Annual: Developing Human Resources,* University Associates, p. 232.

[5] *Ibid.,* p. 229.

■ CHAPTER 9

[1] "Global Work Teams" by Sylvia Odenwald. *Training & Development Journal,* February 1996, pp. 54–57.

[2] "The Hidden Side of Leadership in Technical Team Management" by Gary Gemmill and David Wilemon. *Resource Technology Management,* November/December 1994, Vol. 7, pp. 25–32.

[3] *Caught in the Middle: How to Survive & Thrive in Today's Management Squeeze* by Lynda C. McDermott. Englewood Cliffs, NJ: Prentice-Hall, Inc., 1992, p. 65.

[4] *Ibid.,* pp. 69–70.

[5] "Microsoft Teamwork" by Jeff McHenry. *Executive Excellence,* July 1996, p. 6.

■ CHAPTER 10

[1] *Faultless Facilitation: A Resource Guide for Group & Team Leaders* by Lois Borland Hart. Amherst, MA: HRD Press, 1992.

[2] *The Abilene Paradox and Other Meditations on Management* by Jerry Harvey. Lexington, MA: Lexington Books, 1989.

[3] "How to Choose a Leadership Pattern" by W. H. Schmidt and R. Tannenbaum. *Harvard Business Review,* 1958, No. 36, pp. 95–101.

■ CHAPTER 11

[1] *Caught in the Middle: How to Survive & Thrive in Today's Management Squeeze* by Lynda C. McDermott. Englewood Cliffs, NJ: Prentice-Hall, Inc., 1992, p. 75.

[2] *Ibid.,* p. 77.

[3] "Using the Balanced Scorecard as a Strategic Management System" by Robert S. Kaplan and David P. Norton. *Harvard Business Review,* January–February 1996.

■ CHAPTER 12

[1] *Evaluating Training Programs* by Don Kirkpatrick. Madison, WI: American Society of Training and Development, 1975.

[2] *How to Measure the Results of Teams* by Jack Zigon. Media, PA: Zigon Performance Group, 1995.

■ CHAPTER 13

[1] *Compensation for Teams: How to Design and Implement Team-Based Reward Programs* by Steven E. Gross. New York: AMACOM, 1995.

[2] *The Reward Plan Advantage: A Manager's Guide to Improving Business Performance through People* by Jerry McAdams. San Francisco: Jossey-Bass Publishers, 1996.

■ CHAPTER 14

[1] *The Wisdom of Teams: Creating the High-Performance Organization* by Jon R. Katzenbach and Douglas K. Smith. Cambridge, MA: Harvard Business School Press, 1993, p. 91.

[2] "Building a Learning Organization" by David A. Garvin. *Harvard Business Review,* July–August 1993, pp. 78–91.

■ CHAPTER 15

[1] "The Logic of Global Business: An Interview with ABB's Percy Barnevik" by William Taylor. *Harvard Business Review,* March–April 1991, p. 94.

[2] *No More Teams! Mastering the Dynamics of Creative Collaboration* by Michael Schrage. New York: Doubleday Currency, 1995, p. 33.

[3] "Matrix Management: Not a Structure, A Way of Mind" by Christopher Bartlett and Sumantra Ghoshal. *Harvard Business Review,* July–August 1990, pp. 2–8.

[4] "Developing Collaboration in Organizations" by Udai Pareek. *The 1981 Annual Handbook for Group Facilitators,* San Diego: University Associates, pp. 165–182.

[5] "Collaborative Advantage: The Art of Alliances" by Rosabeth Moss Kanter. *Harvard Business Review,* July–August 1994, pp. 34–46.

[6] Taylor, "The Logic of Global Business: An Interview with ABB's Percy Barnevik," p. 97.

[7] Kanter, "Collaborative Advantage: The Art of Alliances," pp. 34–46.

[8] *The Fifth Discipline: Art and Practice of the Learning Organization* by Peter Senge. New York: Doubleday Currency, 1990, p. 159.

■ CHAPTER 16

[1] *The Interpersonal Underworld* by William C. Schutz. Palo Alto, CA: Science and Behavior Books, 1966.

■ CHAPTER 17

[1] *Technology for Teams: Enhancing Productivity in Networked Organizations* by Susanna Opper and Henry Fersko-Weiss. New York: Van Nostrand Reinhold, 1992, p. 34.

[2] "Virtual Teams" by Beverly Geber. *Training,* April 1995, pp. 36–40.

[3] *No More Teams! Mastering the Dynamics of Creative Collaboration* by Michael Schrage. New York: Doubleday Currency, 1995, p. 33.

[4] Opper and Weiss, *Technology for Teams,* p. 34.

[5] "The Fun Factor in Groupware Design and Implementation" by Bernard DeKoven. 1995. www.california.com/~meetings/funfactr.htm

[6] *Ibid.*

INDEX